CROSSING
THE LINE

CROSSING THE LINE

MY STORY

Luis Suárez

with Peter Jenson and Sid Lowe

headline

First published in Great Britain in 2014
by HEADLINE PUBLISHING GROUP

1

Cataloguing in Publication Data is available from the British Library

Hardback ISBN 978 1 4722 24231

Typeset in Bliss Light by Palimpsest Book Production Limited, Falkirk, Stirlingshire

Printed and bound in the UK by Clays Ltd, St Ives plc

Headline's policy is to use papers that are natural, renewable and recyclable products and made
from wood grown in sustainable forests. The logging and manufacturing processes are expected to
conform to the environmental regulations of the country of origin.

HEADLINE PUBLISHING GROUP
An Hachette UK Company
338 Euston Road
London NW1 3BH

www.headline.co.uk
www.hachette.co.uk

For Sofi, Delfi and Benja.
I love you.

CONTENTS

Introduction: Crossing the Line   1

1. This is a Love Story   18
2. The Dutch School   47
    Referees   71
3. The Hand of Suárez   75
    Fame   104
4. Let's go for 7   108
5. 'Racist'   146
    Fortune   160
6. The Rodgers Revolution   169
    Match Day   195
7. So Close   198
    Friends & Heroes   226
8. That was Anfield   231
    Management   237
9. England, *my* England   239

    Epilogue: The Callejón   259
    Acknowledgements   273
    Picture Credits   274

    Index   275

INTRODUCTION:
CROSSING THE LINE

I knew straight away, as soon as it happened.

When Godín scored I said '*Gol!*' but on the inside everything was shutting down. I was happy that we had scored, and happy for my team-mates that we were going through, but I didn't want to think any more – thinking meant accepting what I'd done and what the consequences would now be.

I had let people down. My coach Óscar Tabárez, '*El Maestro*', was in a bad way in the dressing room because he knew what could happen to me now. I couldn't look at my team-mates. I couldn't look at the *Maestro*. I didn't know how I could say sorry to them. He told me that after the game the journalists had asked him about the incident, and he'd told them that he hadn't seen anything.

My team-mates were trying to tell me that maybe the situation was not so bad. But I didn't want to hear a single word of it. Two more days would pass before I had to leave Brazil, but in my head, I was already gone.

I was at training the next day, still in this unconscious state of denial, not wanting to think about anything, much less face up to the need to apologise and accept the fact that I needed to get some help.

Just as we finished the training session, the *Maestro* called me over. He had news. 'This is the worst thing that I have ever had to tell a player,' he said, hardly able to get the words out. At that moment I thought maybe the ban would be ten, fifteen or even twenty games, but then he said: 'Nine matches'. That didn't seem any worse than I had feared. But he wasn't finished. 'And you can't set foot in any stadium. You have to leave now. You can't be anywhere near the squad.'

I wanted to stay and support my team-mates. Even if I was not playing I wanted to try to make up for things in some small way. But there were representatives from FIFA at the hotel and the team manager, Eduardo Belza, had been informed that I had to leave the squad as soon as possible. They treated me worse than a criminal. You can punish a player, you can ban a player from playing, but can you prohibit him from being alongside his team-mates?

The nine-game ban was to be expected. But being sent home and banned from all stadiums? The only reason I didn't cry was that I was standing there in front of the coach when he told me the news.

There was a meeting with the team afterwards back at the hotel. I wanted to speak to them during lunch, but I couldn't. I was about to stand up and tell them to be strong, to keep going, to keep fighting, but I just couldn't.

Had the ban stopped at nine Uruguay matches – which, as would gradually dawn on me, is a heartbreaking two tournaments and two years out of international football – I might still have challenged it, but I would have understood it. But banning me from playing for Liverpool when my bans in England never prevented me from playing for Uruguay? Banning me from going to watch my nine- and ten-year-old nephews play a game of Baby Football? Banning me from all stadiums worldwide? Telling me that I couldn't go to work? Stopping me from even jogging around the perimeter of a football pitch? It still seems incredible to me that, until the Court of Arbitration decreed otherwise, FIFA's power actually went that far.

They had never banned a player like that before for breaking someone's leg, or smashing someone's nose across his face as Mauro Tassotti did to Luis Enrique at the 1994 World Cup. They made a big thing of saying the incident had happened 'before the eyes of the world'. Zinedine Zidane headbutted Marco Materazzi in a World Cup final in 2006 and got a three-match ban.

I was an easy target, maybe. But there was something important I had to face up to: I had made myself an easy target. I made the mistake. It was my fault. This was the third time it had happened. I needed to work at this with the right people. I needed help.

● ● ●

3

After my ten-match ban in 2013 for biting Branislav Ivanović, I had questioned the double standards and how the fact that no one actually gets hurt is never taken into consideration. The damage to the player is incomparable with that suffered by a horrendous challenge. Sometimes English football takes pride in having the lowest yellow-card count in Europe, but of course it will have if you can take someone's leg off and still not be booked. When they can say it is the league with the fewest career-threatening tackles then it will be something to be proud of.

I don't think I have ever actually injured a fellow professional. I know biting appals a lot of people, but it's relatively harmless. Or at least it was in the incidents I was involved in. When Ivanović rolled up his sleeve to show the referee the mark at Anfield, there was virtually nothing there. None of the bites have been like Mike Tyson on Evander Holyfield's ear.

But none of this makes it right.

When I got home and saw the television pictures of my bite on PSV Eindhoven midfielder Otman Bakkal in 2010 I cried. I had just become a father to a young daughter, Delfina, and the thought that she would grow up to see that I had done this upset me more than anything else. My wife Sofi had been in the stands and she had not realised what had happened at the time. When she saw the footage she said to me: 'What on earth were you thinking?'

I had to start trying to answer that question for myself.

The adrenaline levels in a game can be so high; the pulse is racing and sometimes the brain doesn't keep up. The pressure mounts and there is no release valve. In 2010 I was frustrated because we were drawing what was a very important game and we were on a bad run that would eventually lead to our manager Martin Jol getting the sack. I was angry with myself, and with the situation. I wanted to do everything right that day and it felt as though I was doing everything wrong. The pent-up frustration and feeling that it was my fault that things were not working out reached a point where I couldn't contain it any more.

That is also what happened with Ivanović in 2013. We had to beat Chelsea to still have any chance of making it into the Champions League. It was a long shot anyway, but losing would mean that it was all over. I was having a terrible game. I gave away a stupid penalty with a handball and I could feel everything slipping through our fingers. I could feel myself getting wound up, getting angry with myself, saying to myself on the pitch: 'How can you have been so clumsy there?', or 'How could you miss that?'

Moments before the Chiellini bite I had a great chance to put us 1-0 up. If I had scored that goal, if Buffon hadn't made the save, then what followed would never have happened. I would not have done anything. Nothing.

But I missed the chance.

The pressure builds, the fear and the anger bubbles up inside: 'We're going out here, and we're going out because of me.' It's suffocating. You don't realise the magnitude of what you're doing or what you might do. I'm not justifying what I did – no one ever could – but I am trying to explain what happens. I'm still trying to explain it to myself, to understand what happens and why.

When the heart has stopped racing after the game it's easy to look back and say: 'How could you be so stupid? There were twenty minutes left.' But out on the pitch with the adrenaline pumping and the tension mounting, you're not even really aware of how long is left. You don't know anything. All I could think was: 'I didn't score, we're out of the World Cup.'

There are some players who in that position would have said: 'Well, we're out, but I scored two great goals against England. I'm the star.' I could have asked to be taken off: 'My knee is hurting again, I scored two in the last game, I did my best.' But I don't think like that. I wanted more. The feeling is very hard to explain. After everything you have done, you don't want it to stop there; you want more, you can't bear the thought of failure. It's not that I want to win; it's that I *need* to win. The fear of failure clouds everything for me – even the blatantly obvious fact that I have at least 20,000 pairs of eyes on me; it is not as if I am not going to be seen. Something closes down in my head. Logic doesn't come into it anymore.

Equally illogical is that it should be a bite. There was a moment in a game against Chile in 2013 when a player grabbed me between the legs and I reacted by punching him. I didn't get banned for that. Nothing. Not one game. That's considered a normal, acceptable response. There is no public outcry either. When I called Ivanović after the incident in 2013 he told me that the police had come to see him and asked him if he wanted to press charges and thankfully he had said no. I'm grateful to him because the circus could have gone on for a lot longer. Punch someone and it's forgotten, there is no circus. So why do I take the most self-destructive route?

The problem with addressing this 'switching off' is that the switching off also happens when I do something brilliant on the pitch and, of course,

I don't want to lose that. I've scored goals and later struggled to understand how exactly I managed to score them. There is something about the way I play that is unconscious, for better and for worse. I want to release the tension and the pressure but I don't want to lose the spontaneity in my game, much less the intensity of my style of play.

Liverpool sent a sports psychologist out to see me in Barcelona after the Ivanović incident and we spent two hours talking about what it felt like and what was going through my head at the time. He offered me his services and said that I could see him again if I wanted to, but I resisted. Part of it was the concern that this treatment would make me too calm on the pitch. What if the next time the ball goes past me, I just let it go past instead of chasing it. I'm the player who will kill himself just to prevent a throw-in in the ninetieth minute. That's the way I play. I did not want to lose that.

To a certain extent it's also normal that a striker is irritable and on edge. For those ninety minutes on the pitch life is irritating. I know irritating might sound like a strange word to use, but it fits. I get irritated when the defender comes and pushes up against me from behind. It's normal because I'm playing with my back to goal, backing into him, but it irritates me. I get irritated when I miss chances. Everything is an irritant. Sometimes if my first few touches are good then that bodes well, but if the first few touches are off, then I think to myself: 'What's wrong with you today?' And I know that the first time a player clashes with me, there's a risk I'll react.

Defenders know that too. In the Premier League when I played against someone like Johnny Heitinger, the former Ajax defender then at Everton, or against Philippe Senderos at Fulham when Martin Jol was their manager, I knew the drill. Senderos would step on the back of my ankle when the ball had gone, about five minutes into the game. 'Ah, sorry,' he would say. I just thought: 'Yeah, Martin Jol has told you what I'm like and has told you to do that.'

The irritation comes with the job and to a certain extent it's normal. But when it escalates because of a poor performance in a massive game then I have a potential problem. That day against Chelsea I was awful. I had played badly against PSV in the Bakkal game, and against Italy I had missed a chance that might cost my country its place in the World Cup finals. Each time the irritation levels had gone off the scale, the pressure had got too much, and I had reacted.

It's very easy for someone who is not playing – or who has never played – to say: 'Ah, you shouldn't lose your temper there.' But the pressure makes you do things that you never imagined: eat more, eat less, act differently. There have been games when afterwards I have said to myself: 'Why did I feel under such pressure when all I ever wanted was to play football and enjoy myself'. But the pressure is there. I find it hard not to over-dramatise the big matches. To still be able to give everything, to still care, but to just be able to play the game and not be so intense that I am practically living the match beforehand – that is the place I want to get to.

It seems strange to say it after a third incident, but I have improved, I am calmer. I have matured. When I was a kid, I got sent off once for head-butting a referee. I ran fifty metres to argue a decision, I was shown a red card and so I head-butted the referee. I'm really not proud of that.

My relationship with Sofi has been a massive help in my life. I always said that I had the best psychologist at home. But for a long time she had been telling me that that wasn't enough and that I had to speak to the appropriate professionals.

After my days of not wanting to talk to anyone after the Chiellini bite – back in Montevideo with the shutters down, depressed and not wanting to digest what had really happened – Sofi and I went away to the countryside and gradually we began to talk about everything and I finally began to accept what had happened and what I needed to do. She was annoyed with herself for not having been firmer with me before. She said to me: 'So now are you going to listen to me?' This time it felt like there was no alternative, and I took the initiative.

I did the research and I found the right people. If I had been at Liverpool then maybe I would have gone back to the people that I had spoken to there or if I had already been settled in at Barcelona I would have looked within the club, but I was almost between clubs so I went out myself and found the right people to help me. It still feels like something very private, but I feel that they are helping me to understand that I don't have to hold things in; and that I don't have to feel such a huge weight of responsibility when I'm on the pitch.

Already I feel that the process is helping me. But it's too easy to say: 'Ah look, I'm behaving myself now.' Because if something happens again in the future, then what? I have to understand that this is a process. I have time now to go through this treatment and to start to understand myself better, and to understand what I'm capable of in those moments, and learn how to stay in control. I can also see now that this is something completely normal in the sense that if I have a knee specialist to help me with my knee then why wouldn't I have a specialist in the relevant field to help me with this?

The thing I am happiest with at the moment is that I know I am being sincere and honest with myself. It's one thing to say to people, 'I'll never do it again', because that's what you are supposed to say. It's another thing entirely to really be conscious of what those words mean and properly accept the situation and that is what I feel I am doing. It feels as though I have finally said to myself: 'Luis, you have to realise that you need someone who will talk to you about this so that you can find a way to be able to handle these situations.'

I'm already learning how to deal with these build-ups of pressure. I have always preferred to keep things to myself rather than sharing them with anyone, even my wife who has shared everything else with me, who is my soulmate. But I am learning that if you let it go, some of the tension leaves your body, your mind clears, you feel better for it. Don't keep it all bottled up inside; don't take it all on alone.

When we began to talk things through we had to start with the same old question: 'Why?'

'Why, Luis, why did you do it?' I still don't know. But I'm on the right road to trying to understand that for myself.

● ● ●

As time went by the plain absurdity of the FIFA ban became more and more apparent. We had to plan everything carefully in case the paparazzi, or even just a fan, took a photograph of me doing something remotely football-related. I had to consider what might happen if a picture of me working out in a gym came to light.

Signing my new contract at Barcelona without it becoming public was a difficult operation too. The club had permission to sign me but it had to stay a private matter. It had to be intricately planned so that no one saw us, or worse still, no one photographed us. There was a three-car plan in place with three different vehicles leaving the Camp Nou from three different exits in the event of us realising the press had been alerted. I had already got used to everything being a covert operation. One day I came away from my father-in-law's house hidden in his car to give the paparazzi the slip. Apart from all the things I couldn't do because of the FIFA ban, there was also a lot I couldn't do because of the attention that now followed my every move.

The transfer to Barcelona was very different to the proposed move to Arsenal a year before. Liverpool were more open to the idea because they knew that Barcelona were going to pay what they wanted for me. And there is a big difference between going from Liverpool to Arsenal and going from Liverpool to Barcelona. I will never in my life regret the decision to stay at Liverpool another year. It would have been a huge mistake to leave the season before. If I had not listened to Steven Gerrard I would have made that massive mistake. We spoke about it when I went back to Melwood to collect my things at the end of the summer and he told me: 'You did the right thing, you waited for the right moment.' It brought back memories of being in the gym at Melwood when the Arsenal saga was rumbling on and him saying to me: 'Wait. Play well this season, give Liverpool one more year and next year it will either be Bayern Munich or

Real Madrid or Barcelona that come in for you and then you can go where you want to because you have the quality to play at any one of those three clubs.'

I love English football and I will miss it, but it's impossible to have your dream within your grasp and not grab at it. Not that there weren't tears when the day came for us to move out of our home in Liverpool. A lot of memories came flooding back. My wife was crying; my daughter was saying: 'I miss my home in Liverpool, I remember when it was my birthday, I remember when I had all my toys in my room.' It was emotional.

Predictably, some people were glad to see the back of me. I heard about Richard Scudamore's comments that I had been bad for the image of the Premier League. I thought the Premier League in my final season in England was as exciting as it was because of what Liverpool achieved, so I don't really understand the comment. Maybe he is upset when the league loses its top players to other leagues.

I have come to love all the clubs I have played for, but I don't think I have ever been a badge-kisser – claiming every club I've joined is the one of my dreams. Lots of players say that about lots of clubs: 'This is the moment I've dreamed about.' But with Barcelona it was difficult not to feel that way. There is a video of me as a young kid being interviewed for Uruguayan television, saying exactly that: 'I want to play for Barcelona one day.' A Uruguayan journalist also reminded me recently that when I was at Nacional and about eighteen years old I would turn up at training with a grey Barcelona rucksack with the Barça badge on it.

Visiting Sofi's family who live in Barcelona we saw lots of games together. I saw the 5-0 win over Real Madrid with the famous five-fingered celebration from Gerard Pique. I saw Andrés Iniesta score in a 1-0 derby game against Espanyol. I saw the Barça vs. Madrid game when Fabio Cannavaro scrambled back to clear a Messi goal but only ended up clattering into the post. And I saw Barcelona vs. Arsenal when they won 4-1 and Messi scored four goals.

I went to games but I never imagined I would play for them and throughout the suspension, even once I was allowed to train with the team, I still couldn't quite believe it. When they presented me at the pre-season Gamper Trophy match, it felt like I had been invited to play as a guest, or that I'd won a competition. Sofi said to me: 'How was it? How did you feel?' I told her: 'The truth is, it felt like they had invited me to play a one-off football match.' When I walked out on to the pitch that was the feeling.

It wasn't the most orthodox of presentations to the rest of the squad either, the day I was finally allowed to train with the team. Barcelona's manager Luis Enrique gathered in the players and told them: 'Well, they have finally got him out of Guantánamo to be here with us today for training . . .' Everyone applauded the released prisoner and I did my best not to look too embarrassed about being the centre of attention.

I can relate to what it is the coach and the club are trying to get back to – that attitude, that desire to win. And it's important that the coach has seen those qualities in me, and has the confidence in me to bring those characteristics to the team.

People talk about me being a problem player but speak to my team-mates and try to find even one that feels that way. I can argue with a team-mate like any player; I have argued with team-mates many times, but it's always about football. The one-upmanship and the envy that you can sometimes find in a dressing room has never come from me. Barcelona knew they would have zero problems in that respect. I'm here to do what the coach asks; to deliver what the supporters want; and to work with team-mates who want the same success as I do.

People ask: 'Will it work tactically?' The boss knows that I can fit into any position that he wants me to fill just as I did for Brendan Rodgers. I think to maximise my benefit to the team I know where I need to be on the pitch. With Lionel Messi arriving from deep having combined with the players in the middle of the pitch; and Neymar being a very mobile player who likes to start in wide areas and come inside, or receive the ball inside and then move into space out wide; me being the reference point for the team inside the area is going to benefit us a lot. I'm not saying I'll play through the middle like a typical number nine but, because of the natural movements of Leo and Neymar, I can see that often that will be the space I end up occupying.

Some people have suggested it may end up resembling the Eto'o–Messi–Henry forward line the team had during a period under Pep Guardiola, with Neymar as Henry and myself as Eto'o. To some extent that could be true.

The style of football is similar to the one I experienced at Ajax and then with Brendan at Liverpool – playing out from the back with the ball on the ground, lots of quick movement and one- or two-touch passing. It's the classic Ajax model and it's also very much the Liverpool style from last season. It's the mix of the two in fact – the touch and passing of

Ajax and the 'Dutch School', and the speed of movement of Liverpool.

And the feelings I had on my first day were much like they were at Liverpool, Ajax and Groningen – there was just as much awkward embarrassment. You don't know what you should do, who you should greet and acknowledge or *how* you should greet and acknowledge them. I was very timid in those early days, but the truth is that I had thought it would be a lot more difficult that it was – the players were fantastic.

I had no idea what to expect. Would it be all glamour and superstardom? In fact there was absolutely none of that. All I found was a group of ultra-professionals who want to win trophies working hard for a very good coach. There's a real connection between the players and the manager as well – Luis Enrique is a young coach and there is that healthy balance between the laughing and joking with him and the seriousness of the job that we have to do.

Andrés held my hand on day one because he was the player I knew best and he explained everything to me. And soon I discovered that both Leo Messi and Javier Mascherano take *mate*, the herbal drink so popular with Uruguayans, so that's great for me. I was taking a flask of it to work by my second day. I thought it would be a bit presumptuous to do so on day one, but by day two I felt comfortable.

Dani Alves said he was pleased I had arrived because now he wasn't going to be the only 'bad guy' at the club and that made me laugh. It all helped to make me feel part of things.

Although it would be a long time before I would play alongside Messi and Neymar in the first team, I was soon playing alongside them and Xavi, Andrés, Sergio Busquets and Ivan Rakitić out on the training pitch.

And it really is incredible what they can do to you in a reduced space with a football. The famous *Rondo* passing drills are very tough at first. You have to adapt quickly to this incredible speed of touch or you don't see the ball. But as well as adapting to the Barça style I also know that I had been signed for *my* characteristics and for what *I* do on the pitch and so I have to focus on carrying on doing all those things that made the club want to sign me in the first place.

Sporting Director Andoni Zubizarreta has been asked how could Barcelona still profess to be 'more than a club' after signing me. His reply meant a lot to me. He said: 'We accept human beings with all their imperfections. People get things right and they get things wrong and they have the capacity to learn from mistakes . . . I'm sure that Luis will be a positive force for this club in the future.' They knew they would get that sort of criticism and it means so much that they still went ahead with the signing.

There was a lot of nonsense around at the time of the transfer. I read 'Barcelona have made Suárez sign an anti-bite clause', as if they would do something that ridiculous. Every player that signs a contract signs up to a code of conduct. As if they would put in a biting clause. If they had done that then I would have signed it there and then of course, but there was no such lack of confidence in me.

When I went to have my medical and sign my new contract I told the president about the time I came to Barcelona on holiday to visit Sofi when we were teenagers; we were just ambling around outside the Camp Nou because we didn't have enough money to get into the museum or buy anything from the club shop. On this particular day someone had left a door open – one of the huge gates that leads into the stadium and out onto the pitch. I shouted to Sofi: 'Look over here, they have left one of the doors open.' She was worried that we were going to be caught trespassing and kicked out but I said: 'No, come quickly.' And for what must have been two minutes we were in. I took a picture of myself in the stadium and then we crept out. When Sofi appeared for the official signing one of the directors said: 'Sofi, it's good that you have come because we need you to settle up the bill for the stadium tour you never paid for in 2004.'

Sofi had been by my side on those early visits to the stadium when I was still a young hopeful playing for Nacional in Uruguay and wondering if I would ever play in Europe. She was by my side when I could finally accept and talk about everything that had happened at the World Cup. And she was by my side as I signed for Barcelona – ten years after I had first left Montevideo aiming to join her in Catalonia's capital, I'd finally arrived. It is only right that in telling my story, I should start with her. How we met, and how wanting to be with her first brought me to this city ten years ago.

THIS IS A LOVE STORY 1

It was raining hard and Sofi was absolutely drenched. I was bone-dry and happily playing arcade games inside. How was I to know that she would wait outside the shopping centre where we had arranged to meet for our first date?

Sofi's parents were out of town, taking her brother to play a football match, so I had suggested we take advantage of their absence. She had been waiting outside at a bus stop for me in the sunshine, but the storm clouds rolled in and it poured down. The only phone was on the other side of a busy dual carriageway with traffic lights that meant you had to wait an age to get across. She crossed over to call my house to ask what had happened to me and got soaked in the process.

She spoke to my sister who told her: 'No, he's not here. I think he's gone to meet his girlfriend.'

So not only did Sofi think she'd been stood up, she thought she had been stood up by some scoundrel who already had a girlfriend.

The girlfriend of course was her. It had been love at first sight.

We met through a mutual friend who also played for the youth team at Nacional – the biggest club in Montevideo. I used to say hello to her dad in an attempt to make a good impression. I think she thought: 'Why is this strange boy saying hello to my dad all the time?'

I had spoken to her at a disco before but the shopping centre was our first date. Finally, she came inside to dry off and I appeared, innocently asking where she had been and why she was so wet.

The storm had been so bad her brother's game had been cancelled and when she spoke to her sister a bit later she was told: 'Get back quickly, they're on their way home!'

She was only thirteen and I was just fifteen. More than a decade later, she is my wife.

I was a lot less shy back then. She used to get embarrassed that I would go straight to her mum's fridge as soon as I arrived at her house. Or when she and her mum came back from shopping I would peer into her mum's bag asking: 'Did you buy anything for me?' She thought I was cheeky. Luckily for me, her mum thought I was charming.

Not only did Sofi know me when I was a lot less shy, she also knew me when I had nothing. She lived outside Montevideo and I used to have to ask one of Nacional's club directors, Wilson Pírez, for the forty pesos (about £1) it cost to make the forty-kilometre round trip to see her. If Wilson wasn't around I would hassle another director, José Luis Espósito, for a loan to fund my courting.

I'd look for unofficial bonuses before games, saying to them: 'If I score will you give me twenty pesos?' That would be enough to get me there; I would worry about getting back when the time came. Usually, they would laugh and give me the money and I would get on a bus from Montevideo to Solymar where she lived. I had to find the money from somewhere. I couldn't ask my mum and I certainly couldn't ask my siblings, though sometimes, if she had a little bit more money than usual, my older sister would give me the fare for the trip.

Wilson and José Luis were very good to me. I still speak to both of them and what I most value about our friendship is that they have never asked me for anything in return for all the favours they did me.

Then there was a local man who collected old telephone cards and if you had some then he would buy them from you, so I would keep my eyes peeled, checking all the phone booths for these cards and then sell them to him. Sometimes my mum would collect them for me.

It would have been easy for Sofi's parents to reject this little rascal. When my daughter is thirteen, if she brings home a fifteen-year-old boyfriend who looks like he might be from the wrong side of the tracks I might not take so kindly to him. Not only did they seem to accept me, they actually appeared to like me. When Sofi's father went away for work I would help her mother out with jobs around the house such as lighting the boiler. Sometimes Sofi and I would have disagreements and her mum would defend *me*. I suppose they valued the effort I put in just to see Sofi. Here was this kid from Montevideo who couldn't afford the bus journey to Solymar, but he always found a way to see their daughter. I think they realised I would have walked if I'd had to. There were days when I had the money to get there but not enough money to get back and so I used to hitchhike home in the early hours. I had to be at training at Nacional the next day after all.

Sofi saved me from myself. Before I met her I had got into the habit of staying out late and not worrying about training. Sometimes I would turn up still tired and not in the right frame of mind. I always regretted it, especially when team-mates who hadn't gone out trained better than me and ended up in the team at my expense. But I always fell back into the same habits. In the season when I was thirteen and fourteen years old I only scored eight goals in thirty-seven matches and Nacional told me that they wanted to let me go because they knew that I was going out at night and I was not behaving as I ought to. It was Wilson who persuaded them to give me another chance and sternly told me not to waste it. Sofi showed me another way. Without Wilson and Sofi, my career might have ended right there.

My friends would meet up in the street or go to the local disco and I wanted to do the same. I knew it was damaging but when you're a teenager, just a kid, you're not aware that you are at a crossroads in your life. The fact that I was able to choose the right path owes so much to Sofi; if I had not met her I don't know what would have happened to me.

By the time I reached my sixteenth birthday I was totally focused on my football. I used to play on Saturdays and I would stay at Sofi's house on Saturday nights and spend Sunday with her. If I had not met her I would have been out, mixing with people who I shouldn't have been mixing with. I might have done very different things and ended up a different person.

Sofi's world was very different to mine. I had been forced to leave Salto, a smaller town with wide open spaces, for the city at the age of seven and then lived through the separation of my parents when I was nine. I was on the street a lot of the time. Between where I lived in Montevideo and her home lie some of the roughest neighbourhoods in Uruguay. When we were both a little bit older we would take that bus journey together and she was surprised that I knew those parts of the city only too well. She would say: 'But how do you know these places?' When I was younger I would be walking those streets with my brother as we went to and from training.

My mum, Sandra, accompanied us whenever she could but she was busy working as a cleaner at the local bus station in Tres Cruces. My father, Rodolfo, would go to some of my games but he couldn't go to any of my training sessions because he had to work long hours too. He was a former soldier who, having left the army, had to look for work wherever he could find it. He worked in the local biscuit factory and then later as a concierge, sleeping in the apartment blocks where he worked when he had no money for rent and nowhere else to stay. I know my parents had it tough and I value all that they did for me and my brothers and sisters. But it was an anarchic upbringing at times and Sofi's life seemed so much more stable and structured by comparison.

I had never really studied either. I went to school but that was as far as my commitment to education went. I was a terrible student. I never paid attention and I never wanted to learn; I couldn't be bothered. I just misbehaved.

Sofi would say to me: 'How come you're still in the first year of secondary school?'

I had had to repeat the first year twice and so I was two years older than everyone else in my class. In the end I had to go to night school to catch up. I would train in the afternoons and then I would go to study. At least at night school I was the youngest instead of being the oldest. Sofi couldn't understand it. She had come from a world where you *had* to study. She used to help me with my homework and she would say: 'But you're not stupid, you're just lazy! You can do this!' It was the first time someone had encouraged me. My mum did all she could but she had a house full of children to care for.

I would come home from school and she would say: 'Did you study?'

'Yeah.'

What was she going to say? There was no time for further questioning.

Sofi wanted to help me. She wanted me to see that life was full of opportunities. Life wasn't just football; you could study as well. And she didn't just advise me to study; she *made* me study. I had to show her my homework. She was bright so she was able to correct me. I was embarrassed when it came to schoolwork, having fallen so far behind, and she helped me overcome that. I was discovering another world, one beyond selling telephone cards for my bus fares and staying out late. I started to study harder under her guidance. What I really wanted was to earn more money so that I could look smart for our dates and buy her gifts too.

I didn't just want to be able to travel to see her, I wanted to take her a present from time to time. And while it wasn't quite a case of having just the clothes on my back, I certainly didn't have the latest fashions.

At Nacional, players had to get to the stadium so that they could then be taken by bus to the training ground forty-five minutes away and if you lived far enough away from the stadium then the club paid your bus fare. I tried to pull a fast one, saying I had moved away so that I could get free transport to and from Sofi's house. It would have been perfect – my travel to and from Sofi paid for by my club would leave me with some money to spend on her. The scam failed, though.

The struggle to see her was about to get much worse with the news that she was moving to Europe to start a new life.

I was devastated.

It felt like my world was falling apart, and not for the first time; everything was being taken away from me again. Moving away from my childhood friends in Salto and from the countryside to the big city where I knew no one and where the other kids would laugh at my strange accent was hard enough. To then have the family torn apart by the break-up of my parents in 1996 was almost more than I could take. We could feel that things were falling apart, breaking down. Now this. My family knew what I had found with Sofi and my mother appreciated what her family had done for me, looking after me, and helping me to stay on the right track. They knew how I would suffer when she went away.

Her dad worked in a bank in Uruguay that closed down in the crisis in 2002 and because he had a brother in Spain he said: 'Right, let's go there.'

They went to Barcelona in October 2003. Sofi was everything and everything was taken from me. When I said goodbye to Sofi at the age of sixteen I thought it was the last time I would see her. The day before she left, her house was packed with friends and family and we took a stroll to get away from everyone. I remember us standing at a bus stop and me saying to her: 'I can't believe I'm never going to see you again.'

There was no way she could stay behind and live with me. Her mother had said: 'You can study something and if you get a qualification then you can go back to Uruguay to be with Luis.' She asked around to see what was the quickest thing to qualify in and they said hairdressing, so she decided she would study to become a hairdresser. It was never what she wanted to do but she was smart enough to know that it was the fastest track back to Uruguay to be with me.

I cried the day she left. She gave me an exercise book in which she had written the lyrics of songs and I read them and sobbed. I thought it was the end of our relationship and the end of my world. How was I going to be able to go to Barcelona from Uruguay if I could hardly raise the funds to go from Montevideo to Solymar?

From now on it would no longer be about scraping together enough money to visit Sofi by gathering up telephone cards; it would be about scraping together enough money to call her on the telephone.

A month after she left, she called me to tell me how sad she was feeling and she said: 'If you don't come at the end of the year, we won't see each other again.' She said I had to do all I could to get there; I had to try everything.

Thanks to my agent at the time, Daniel Fonseca, I was able to visit her. Of all the players that Fonseca had I was his least important but he still paid for the trip and my older brother gave me about $60 to travel with. I had no idea how little that was. I was sixteen and it was my first big trip to Europe. I travelled in December 2003 with this money burning a hole in my pocket, feeling like the richest man in the world. It didn't last long but at least I now knew, during that first New Year's Eve together, what I really wanted to do with my life and my career.

I wanted to play in Europe to be with Sofi.

● ● ●

There is a team in Uruguay called Liverpool FC. They play in Montevideo. The club was founded in 1919 at a seminary and the students there named it after the English port because the boats carrying coal that used to arrive in the city had come from Liverpool. Before the 2005/06 season they even changed their away kit to all-red as a further tribute.

In 2006 some representatives from the Dutch club Groningen came to watch a Liverpool striker by the name of Elías Figueroa. They stayed an extra day and watched another striker, a nineteen-year-old called Luis Suárez.

It wasn't that this 'Suárez' was a little bit further down on the Groningen scouts' list; he wasn't on *any* list. Grads Fuhler, the scout, and Hans Nijland, the director of sport, spoke to people in Montevideo and everyone they spoke to told them how good this Suárez was. Having come so far, they felt that they had nothing to lose. They were there in Uruguay, there was a game on, the flight wasn't until the next day. They might as well. It was chance but it worked out perfectly.

'No, we want this other player,' the Groningen delegation told their hosts when they were asked about Figueroa. They had only seen me play one game and it was hard to invest in a player on that basis but they had seen enough. The one game in question had been Nacional against Defensor Sporting. We were fighting it out for the title and I put in my best performance of the season, scoring a goal. I had no idea they were watching me and I'd never heard of Groningen but I knew it was closer to Barcelona than Montevideo was.

Playing so well and scoring such a good goal in front of scouts who weren't even meant to be watching me was just the stroke of luck I needed. I felt I had earned it too.

It had been a long hard road through the youth ranks at Nacional. I had survived that career blip when it seemed they would be letting me go because I wasn't sufficiently focused. But for Wilson Pírez's intervention, they probably would have done; but for Sofi I probably would have wasted that second chance. But they were there for me and my form after that was good enough for me to be called up to join pre-season training with the first team when I was just sixteen. That call came in the middle of that first trip to Spain to see Sofi.

Wilson had known me for a long time, both as a player and as the kid who wanted to borrow some money to see his girlfriend. He was the father of another boy in the Nacional youth system and having seen something in me he had become determined to guide me in the right direction. It was Wilson who rang to tell me that Santiago 'El Vasco' Ostolaza, who was the coach at the time, wanted me to join the pre-season. Sofi couldn't believe that I had come all that way and would now be going back again ahead of schedule. I said to her: 'I have to go; and when I'm in the Nacional first team I will have more money than ever before to come and see you.'

Having flown all the way back I ended up taking part in just three days of pre-season before going back down to the youth team, but I wasn't going to complain – this was just an indication of how tough it was going to be.

The following year I was called to train with the first team again, but this time I stayed with them. In March 2005, aged seventeen, I made my debut in the Copa Libertadores, playing fifteen minutes. Then when the league season started in August I played and scored after just five minutes. Sofi was there to watch me because she was visiting for her birthday. That season I got used to playing in Nacional's first team but the explosive form that would get me my move was still some way off.

At first, I missed chances. Lots and lots of them. It reached the point where people insulted me and whistled me. They called me *pata pala*, club foot. Others called me a *burro* or donkey. The coach, Martín Lasarte, defended me, saying the work that I did on the pitch was brilliant even if I didn't score. He told the supporters to be patient and encouraged me not to let my head drop. I started one game against Atlético River Plate and we created thirteen chances and I missed nine of them. It finished 0-0 and of course I got the blame – the kid who ran around a lot but couldn't score.

The good thing was that I always thought that if I was wasting chances it meant I was at least creating them. I always had the mentality to keep on chasing, looking for the opportunities. I didn't want to be missing the chances in my head because I hadn't even made the run. The lower my head drops the more I fight to lift it up again. I think at the time most people thought that I was going to be just another average player. Even now I meet people who say to me: 'I used to insult you, I used to shout at you, I was one of those people who thought you were never going to score any goals.'

But I had scored a big goal that night against Defensor Sporting and in front of the Groningen scouts. Now I was off to start my European adventure – not that it is ever as simple as just turning up at your new club and signing on the dotted line.

First, I travelled from Montevideo to Madrid with my agent Daniel Fonseca and another of his players, Juan Albín, who was being moved to Spanish club Getafe. We had to stop there for a couple of days until Juan's deal was finalised. I had travelled with no guarantees and that made it seem like the longest flight I had ever taken. Normally, I sleep on flights; that time, not a wink.

Then came the waiting. Sofi had taken a job in a McDonald's in Barcelona and she almost quit so that she could come to Madrid to see me. We had not seen each other for six months and we were now so close, almost within touching distance. She tried everything she could to get the time off but they wouldn't let her. Eventually, she had pleaded so much that they said yes. By then, though, there were no flights available. Meanwhile I was in limbo, staring out of a Madrid hotel window, waiting. Finally we travelled from Madrid to Amsterdam and the move to Groningen appeared to be getting closer.

You're totally at the mercy of others in those situations. In Uruguay they had said: 'Travel, you're going to sign.' And so I had travelled blind. Groningen had been the only option but there was now some new problem. The closer the deal got the more agents seemed to be involved, the more hurdles seemed to appear. I was told by my representatives that the signing wasn't happening because the club didn't want to make some payment or other. As a young player it's hard to keep track of who's who in a transfer. There are agents, and this guy and that guy, and the problem seemed to be with these other parties and not with Groningen. My representatives now seemed to be saying the deal was off.

'Luis, we've got to leave.'

'What do you mean "we've got to leave"? Where are we going?'

They told me not to worry and that there was a chance of going to Getafe instead with Albín because their manager, Bernd Schuster, was looking for another striker. That sounded even better: it wasn't Barcelona, but I'd be in the same country as Sofi. And if we were leaving Holland and heading back to Madrid now, then I could even arrange to see her. But no sooner had I started thinking about that possibility than things changed again and that door was slammed shut, too. Finally, I got my move to Groningen.

It had been six anxious days in total – in hotel rooms, first in Madrid and then in Amsterdam, with nothing to do but watch the telly and listen to the clock ticking. Stuck, nervous and unable to speak the language. In Amsterdam, I was sending messages to Sofi asking her how to ask the hotel to wash my clothes or how to get something to eat. She sent me back two messages: one with my request written in English and the other with the phonetics so I would know how to pronounce it. I was reading 'ies plís' and trying to say 'yes please'. I didn't understand the messages and in the hotel they didn't understand me. In the end I just had to hand them the phone and let them read the texts. I was helpless; completely reliant on other people and trying not to think about the worst scenario: the deal falling through and having to go back home, back to square one, back to a different continent from Sofi.

At the time I thought that either I signed for Groningen or I wouldn't make it at all. I think Nacional had sold me to my agent which would have made him my new owner. So if I hadn't signed for Groningen I don't know if I would have returned to Nacional, or if he would have done everything he could to sell me to another club. I would have gone to any club, so long as it meant coming to Europe. And I don't know what I would have done if for the sake of 60,000 euros the deal had not been done. During those days I was powerless, my whole life in someone else's hands. Finally, on the road from Amsterdam to Groningen in the north of the country, it began to sink in that there was now nothing to stop the transfer going through. It was a huge relief.

It was July 2006 and I'd made a small step up in my career and a huge step closer to Sofi, albeit not quite as close as I had imagined: one of us was in Spain and one of us was in Holland. So now we had to bridge that gap too. I went to Barcelona on holiday to visit Sofi for ten days after I signed and we talked about how we would try to resolve the situation. Her mother and sister were back in Uruguay at the time visiting family. I called them to say: 'I'm taking her with me from Barcelona to Holland.'

Her mum said to me: 'Well, if you are, make sure you look after her.'

I'm not sure she realised I was serious. I'm not even sure if I knew how serious I was. But when we were saying goodbye to each other at the airport, I was overwhelmed by a sense of 'now or never'. I had come all this way, I didn't want to leave her now. Not for a moment.

'Come with me,' I said. 'Now.'

'You're mad. How can I just come with you? I'm sixteen. We don't even have tickets. What about my dad?'

'Come with me now. I can buy the ticket.'

She phoned her dad right there and then in the airport and she said: '*Papá*, I'm going to Groningen with "*Salta*".'

(*El Salta* was my nickname, taken from the name of my home town, Salto.)

Her dad said: 'Okay, when are you coming back?'

She wasn't. She was only supposed to be staying until the following week but she ended up staying for good. And now she was boarding a plane, just like that. She had no bag, no clothes, nothing. We went and bought a ticket and she travelled with me just with what she had on – she went back to Barcelona a week or so later to get the rest of her things. We were together at last. It was a gamble but it just felt right. It was that feeling of saying goodbye at the airport again after so many other good-byes and thinking: 'Right, we've waited long enough, we have to give this a go and we have to give it a go now.'

● ● ●

Holland was a wonderful football education for me; it was an education in life too. And Groningen was the beginning of that education.

When you are in Uruguay, you don't have people on top of you, guiding you. You don't have people controlling what you eat and drink. I arrived in Holland five or six kilos overweight. I was *fat*.

The coach, Ron Jans, who still ranks as one of the best that I have ever had, said to me: 'Your target weight is 83 kilos – any heavier and you won't be in the team.'

I didn't know anything about diet so I asked people at the club how to go about losing the weight.

The first thing I did was stop drinking cola. I did not understand that drinking cola could have such an impact. Sofi suggested that we started to only drink water and I got used to it. Now I can't drink anything else.

When they weighed me the next time I was 83.4 kilos and Ron let me off that point four of a kilo. He said that he had seen that I had set about the task and tried to do the right thing.

That's when I realised what I had to do to make it. And that is also when I learned that I could do it myself; I didn't need anyone on top of me. I could set targets and work to them on my own. I had that discipline.

When we first arrived in Holland, neither of us knew how to cook. Ronald McDonald was our friend and I bought this electric grill to cook steak on. The house would fill with smoke. At the time, we thought the steak was great, but looking back on it, *madre mía!* How did we eat that?

Sofi already had better eating habits than me and living together seemed to make those habits rub off on me. She also got me house-trained. I was used to living with my mother and my sisters and they would make the beds and tidy the house. Now in Holland we were in it together and I had to take responsibility. We would split the cooking and the chores and we grew up fast together. Groningen was a city of 200,000, around 50,000 of which were students. Everyone went everywhere by bike. So did we, a lot of the time.

We also had a crash course in basic finance, learning the difference between 'net' and 'gross' the hard way. When I signed for Groningen I thought: 'You're going from Uruguay to Europe, that's your economic situation resolved for ever.' But of course that wasn't the case. I was nineteen, I didn't know what was going on.

There were things that the people negotiating the contracts had not told me. They never said *this* was net and *that* was gross. I thought the *gross* was what I was taking home and they let me think that. Wrong. I got played. I felt conned.

And of course the family thinks you're going to Europe and you're going to be a millionaire. When I went to Groningen they thought I'd be the richest man in Uruguay. I have never told them what I earn and they have always respected that but there are people who surround the families of footballers and they are much, much worse. Your family knows where you've come from and how you've struggled to get there, the sacrifices you have made, but the people who try to take advantage of you don't care about that.

The man who explained the difference between net and gross to me, and much more besides, was Bruno Silva. Bruno would be our salvation at Groningen in those first few months. I remembered him as a Uruguayan international and as a player for Danubio – one of the third teams in Uruguay along with Defensor, behind Nacional and Peñarol. We used to get together to watch games from the Uruguayan league or we would meet up for family barbecues. We couldn't find any Uruguayan steak so we managed to get hold of some Brazilian meat instead from a Brazilian who had played for many years in Groningen called Hugo Alves Velame. He was coaching in the academy at that point and he was someone else who was great with Sofi and me, becoming our translator whenever we had to deal with the club.

Bruno told me what he knew about Groningen. It was a club in mid-table that was trying to establish itself in European football having qualified the season before for the first time in fourteen years. They had an impressive new stadium that held 22,000 and they were financially solvent so I was always going to get paid on time. It was lucky for us that Hugo and Bruno were there; they made things so much easier. The three of us and our families would get together on a regular basis. They both helped me on the pitch and their families helped Sofi and me off it too. The way they treated us was incredible, especially when you think that we turned up as kids who didn't have a clue about anything. They had no way of knowing I was going to make it either; their support was entirely unselfish.

When I arrived Bruno wasn't playing because he was injured. Sofi asked him if he usually played in the first team and when he said he did we were star struck – someone who played in Groningen's first team? Wow. Everything was an adventure.

Like any good Uruguayan, Bruno loved his *mate* (pronounced 'mah-teh'). I started drinking *mate* very occasionally in Uruguay when I was eighteen or nineteen, with my dad or my team-mates. But once I left Uruguay I became more Uruguayan than I had ever been before. It's hard to explain exactly what *mate* is. I always told people at Liverpool that it's like a bitter green tea that we add hot water to and drink through a metal straw. Whenever you see a group of Uruguayans you'll probably see one of them with a flask of hot water, pouring it into a small cup, sucking from a straw and then passing the cup on to his friends. With Bruno we got used to taking a lot of *mate*. I didn't know too much about what we call '*cebar el mate*' which is to 'load up' the *mate* cup. I didn't even know how to heat the water. I learned a lot from Bruno.

He was twenty-seven when we arrived and I can remember him blowing out his cheeks and telling me: 'I don't have long left of my career.' I was thinking how far away I was from being that age, and now here I am telling this story aged twenty-seven.

Becoming more Uruguayan than ever after leaving the country extended to religiously watching my beloved Nacional and the Uruguayan league games. At first I would say: 'Right, at eight o'clock I'm watching the game so I don't want to be disturbed.' Gradually, I got used to not seeing all of the game, though, until I was happy just to check the results. Bit by bit you disconnect. It's sad in a way, a little part of you slipping away, but it's inevitable.

When the Uruguayan Sebastián Coates first arrived at Liverpool, he would say: 'No, at eight o'clock I can't do anything else because I want to see the game.' And I would say to him: 'It won't last.' I knew; I had been through the same process.

I'm still in contact with Bruno. He's a very important person for me. He is back in his home town of Cerro Lago now, and still playing, but prior to that he would follow me to Ajax. I went in August 2007 and he joined me the following January. They asked me about him before signing him and, of course, I spoke warmly about him and told them how much he had helped me at Groningen. It wasn't just him but his family too.

Then we played together in the national side. I'm not going to claim Bruno played for the national team because of me, but when they asked me about him I told them what a very good player he was and the coach, Óscar Tabárez, had a look at him and brought him into the squad. Bruno appreciated the way I gave him a good reference but that was nothing compared to everything he did for me in Holland and the way he helped me in things that I never imagined someone who had known me for such a short time would do.

When I joined Liverpool, Bruno was having a difficult time after a shoulder operation in Holland that went badly wrong. He said he 'went up to heaven and came down again', that's how bad the operation was. He jokes about it now but it was a big concern at the time. There was an infection and because of the complications he was in real danger.

Bruno knows me as well as anyone in football. If ever I say to him: 'Did you see that goal I scored?', he'll say to me: 'Calm down, kid, I remember what you were like in your first week in Holland.' He still sends me messages from time to time saying things like: 'You should have put more curl on that free kick.' He also taught me a lot about Uruguay because, leaving Salto so early, I grew up in Montevideo and as he lived in Cerro Lago he was more from the country. So Sofi and I learned about what people were like outside of the capital.

It's difficult to make true friends in this game but Bruno is definitely one of those that I have made along the way. And he still treats me the same way as he did when we first met at Groningen. I prefer it that way. I value the friendships that I have from the time when I was trying to make a name for myself in the game.

Dutch football was great. The games were spectacular, the stadiums were wonderful and gradually I started to find my way on the pitch, albeit only after a spectacular fall-out with the manager. It was September 2006. We had a UEFA Cup qualifying game against Partizan Belgrade and we lost 4-2 over there in the first leg. I scored a goal having come off the bench for the last fifteen minutes. In the return game I played from the start, but with the score at 0-0 Jans had taken me off midway through the second half. We were going to be knocked out. I left the pitch in a mood. I didn't like being taken off, and it was raining. I was also not used to the convention in Holland that you have to shake the manager's hand when you go off. I did a gesture as if to say: 'No way am I shaking hands with you.' I threw my hand up in anger. He furiously threw down the umbrella he was holding at my lack of respect. It broke.

So it was my fault it was 0-0, it was my fault that his umbrella was broken, and it was probably my fault that it was raining too.

The show of dissent upset everybody but I did not have to wait too long for redemption. The following weekend we were playing Vitesse Arnhem and we were winning 1-0 before they turned it around to make it 3-1. Then we pulled the game back to 3-2 after I won a penalty on eighty-two minutes. I scored the next goal to make it 3-3 with a minute left and it seemed that we had salvaged a point, but there was more to come. In injury time, another cross came in from the right and was headed back across the six-yard box to me. I took a touch with my right foot to send the last defender and the goalkeeper the wrong way and hit the ball into the roof of the net with my left for what was the winning goal. The place went wild.

One of the traditions at Groningen was that whenever you won a game you had to go around the pitch, applauding the fans. The game was at home, it was my best performance since arriving two months earlier and, with the fans celebrating and the cameras all focused on me, Jans came out and handed me his umbrella. Everyone knew what had happened the week before because it was all they had been talking about in the build-up to the game. I jigged my way around the lap of honour holding the manager's brolly and with a huge grin on my face.

After the game there was a meal at the club and the directors who had come to see me in Uruguay told Bruno Silva they were breathing a big sigh of relief. It was starting to look as though the money they had invested in me was going to be worth it. They had taken a huge risk and now it was paying off. Remember, they had only seen me play one game in Uruguay. The umbrella game changed everything. I started playing more, everyone seemed happier with us, and we were happier with our new life. The early days, when I had been out of shape and out of the team, were gone. The Groningen fans had been incredible with me and I was now giving them something to smile about.

Off the pitch, I started learning Dutch to further integrate myself into Dutch football. On the pitch, I had to learn something that was similarly alien to me – not going down in the area as soon as I was touched.

Football in Uruguay is different. In Uruguay if they touched me, I went down and everyone accepted that. They expected it. At first in Holland I was getting penalties that weren't penalties. But then I started not getting the penalties that should have been awarded. It would be that way later when I moved to England. It wasn't that I dived in the sense of inventing fouls; it was more that if I felt the slightest touch then I went to ground.

I learned to adapt and the adapting would continue in the Premier League. I had to: the manager even asked Bruno to have a word with me to tell me that I couldn't dive and talk back at the referee so often. It just wasn't done here. I was different to what they had been used to.

I started learning Dutch to speak it in training sessions and because the Dutch themselves really appreciated the effort. I would do interviews in Dutch. Whether they were good or bad was another matter, but it mattered to them that I tried. I should probably have learned English instead as most foreign players do, certainly in the bigger cities of Holland. It would have helped me handle certain situations I would later face at Liverpool. But I chose Dutch and it's still nice from time to time to surprise someone from Holland who would never believe I might speak their language.

It took a while for the lessons to really start to take effect and so to start with I didn't understand anything. Ron Jans would tell Bruno Silva, who would then explain things to me. I remember in one game, I was playing very badly and when the coach said something to me at half time about how badly I was playing, I said: '*Sí, la concha de tu madre.*' It's a very rude Spanish phrase that makes reference to someone else's mother.

'Not my mother, your mother,' Jans replied in perfect Spanish.

It seemed the communication barriers were coming down on both sides.

I played alongside Erik Nevland who later played for Fulham and he was a massive help. The Norwegian striker was the star of the team at the time but he helped me no end on the pitch, much as Steven Gerrard would later do at Liverpool.

I also have to thank Groningen for putting me on the international stage and the radar of the national team coach who called me up to the senior squad in February. That was incredible for me. When I moved to Groningen I thought I would be forgotten about; I would have no chance of getting into the squad because I didn't think anyone knew anything about the club back home. When I first heard about their interest in me I got straight on to the PlayStation with my brother to find out what players they had and there was no one either of us had ever heard of. If you say 'Holland' to a Uruguayan then they will say Ajax, Feyenoord and PSV. And the rest don't really register, not even AZ or Twente, who have both won the Eredivisie, the top league in Holland. Groningen would have been in there with the teams that I had never heard of in my life such as NAC Breda, Roda and RKC Waalwijk – teams I couldn't pronounce, never mind tell you anything about.

If I had never heard of Groningen, I assumed the technical staff of the national team would not have either. But I was wrong. I started seeing on the internet: 'Luis Suárez scores for Groningen.' And I thought: 'Well, if I can see it then there will be people in Uruguay who will also be able to see it.' And there I was, nineteen years old, playing for Groningen and being called up by Uruguay. In the last few minutes of my international debut I got sent off in a friendly away against Colombia for a second bookable offence, for dissent. I had been protesting some of the decisions and eventually, in the eighty-fifth minute, the referee Jorge Hernán Hoyos lost his patience with me. Tabárez was not happy but I had made my international debut and Groningen had helped me do that.

The club were happy with me too, and I wanted to repay that. I don't usually make promises about how many goals I'm going to score, but when I was presented to the fans in the middle of the pitch having signed my contract the chief executive asked me how many goals I was going to score in my first season. I was just a kid, it was my first transfer, and I had been put on the spot. What was I going to say? I plucked a figure off the top of my head: 'Fifteen goals . . .' I said, before making a joke to try to back myself out of it: 'Fifteen goals . . . but across the next five years.'

But we settled on fifteen and, incredibly, by the end of the season I'd hit my target. I scored twelve during the season, and we finished in the play-offs for places in Europe for the following season and that meant two more games. After scoring two more in the play-off semi-final I got another in the play-off final to give me my fifteen goals.

I was playing so well that the country's biggest clubs had taken notice and decided I was the striker they needed. Of course in that situation you have a sense of loyalty to your club but your greater sense of loyalty has to be to your own career and when Ajax came in for me it was an opportunity that I did not want to pass up.

The move from Groningen to Ajax proved to be very difficult. I had to fight to get out. Groningen bought me for €1.4 million and Ajax were offering €5 million. I was going to earn about six times more than I was earning at Groningen – and, of course, by now I knew the difference between net and gross.

In Holland there is a rule that states that if there is a bigger club that is going to play in the Champions League and will pay you double what you are currently earning then your club is obliged to accept the offer and sell you. Ajax were going to be paying Groningen more than three times what they had paid for me. In theory Groningen had to let me go, but they wanted to take the case to the Court of Arbitration. My agent told me: 'They don't want to sell you, they are trying to be clever.'

So I had to go to court and listen to my lawyer present our case. The problem was that Ajax still had not qualified for the Champions League proper.

Jans said to me: 'Luis, they don't want to sell you but I am trying to help you.'

I told him that I was missing out on the opportunity of my life with the biggest team in Holland wanting to sign me and I think he understood.

'Yes, I know but it's the directors; they don't want to let you go.'

It was about a five-day wait for the Court of Arbitration to make their decision. In the meantime, I had to carry on training at the club. You can imagine what the fans were saying to me. One morning they told me that I had lost the case. I had two training sessions ahead of me and I just couldn't move, my head was gone, my thoughts elsewhere.

'Luis, don't you want to train?' asked Jans.

I told him that, no, I had no desire to train after receiving the news. I didn't feel like doing anything. I felt sunk. I just wanted to go home and cry. I couldn't believe what the club was doing to me.

That was when the club's technical director Henk Veldmate said to me: 'Get yourself home and don't worry. I'm going to sort it all out for you and you are going to be allowed to leave.'

I went home at midday and by five o'clock in the afternoon my representative Fonseca called me to say: 'Luis, everything is sorted – for €7.5 million they are going to sell you. You need to get yourself to Amsterdam.'

Then I had a phone call from a director of Groningen who said: 'Luis, congratulations, you're going to Ajax. Thanks for everything.'

They'd only been fighting for the best price and now they had it.

In Holland whenever a player leaves, the club gives him a special send-off so the supporters can say goodbye. Of course 'goodbye' wasn't exactly what they wanted to say to me. They were shouting 'huurling' ('mercenary') at me, accusing me of only going for the money.

The truth was that I was going because I wanted to be a success at the biggest club in the country, but people were burning my shirt and the scarves and banners that had my name on them. There would be no special send-off match for me.

When I came back to play for Ajax against Groningen the following season, in April 2008, feelings were still running high. The supporters organized 'anti-Suárez' T-shirts and were still shouting 'huurling' at me. There were banners and flags against me with dollar signs on them.

Bruno had also left to join Ajax by this point and he said to me: 'Ufff, this is going to be difficult.'

At Groningen's ground the bus usually leaves players at the main gate of the stadium and from there you walk to the entrance and down to the dressing room. This time they had to park the bus inside the outer perimeter, otherwise we might not have made it from the bus to the entrance in one piece.

In the warm-up the fans were insulting me and there were banners everywhere. As we ran out on to the pitch at the start of the game there was a sudden crowd surge and people started pouring on to the pitch because fires had been started in the stands. A lot of paper had been thrown along with some fireworks and some of the paper had caught fire. Soon some of the plastic seats were on fire too. There was black smoke billowing out and panic took hold. Twenty people were injured. We had to get ourselves into the dressing room as quickly as we could, and there were also quite a few Groningen supporters who had the same idea.

The corridor to the dressing room was full of upset fans shouting: 'Luis, Luis why did you have to leave?' Then they started asking me for photographs and autographs. They had gone from causing fires in the stadium and insulting me to wishing me luck and asking for a souvenir. It sums up the passion of the fan – to have all that rage and then, in a second, it changes.

Sofi was at the game with her dad and couldn't believe the scenes. In the end the match had to be postponed and played four days later. I scored but I didn't celebrate. I scored goals in the three or four games against them after that. When I scored at home I did celebrate but still in quite a restrained way. The Groningen supporters had been incredible to me in the beginning and I was grateful to the club for bringing me to Europe.

Feelings towards me had changed towards the end, but that was to be expected. When I had first arrived at the club I had to go back to Uruguay to get some papers signed. Sofi was left for four days in Groningen on her own in the apartment we had in the centre of town. She didn't know what to do with herself so she went out and bought some albums and the most recent newspapers to start a scrapbook of photos and match reports. She kept on filling them up during my time at Groningen, though it's a good job she started it at the beginning of my time there because the stories weren't so nice towards the very end.

In Groningen there was a big statue of what looked like a chicken in the centre of town. When we had just arrived I used to joke to Sofi that they would end up replacing the chicken with a statue of me. That wasn't quite how it worked out. Instead they ended up burning my shirt. And yet, I had passed an important career landmark – my first club in Europe. The club I had joined to be closer to the love of my life. When I was a kid two things saved me: football and Sofia Balbi. In 2007, we were off to Amsterdam together, where we would marry and have our first child; and where I would go on to captain one of the greatest clubs in European football.

THE DUTCH SCHOOL 2

'No, no, no! Are you mad, Luis? Don't mention that ever again. We don't do that kind of thing in Holland.'

It was nearing the end of the 2009/10 season – my last full season at Ajax – and if we won our final game and Twente lost theirs then we would be champions. The idea occurred to me that we should offer the team that had to play against Twente a win bonus.

It was just an idea and nothing more and I certainly wasn't suggesting paying anyone to lose. That would be fraud. This was just offering an incentive to the opponents of our title rivals. But the response was emphatic. The Dutch and Uruguayan mentalities are not the same and I quickly discarded my idea.

Twente won their final game against NAC Breda. We beat NEC Nijmegen and I scored twice to make it 35 league goals in 33 games for the season. I had also made it to a century of goals for the club.

But we had fallen short of winning the league for the third season running.

I was desperate to win the Eredivisie. It was a great period of my career at Ajax. The supporters were brilliant with me from the very first day. Sofi and I were happy off the pitch enjoying life in Amsterdam, and on the pitch all that was missing was the league title.

Losing out in 2010 was especially tough because the manager Martin Jol had shown so much faith in me by giving me the captaincy and it would have been the greatest way to pay him back. He had been like a breath of fresh air after Marco Van Basten's time in charge.

Jol's style was not unlike my first coach at Ajax, Henk ten Cate. I would have liked Ten Cate to have stayed for longer, but he moved to Chelsea to become their assistant manager when I was barely into my first season. He had brought me to the club and that made me feel that he trusted me. He had come from Barcelona with a philosophy that suited me. I felt comfortable in the first games for him and he also spoke Spanish, which made things much easier when I arrived in 2007. I signed on a Friday and the paperwork didn't come through in time for me to play in the Dutch Super Cup that Saturday but the following Tuesday we had a Champions League qualifier against Slavia Prague and he didn't hesitate to put me straight in. I scored on my league debut and on my home debut and it was just a great start under a manager I instantly clicked with.

With the Ajax supporters right behind me from the start, grateful for the way I had pushed for the move while at Groningen, I felt very much at home. And with a manager I could relate to I made a very good start. I also quickly became good friends with Gabri who Ajax had signed from

Barcelona and who I would later be reunited with in Spain, because he is now coaching Barcelona's B team.

Gabri had played under Ten Cate and Frank Rijkaard at Barcelona and told me the two coaches were alike in terms of how they wanted their sides to play. Had Ten Cate stayed I think we would have worked well together but by October he had had an offer to become assistant coach at Chelsea under Avram Grant and so he left. It was a shame – I had lost a coach I was developing an excellent relationship with.

Adrie Koster came in until the end of the season as interim coach and we just missed out on the league, losing our last match. He was a very calm and straightforward manager and that was a good season for him to mature and grow as a coach. I learned under him, but I didn't feel quite so much support, technically, as I had with other coaches.

Ajax went for a big name at the end of my first season. It was July 2008 when the club appointed Van Basten. I went on to score 28 goals in 43 games under him that season, which was an improvement on the 22 in 42 in my first season, but we would only finish third and the chemistry between me and the man who should have been my dream coach was just never right.

The prospect of being coached by someone who had been a great player – one of the best strikers there has ever been – was exciting and the first impressions were good. He was very strict as a coach and I liked that. If he had something to say, he didn't hold back, and he had everyone very focused from the beginning. But as the weeks went by I realised his methods were not for me. He was very rigid tactically and I did not always fit in to the system he wanted to play.

He was especially keen on us doing group activities to bring the squad together during the week. The way I saw it, we had to be united on the pitch; there was no need to obsess about being united off it. It felt forced. It felt like he was asking too much from us.

I didn't agree with his methods and he knew I didn't. He also knew that I was not the only dissenting voice in the dressing room – there were other players who also would rather have been at home with their families than 'bonding'. One day we went to an art workshop to paint together. The only unifying feeling that created was: 'What are we doing here?' We all felt the same way, at least.

I was on the same flight as former Ajax team-mate Dario Cvitanich recently and we got talking about those days and the things that Van Basten made us do and how half the time we wanted to curl up and die. It was incredible.

During these 'art classes' we would have random words thrown at us and we would have to paint whatever came into our heads. There would be five or six of us there trying to find our inner Van Gogh. It was just the wrong sort of Dutch Masters for me. I didn't get it.

We didn't win the league that season but there was still no let-up in this idea that you could force a group spirit on the team by getting them to do things together off the pitch. I remember when there were just three weeks left of the season and AZ Alkmaar had already won the 2008/09 title. Van Basten sent us out on a treasure hunt . . . yes, a treasure hunt.

I was in a team of five crammed into a Citroen 2CV and we were driving around Amsterdam looking for magical mystery clues while just thirty-five kilometres away AZ were celebrating winning the league. The contrast said it all. They win, we drive about in tiny cars.

There were just some things that I really didn't understand. I can make light of it now but it upset me at the time.

My relationship with Dennis Bergkamp was better. He came in from time to time as an assistant and he would join in the passing drills with us; he was fantastic to watch and to train with. I grew up watching Dennis for Arsenal and he was a wonderful player. I also remember him scoring one of my all-time favourite goals against Argentina in the 1998 World Cup; controlling the long ball forward and getting the better of Roberto Ayala, cutting inside with a sublime touch, to score and knock out Argentina.

Being a twenty- or twenty-one-year-old kid and playing alongside him was incredible. Frank de Boer was there as well and when they got the ball out and started playing, it was something else. I could see that these were guys who were on a different level. Van Basten was as well, of course, and he would join in the football tennis too in the early days. But it didn't feel the same; there wasn't the same warmth or ease to the way he acted. Our relationship deteriorated as time went by and, oddly, the more goals I scored the worse it seemed to become.

It was eventually suggested to me that one of the reasons why Van Basten didn't like me was because I was coming close to breaking some of his scoring records. I remember not being picked in one Europa League game when I was on the verge of overtaking his European goals tally. Maybe it wasn't the case, but I did wonder whether it was more than just a coincidence. The supporters loved me and I was doing my job

– scoring goals. But he would always focus on the things that he thought I wasn't doing well. We never had a big falling out; I just never really understood his attitude towards me and we just didn't seem to connect.

Perhaps it was also because I was not a typical Ajax player with a nice, even temper? I picked up a lot of yellow cards that year and he became frustrated with that. Maybe it was a personality clash? Or he didn't like the way that I played the game? He liked neat, tidy football, technical and thoughtful. I was much more the kind of player who would go at people, who wanted to take everyone on, chest out, refusing to stop, always going forward.

I never had any real conversation with him and so I never found out the truth.

I was talking to some of the directors and they told me things about the plans he had for me; there was a suggestion that he wanted to sell me and that hurt.

What I do know is that it was a missed opportunity. I would have liked him to have helped me more as a player. If you are a striker and Marco Van Basten tells you how to do things then of course you are going to listen. You'll do what he tells you. He knows. I would have loved to have learned more from him and had a better relationship but it seemed there was another agenda. Things fell into place for me a little bit more after he left.

● ● ●

Sometimes the trials of adapting to another league are exaggerated. That, at least, has been my experience. To a certain extent I played the same way in the magnificent Amsterdam Arena as I had done on the streets of Montevideo. But it is also true that there are little differences and that if you want to keep on improving you do have to take them on board and learn. For example, I became a better trainer at Ajax and also a less chaotic player during matches. I learned to be much more intelligent; to *think* about the game. In Uruguay we would be out on the training pitch for two and a half hours with thirty minutes of that taken up just with running. I arrived at Groningen and there would be sessions of just an hour or seventy-five minutes. At Ajax things were even calmer.

I learned that you have to train well, but 'train well' did not always translate simply as working hard; intelligence was as important as intensity. And, besides, the most important thing is the match itself. I learned to put more order into my game. When I first arrived in Holland I would run all over the place for ninety minutes. If I felt like pressing then I would go and press. I would hunt down the ball on my own if necessary. I learned to temper that a little and play more to the needs of the team. Tactically, I improved.

The coaches at Groningen would say to me: 'No, no, Luis, stay where you are and let Erik Nevland press. And then the next time when he sits, you go and press.' I learned to wait for the right moment. You would always get a shout from the midfielder: 'Now!' And then you would press. The central midfielder would be the player giving the order and you would follow it. There was no point in going it alone; you would just tire yourself out for nothing. Instead we coordinated the moves, choosing our moments carefully.

I also preferred running forward to running back. Klaas-Jan Huntelaar was the number 9 at the time so I would play to the left or the right of him and of course the wingers in Ajax's 4-3-3 system have to track back and follow the rival full-backs when they go forward. If the opposing full-back ran forward seven times in a game I would probably track him once. I used to tell the coach that I couldn't track back because if I did I wouldn't be able to attack with the same energy. At times that could cause problems, and with Van Basten it probably did, but sometimes there was a compromise. Some of the coaching staff even ended up coming down on my side and saying: 'Luis, don't go following their forwards, you stay high up the pitch and save your energy for making sure you take your chances.' But I was learning to think about what best suited the team at any given moment.

The training methods suited me. You look at the kids in Holland and it is all about the ball. They work with the ball the whole time. If you go to a football school for kids in Uruguay the first thing they do is send them out running. They have seven-year-old kids and they send them out for three laps around the pitch and when they've finished maybe throw them one ball between the lot of them. You can see why such a high proportion of players in Holland have excellent technique compared to Uruguay. Instead, we produce a lot of players who will put their foot in and scrap for everything, as if their life depends on it. It's not easy developing fantastic technique if, aged seven, you turn up for training and they send you out for a run.

I noticed the difference in pre-season as well. For many years a Uruguayan pre-season would last a month and for twenty days of that time you would be running on the beach with sandbags strapped around your shoulders or charging up steep banks of sand until your legs were like tree trunks. Sometimes I would be sent out for a long run the day before a game and think to myself: 'How am I going to run today and then play a match tomorrow?'

But that is how it was: running and weights for twenty days of pre-season.

At this point, I should own up and admit that I'm not the best trainer. Mario Rebollo, the number two with the national team, nicknamed me '*Gruñón*' ('Grumpy', as in Grumpy from the Seven Dwarves) and the name has stuck. I'm always the one who says: 'What, we have to go for a run?' But then I do the run. Or we are told to do thirty repetitions on the weights and I'm the one who pipes up: 'What, thirty?' But then I do the thirty.

I'm still Grumpy today, but no one can ever say, 'Ah, look at him, acting the big star,' because I've always been a moaner. All my coaches will testify to that.

At Ajax, I found a method that I was more comfortable with: match-orientated training sessions suited me far more than some of the sense-less slogs I had endured before. There was also a slightly more relaxed attitude to gym work. I don't like being obliged to do gym work. The way I see it a player knows his own body better than anyone else. At Nacional I would say: 'I can't today because I did it yesterday.' That never worked and there was no way of getting on the exercise bike and just going through the motions because the fitness coach would be on top of us telling us what exercises to do and with how many repetitions. At Ajax no one forced me to do gym work. Being guided but also trusted to judge for myself and choose what was best for me was something new.

At Ajax, the ball was what mattered – the ball and passing it well. And you didn't only pass it if you couldn't run with it or shoot, which had pretty much been my attitude before. Instead, you passed it because passing was, they said, the right option. It lay at the heart of everything they did there. It was hard for me to fit into that idea at first. I liked to fight for the ball, turn and get a shot away. That was my game. At Ajax there was adaptation on both sides. They started to get used to the way I played, but I had to change and improve too to fit the system.

I would stay and work on my weaknesses: my left foot; my jumping; my shooting. I still do that now. I want to keep on improving. I could have gone to Holland thinking: 'I've scored a lot of goals, I'll just carry on doing what I have been doing up until now', but I have never liked to settle for that or to look back on what I've done. I have seen a lot of players make the mistake of thinking that they have already made it – often encouraged to think that way by getting a big bonus at too young an age. I even saw it at Nacional in Uruguay. There were players who, at the age of sixteen or seventeen, lost sight of the value of money because they were suddenly earning a relative fortune in the first team. Three or four years later the players who have made steadier progress, gradually earning more as they move up through the ranks, are thriving, and the kid who got the big pay-rise is now playing for a second division side. It's too much too soon.

I saw players at Nacional go up to the first team and they would buy a car with the pay hike – not as big a car as the Dutch players when they 'made it' at Ajax, but a car all the same.

I used to say: 'Ah, I see you've bought a car!'

'Yeah, yeah, I've bought a car,' the player would reply.

'And does the car have a bathroom?'

The priority for me was always a roof over my head. And once you have a home then you can have a car.

Of course, a lot of the kids at Ajax had the car and the house with a bathroom. For many of the players who were around my age-group, daddy was there to buy them whatever they asked for. It was a world away from what I had grown up with in Uruguay. I had never been able to say to my parents, 'Can you buy me this?' and expect them to be able to do it. I couldn't get a pair of trainers, let alone a car. But while that seemed like a problem, it might have been a good thing. It might have helped me make it. If Daddy is buying everything for you off the pitch then why run your guts out on the pitch during the game? There were players who didn't give everything because they had it all so easy.

It is not just Holland. That's my example because that is where I played but I imagine it is the same in many other places. The hunger makes a difference and if you don't have it because you have been spoilt then that shows on the pitch. The hunger to want to succeed had got me to every single loose ball in Uruguay before the other guy. Even now, I can't bear the thought of wasting a second of any game. If the ball is going out for a throw-in in the eighty-ninth minute, I'll chase after it. That's the way I see football and it's hard to watch players giving up a ball for lost that I think they can reach. I had that desire inside me and I never suffered gladly those who didn't. When Martin Jol replaced Van Basten as Ajax manager I finally felt I had a coach who was on the same wavelength.

and Jol said he liked the way I carried the team forward and he told me I was capable of doing the job. It wasn't an easy decision because lots of people thought that he would give the armband to a Dutch player such as goalkeeper Maarten Stekelenburg, or to Jan Vertonghen who was another strong candidate. But he took me to one side in training one day and said that he was thinking about giving it to me. He saw from my reaction that I was not going to be afraid of the responsibility in any way and after a pre-season friendly he announced to the rest of the team that I would be Ajax captain for that season.

I was extremely proud. I was proud enough just to play for the club; I never thought I would end up with the armband. I never lost sight of the importance of the team and I certainly didn't suddenly feel superior to anyone else. I was not going to change the way I spoke to my team-mates just because I had the armband but I felt the added responsibility and it inspired me.

Martin improved my game too. What most defines me as a player is my instinct. They used to say at Nacional that I would still be able to score if you blindfolded me – it's the way I feel the game. Martin knew how to develop that. He corrected aspects of the way I played and made me slow down at certain moments in a game. Sometimes I would try to do every-thing and he told me that I had to try to stay calm because I was driving the rest of the side crazy. There were spells in games when my team-mates needed calm, not perpetual motion. But he didn't want to take that away from my game entirely; it was what made me the player I am.

Jol changed the formation, switching to a 4-4-2 that suited me better instead of Ajax's traditional 4-3-3. I had to be the reference point at the top of the eleven and give the team what it needed in any given moment. I found it difficult then and I still find it difficult sometimes, but as time goes by I have learned that there are moments when you have to just think for a second longer than you would otherwise do. Martin helped me do that.

There were responsibilities that came with the captaincy. Before going out on to the pitch at Ajax the captain has to address the team – in Dutch, obviously. I had continued to make progress in learning the language, but this was tough. Before every game I had to give the team-talk. I had to think of something to say to try to inspire the rest of the side. Jan Vertonghen always had a good laugh at my expense saying that he knew exactly what I was going to say every week, because I always said the same thing.

But it was working.

In May 2010, we won the Dutch Cup, beating Feyenoord 2-0 in the first leg and then 4-1 in the second leg at their place, where I scored twice – the first after just four minutes, which effectively killed the tie as it meant Feyenoord needed to score four, and the second right at the end of the match which meant I ended up top goalscorer in the tournament. I lifted my Ajax shirt to reveal Nacional's colours below. The Dutch Cup Final would often be played in Feyenoord's stadium in Rotterdam and the Super Cup curtain raiser would usually be played in the Amsterdam Arena, but with concerns about so many Ajax supporters travelling to Rotterdam it was played over two legs, giving both sets of supporters the chance to see the game in their own ground. This made it even better because we were able to beat them twice. My team-talk, as Vertonghen would say, was the same both times: we play with our hearts, we give absolutely everything we have, and most importantly, we win.

After scoring two goals, to be able to lift the trophy as captain in the De Kuip, Feyenoord's stadium, in front of around 10,000 travelling supporters was very special. It was probably the peak of my time at the club although winning the Player of the Year vote was also very special and a surprise because Ajax had not finished as champions – we were second, behind FC Twente – and I was a foreign player which seemed to make it even more of an achievement. The award was given on the basis of ratings awarded by match reporters after every game throughout the season. It was an accumulation of positive verdicts on my performance, so it showed the consistency I had found under Jol. Despite not winning the league, his decision to give me the armband had been vindicated. I had notched 49 goals in 48 games in all competitions, the most that I'd ever scored in one season, and had driven the team on as he had wanted.

Things seemed to be getting better all the time, but the following season came the worst moment of my time in Holland.

It was during injury time of a goalless draw against PSV Eindhoven that I had the argument with Otman Bakkal. The referee had just sent off my team-mate Rasmus Lindgren for a foul on Ibrahim Afellay. There were several players arguing. Bakkal had stepped on me and I bit his shoulder. I actually put my arm around him when the final whistle was blown and said sorry. We left the pitch together but the damage had been done.

Jol backed me as much as he could. One paper called me a cannibal but he tried to make light of the incident by calling it a 'love bite'. He also understood that I had been frustrated. He knew that while that didn't excuse my actions, it at least helped explain them. I don't think he felt I had let him down, more that I had let the club down. It was not the image the captain should be projecting. Especially not at a club like Ajax, so proud of what it represents.

The club fined me, which of course I accepted without complaint because they had every right to do so. Subseqently, I received a seven-game ban from the Dutch Football Association.

Soon, it got worse: having drawn the PSV game 0-0 – our third game in a row without scoring – there was no let-up in our dismal run and not long afterwards Jol left the club. We were third in the table, just six points behind first-placed PSV, but the expectations raised by the previous season were not being met.

Despite my ban I was allowed to play the last group game of the Champions League against AC Milan. Our fate was already sealed – we were lodged in third place, four points behind second-placed Milan, and with no hope of qualifying for the knockout phase, but it was a sign of what might have been if I had stayed playing under Frank de Boer, who had taken charge following Jol's departure. I set up the second for Toby Alderweireld and we won 2-0. Frank was from the Barcelona school, like my first Ajax manager Henk ten Cate, and the style he wanted us to play was ideal for me.

He was tough but fair, never more so than when he wanted to talk to me about my situation and about what had happened with Bakkal. Jol had given me permission to go to Uruguay after this game. Frank told me he didn't agree with the decision to let me go on what could be seen as a holiday after what I had done because he felt that the ban should be a punishment. But he said that because Jol had authorised it, he would respect the decision of the last manager.

One decision he would be taking himself was about the armband – he told me that he wanted a Dutch captain for the team which I completely understood and respected.

When I came back to training in January I spoke with him again and the relationship was a good one, but then came the offer from Liverpool.

If I had stayed, I know from the way that Frank had dealt with me that I would have learned a great deal and really enjoyed working with him.

● ● ●

Through everything that happened in my three-and-a-half years at the club the fans at Ajax never turned their back on me. As captain, the standard-bearer of the club, I had let them down with the biting incident. Yet, they had also seen that I played to win to the extent that I felt this tremendous responsibility to transmit that desire to win to the rest of my team-mates. There was no excuse for what I had done, but they appreciated that I always gave everything and many felt that I had instilled that winning mentality into the team. They liked me precisely because I was not what they were used to. I had supporters writing to me to congratulate me on how I had played as their captain and I will always carry that in my heart. They sang my name from my first game, and they even sang it after I had left the club. When Ajax were drawn to play Manchester United in a Europa League game in February 2012, I had just come back from my eight-game ban at Liverpool. Around 4,000 Ajax supporters sang 'There's only one Luis Suárez' throughout the game at Old Trafford. When people told me about it I was overwhelmed; it's something I will never forget.

Another reason why the club will always be special to me is because of the way they treated my family. We loved living in Amsterdam. It was a big change from Groningen; it is a much more international city, and one that had a lot of tourists and much more going on. The club advised us that we should be careful when we were out and about – the sort of warning locals might give any young wide-eyed tourists in a big city – but we had a wonderful time. Sofi and I picked out a loft apartment in a converted warehouse on Amsterdam's IJ lake waterfront and, as busy capital cities go, it was a relaxing place to live. Above all, that was because of the attitude of the people. For a player it's perfect because you are at a top European club but away from the pitch there is maximum respect for your personal space. No one bothers you for pictures or autographs if they see that you're with your family. It couldn't have been better.

We also got married in Amsterdam, on 16 March 2009, and if it hadn't been for the club's support – even laying on a private jet for me – I would not have made it to the birth of my first child. I was so proud when Delfina made her 'debut' in the Amsterdam Arena aged two weeks and a day.

Martin Jol had given me a few days off in Barcelona to be with Sofi and the baby and the plan was then to all head back to Holland. Delfina still didn't have a passport, though, and it was going to take fifteen days to get one. So, with Delfina aged thirteen days, Sofi travelled in the car from Barcelona to Amsterdam, driving for a whole day.

'Are you mad?' I asked her. 'Twenty-four hours in the car. With a two-week-old baby?'

'You're there alone and we want to be with you, so we're going,' she told me.

They arrived in Amsterdam the very next day and were both at the ground for the game that weekend.

The Amsterdam Arena is probably the best stadium I have played in. It has all the benefits of a modern stadium, but because of the supporters you can feel the history of the club when you play there. It makes me very proud to think that if those supporters were asked today about the top players that have played for the club they would include my name. In fact, just having been part of Dutch football is incredibly special to me. If my Uruguayan roots taught me to never stop fighting on the pitch, then my Dutch education taught me to never stop thinking.

The reputation Dutch dressing rooms have for in-fighting is misleading because it is more a product of that thoughtfulness. The only dressing room row I was ever aware of was the one I had with Albert Luque when we started pushing and shoving each other at half time over a free kick and were subsequently both taken out of the team. There was not much in it really and the comical thing is that Albert and I were good friends – a Uruguayan and a Spaniard giving a Dutch dressing room a bad name.

The Dutch don't fight, they argue – and what they are nearly always arguing about is tactics. Everyone has an opinion on the way the team is playing and no one is too shy to tell everyone else what it is. In Holland I learned to discuss things more, to talk about them and to argue tactical points. Players are constantly discussing ways of approaching the game. The non-stop tactical debates where everyone has a voice is something that almost never happens in England, for example.

In Holland it would be: 'No, you have to close off the space to the left' ... 'No, but if you play *this* pass, I can then go there.' The goalkeeper would be talking to you constantly too. You can see that it's part of their footballing culture from a very young age. There's always a counter-argument and I think that's enriching. They're always thinking about the game, going through the options, and discussing alternatives.

It is perhaps because of this contrast with Uruguay that going to Holland was the best footballing decision I have made in my life. I improved technically and I made great strides in terms of my football intelligence there. I *understood* the game much better at Ajax. In Uruguay I had always played on the edge and to the limit. I did everything with the accelerator pressed to the floor. Dutch football taught me to put the brakes on and to read the game much better. I feel as though I have had the best of both worlds. In many ways Holland and Uruguay are football twins. Both have spectacularly over-achieved in terms of the sizes of their populations, but they are also at two extremes; their success has derived from almost completely opposite approaches. There are many ways to win and Holland and Uruguay represent two of them, from either end of the spectrum.

In Uruguay, we know that technically we're not the best, but we also know that for desire and balls, no one can beat us. We may be second best in terms of skill, but when it comes to sticking the foot in we always get there first. And we are taught to get there first from a very young age, regardless of who we are up against. They teach you that you have to compete, that you can't lose. That happened to me playing in the back streets against kids that were much bigger than me. I did not care. I went for them; I took them on. I wouldn't let them beat me.

In Holland, you are also taught that you can't lose. But you can't lose because of the way you play. It's not that you are tougher than the other guy or street-smart enough to think about paying your rival's rival a bonus. It's just that you are two passes ahead of him because of how sound you are tactically and technically. They think more, they're more technical and they're more intelligent. We're the opposite: it's what comes from inside with us. I've been nurtured by both cultures and I feel privileged for that.

When it finally came time to leave, I could not have wished for it to be handled better by Ajax. I felt privileged to be given such an incredible send-off. There was no recrimination that I had chosen to go to Liverpool; they were just grateful for what I had achieved while I was there.

They asked me if I could go to one of the matches and I went along with Sofi and Delfina one weekend in February when Liverpool were not playing. At the end of the game I was presented to the supporters. Sofi and Delfina were with me as I went around the pitch on my lap of honour greeting people and kicking footballs into the crowd. There were fireworks and video footage of my goals on the big screen. The supporters even sang 'You'll Never Walk Alone'. Rarely in my career have I been so emotional on a football pitch. It was the goodbye game that I had missed out on at Groningen.

It was a very special day for me and Sofi. Dutch friends told us they had never seen anything like it, with so many people waiting until after the end of the game to applaud me, and that made me so proud. I had experienced a lot of send-offs for various team-mates while at the club, and I had often thought about what it might be like when it happened to me.

I'm someone who likes to keep mementos from my career and I have a lot of keepsakes from Ajax. My house in Uruguay is full of shirts, many of them from my spell in Holland. I still have the shirt from my Ajax debut framed on the wall, and the shirt I wore the first time I captained the club is in the collection too. I kept my entire kit from the day I scored my first Ajax hat-trick. I also kept the full kit when I scored four goals in one game – boots and all. And I have the commemorative boots that Adidas made for me when I scored my hundredth goal for the team.

The memories are very much intact too. I went out onto the pitch against PAOK FC on ninety-nine goals and I had asked the players' supervisor Herman Pinkster, who had helped Sofi and me so much in the early days, becoming a good friend that we would eventually invite to our wedding party in Montevideo, to write a message on the vest underneath my shirt. It read: 'Gracias Ajax por 100 goles'. I had wanted it in Dutch, but I think he was so used to speaking with me in Spanish, that's the language he had written the message in. It didn't matter, a hundred sounded good in any language.

A century of goals for a club as big as Ajax, one with such a rich history, meant the world to me. Incredibly, some fans even started to put me right up there with the best players they'd had: Cruyff, Van Basten, Suárez . . .

It was a shame that while I was at Ajax the great Johan Cruyff was not on the best of terms with the directors and was not going to matches. I ended up meeting him for the first time on a flight from Barcelona to England after joining Liverpool and I was thrilled because he is an Ajax legend and also because of the complimentary things he had said about me: that I had done so well at the club having come from outside of Europe. Now I find myself following in his footsteps as a former Ajax player moving to Barcelona. I'm sure the fact that the two teams share a style of football that owes so much to him will stand me in good stead.

I had scored seven goals in thirteen games before the ban and my departure to Liverpool. That season, the team would go on to win the league. I called Herman at the pre-match meal before the last game of the season. Ajax were a point behind Twente who they had to play at home on that final day. Herman put me on the phone to my good friend Jan Vertonghen so I could give him one of those rousing speeches I knew he missed so much. 'You have to win this title,' I told him. There was a real belief in the squad going into the last game and they duly beat Twente 3-1 to finish as champions. It meant I was given a league winner's medal.

I left the club having scored 111 goals in 159 matches and it had been a great time for me. Not perfect because I hadn't won the Eredivisie in one of my full seasons and because of the ban, but still a wonderful period of my career.

I always say that I would love to go back to Ajax at some point in the future and play for them again because, in terms of my development as a footballer, it was my defining era.

REFEREES

This might be hard to believe, but I actually quite like English referees and the sense of fair play that I found in England.

If I lose a game in Uruguay and you come to shake my hand at the end, I'm off. I'm not going to shake your hand. In England, you were expected to do so and I tried to make an effort, although I admit that there were times when the final whistle went and the last thing I wanted to do was congratulate my opponent. I needed time to calm down first and would rather just get back to the dressing room.

Some people say that the fair play in England is a bit superficial – you kick and insult each other and then at the end you shake hands – but I like it. The game's over, we're not rivals any more.

In the middle of it all is the referee. People say the answer is players becoming referees when they retire but there's absolutely no chance of that: if anyone knows that referees have an impossible job, it is the players. Become a referee? No thanks. They have to be in the right position, they have to take the abuse, they have to make the right decision and they are under constant pressure. He has a hard job. I can miss a clear chance, and if I can make mistakes, why shouldn't the referee too?

And whenever they make a mistake they are in the eye of the storm.

A lot of referees make different decisions depending on the situation they're in . . . and the stadium they're in. Then there are fouls that are always given outside the area and never given inside it.

Referees take on board all sorts of factors even if only subconsciously: where the foul is, who it is. If thousands of people are shouting for a penalty, of course it's going to influence him, that's human nature. For example, if the foul that Samuel Eto'o committed against me at Stamford Bridge early last season had been at Anfield, I think a penalty would have been given. The player knows where he is too: there are some games where you might try to stay on your feet more because you just don't trust them to give the penalty. Not that you're always right. I must admit, I never thought I would see three penalties given against Manchester United at Old Trafford.

I certainly didn't think we would get the one given to Daniel Sturridge. He threw himself down. But then it was such a good dive that even I thought it was a penalty. I saw it and thought: 'Penalty.' But then I also saw how annoyed Nemanja Vidić was, which made me think that perhaps it wasn't a foul. When I saw the replay, I realised that Daniel was about a metre away from Vidić.

I said to Daniel later: 'Can you imagine what would have happened if that had been me?'

He said: 'I felt him touch me,' and started laughing.

Referees have to make decisions like that instantly. It's no wonder they get it wrong sometimes.

At least English referees admit it. Sometimes they even admit it during the game and I like the fact that they talk to you. And that means you can talk to them too.

I remember one game with Mark Clattenberg. He had been a bit quiet in the second half. He had also booked me and I had protested. About five minutes later, he came past and said: 'It was a yellow, you can't say that it wasn't.'

I said: 'Yes I know, it was my fault.'

Then I played the pass for a goal and he came past:

'Different class, Luis.'

Dialogue is a good thing and a bit of fun with the referee does no harm.

Referees are different in England. They call you by your name. Sometimes, they don't give you a free kick and then a couple of minutes later they realise they were wrong and they might tell you so. That happens more in England than anywhere else. My friends in Spain have told me that over here, you can't talk to the referees, so I will have to adapt again playing in La Liga.

In England, they're much more talkative, almost to the point of distraction. When you're standing over a free kick, some would ask you who's taking it or say: 'Don't let him shoot, the last one went miles over.'

Communication helps and is a two-way thing. To start with at Liverpool, I had to rely on gestures to communicate with referees. I didn't really understand anything they were saying to me and I couldn't make my point without waving my arms at them. That annoyed them. I'd start gesturing and they were imagining an insult, even if there wasn't one (okay, sometimes there was). They would gesture back at me, signalling for me to stop and then pull out the yellow card. As I got better at speaking English, it became easier for me to maintain a degree of dialogue with them, to be able to explain my point of view.

English referees appreciate the speed of the game, the tension. Afterwards, they'll say 'well done' and tell you that you played brilliantly, if you did. Deep down, they know that in part you're playing a role: appealing, putting pressure on, trying to gain an advantage.

Over time, you get to know most of the referees, the ones you can joke with and the ones you can't. Sometimes they're friendly and open before the game and then they close up during the game and you get no dialogue with them. But there's no reason why you shouldn't have a perfectly normal chat before the game and after it

Before one match, a referee said to me: 'Last time I was here, you scored.'

You can't remember the goal, but he can. That reminds you that, above all, these guys are football fans. If they weren't, the job would be unbearable.

In England, they're still a bit more distant than in South America, though. I once had a linesman there asking for my shirt after the game. Then you know they're football fans. There's nothing wrong with that. I asked a referee for his shirt once. He'd asked for mine, via one of the club officials, and I said: 'Okay . . . if I can have his.'

He never sent me it. That was a pity. I would like to have had a referee's shirt to wear on my days off.

THE HAND OF SUÁREZ

3

When Uruguay beat Ghana in a dramatic penalty shoot-out to reach the semi-final of the World Cup for the first time in forty years, my heavily pregnant wife watched nervously on television . . . and so did I.

I had been sent off for saving a shot on the line with my hand, denying Africa its first-ever semi-finalist, and now I was in a quiet, virtually empty dressing room at Soccer City, Johannesburg, my pulse racing, barely able to peer between my fingers at the screen. I just had kit man Guillermo Revetria with me there, but I was also swapping text messages with Sofi who was watching the game with her family in Barcelona.

With each penalty, the tension got worse. Then up stepped my idol, Sebastián Abreu. They call him 'El Loco', the madman, and he lived up to his name. It was classic Loco. He dinked his penalty gently into the net.

Incredibly, Uruguay were through. No one had seen anything like this in generations. No one had expected it either.

At the end of Uruguay's first game at the 2010 World Cup finals – our worst performance of the tournament – Sofi had left South Africa for Barcelona. 'Adiós,' she said, kissing me goodbye. 'See you next week.'

'Yes,' I said.

She was seven-and-a-half-months pregnant and she was heading home to her parents' house. She thought I wouldn't be far behind and I thought so too.

The way we had played in that first game against France we looked like a team that would be going home soon. It finished 0-0 and it was awful; we were awful.

The dressing room was quiet after the game, flat. It was hard to take. The fans had been on our backs during qualification and at times there'd been tension but we'd eventually reached South Africa. We had finished fifth in our qualification group and had to beat Costa Rica in the play-off to get there. From October 2007 to November 2009 we'd been fighting for this and we thought we had left those problems behind. But after that first game it felt like we were going to let everyone down. All that work for barely a week at the World Cup.

Then we beat South Africa 3-0 in Pretoria and the confidence came flooding back. We thought: 'If we can beat the hosts and if we can keep playing as well as this, who knows what can happen?' Suddenly we had belief in ourselves. Our World Cup over? It had only just begun.

Diego Forlán scored the first that night and I won the penalty from which he got the second. Their goalkeeper brought me down and was sent off. Then I set up Álvaro Pereira for the third. Next, we beat Mexico 1-0 and I scored my first goal at a World Cup, celebrating by miming a bump in my belly. Both Uruguay and Mexico knew we were through before the game, but winning meant avoiding Argentina, so neither team wanted to lose. We wouldn't be heading home after the end of the first round after all. In fact, we might even be going further. In the end, we were in South Africa until the very last day.

We got better and better. Meanwhile, Sofi got bigger and bigger.

It was a weird sensation for me. I was fulfilling my dream of playing for Uruguay at the World Cup but I was terrified of missing the birth of my daughter and desperate for Sofi to hold on. I missed her too. Sofi normally goes to all my games but she had gone home because I wanted her to have her family around her, doctors too, and I didn't want her to get nervous. That didn't exactly work: I'd phone her constantly and she told me she was having contractions after every game.

Uruguay were based in Kimberley, which was in the middle of South Africa, although we had to change cities after the group stage. There was nothing much there and so the families never came to see us. We were isolated but that suited us fine because we were there to work. We also didn't feel under pressure; expectations were low after the way we had qualified and even more so after the game against France. No one talked about us and that was the way we wanted it.

Near our Kimberley base, there is a big hole. It's actually called that: Big Hole. An old diamond mine, it lives up to its name; it's like a gigantic vacuum. We all went to see that and it's really striking, unlike anything I had ever seen before. Two-hundred-and-forty metres deep and as wide as a dozen football pitches. Our guide told us that it was the biggest hand-dug hole in the world. *They'd dug that by hand?*

We also went on an excursion to see lion and tiger cubs. Diego Forlán reckoned he knew the answer to the trivia question: who'd win a fight between a lion and a tiger? He'd seen a documentary, he said. Apparently, it's the tiger. Either way, I was terrified. They took the cubs out and brought them to us. Everyone was loving it and it was the kind of incredible experience you could only have in South Africa, but I was scared stiff. I sent Sofi a message saying: 'I can't believe this, we're here with a load of lion cubs and some of the others are going up to them and holding them, cuddling them. There's no way I'm doing that.'

'What are you talking about? You've got to get a picture.'

'You're mad!'

'Please, take a picture.'

So I did. But if you see the picture you see that I'm trying to hold this lion cub out of the way. I'm looking at him sideways, my head turned to the other side, frightened that he's about to go for me.

We were also visited by Alcides Ghiggia, who had scored for Uruguay against Brazil in the 1950 World Cup final at the Maracanã. Ghiggia is the only survivor of that team. It's hard to quite do justice to what their victory means for Uruguayans; it's not that we learn about it, it's that it feels like we're born knowing about it. Ghiggia told us stories about his experience. He told us what the *concentraciones* (team get-togethers before games) were like for them. And I thought *ours* were bad. For them, it was like they were locked up in military barracks: they had no contact with the outside world, they couldn't see or speak to their families and they were there in huge dormitories. He said that in the Maracanã they saw people throwing themselves from the top of the stands. These were images Ghiggia would never forget.

Spending time with Ghiggia was unforgettable for us, too, but mostly it was just us, alone. We weren't really able to see much of South Africa; there was no real chance to visit other parts of the country or to take advantage of being there to learn more about its history or culture. That's always the way it is. Footballers go to a lot of places but actually seeing them is a different matter. On one level, that's a pity. And yet, I don't really feel like I'm missing out. When I go to a game, or a tournament, I know that I'm there to work. If I can see something or go on a trip or a stroll, then fine. And if it's an obligation, I'll go. But the truth is that, if not, I prefer not to.

Sofi always says: 'Did you see . . .'

And I say: 'No.'

'What's the city like?'

'Well, to tell the truth, even on the bus going through the streets, I wasn't really looking. I was chatting to my team-mates and I didn't see anything.'

If I want to see somewhere I would rather go with my family and enjoy it properly.

Personally, I hate *concentraciones*; I prefer to be at home with my wife and now with my kids too. I don't see the sense of it: the time passes much quicker for me at home than locked up in a hotel waiting for the hours to tick down before the game. But you have to get used to it. I accept it. And at a World Cup it is different, of course. It's not like you can go home between games and, when you live away from your own country, as I have done since I was nineteen, there's something special about it. We made a Little Uruguay in the middle of South Africa.

I think when you're away from home, you miss the good things and you forget the bad ones. With the Uruguay national team, we'd sit around together for hours, chatting, sharing stories, telling jokes. Or asking Nacho González, who had played at Monaco not long before, how you say *bonjour* in French. He was baffled.

We'd been there for two days and I was in the shower when Sebastián Abreu appeared. I was sharing a room with Martín Cáceres and he was with Edison Cavani. He came in looking confused and said, 'Are you getting hot water?'

'Yes.'

'But how? Mine's really cold.

'It's H for hot and C for cold.'

'Ah, I thought it was C for *Caliente* [hot] and H for *Helada* [freezing].'

I was like: 'Donkey!' We all fell about.

'Don't tell anyone please,' he pleaded. So of course we told everyone.

When it's the national team, especially one like ours where everyone plays abroad – only Egidio Arévalo and Martín Silva were playing in Uruguay at the time – you only see each other every couple of months so it's special. You share a *mate* and you talk, talk, talk; it's a real coming together of old friends. I don't remember a single problem with any player fighting with another or getting upset and I think that was one of the secrets of our success. There were no confrontations and no one thinking they were better than anyone else.

That was one of the things that had always struck me about Uruguay, from the very first day I got called up. Diego Forlán was the star but in the dressing room he was exactly the same as everyone else. Lugano, Cavani, everyone: there's a genuine equality. No one ever thinks, 'I'm better than you.' Never.

It's the same with the staff: they know we're not the typical players who think they're great, strutting around with our chests puffed out. We all come from the same kind of families, that struggled and fought. And if you bring together people whose mentalities and experiences are the same, whose obsessions are shared, you have a big advantage.

We had the hotel to ourselves so we played pool, there were marathon hands of *Truco* (a Uruguayan card game) and someone organised football tournaments on the PlayStation. It got quite competitive and I had a pretty good record.

There would be tournaments on the training pitch too: one day my team lost in the final. Or there would be free-kick and penalty competitions, where the loser had to be everyone's slave for a day. I've served team-mates' dinners dressed in chef's hat and striped apron. Sometimes it's much worse than that.

It was like a family. Aldo – '*El Cachete*' – the chef. Guillermo and Minguta, the kit men. All the staff. They'd be up at five o'clock every morning to make sure that we had everything we needed; they were friends and confessors, a support network. We really appreciated that, like us, they were miles away from their families and they were working much harder than us. We had more responsibility, sure, but they definitely worked harder. When it came to eating and playing games etc., they were part of the group.

The coach was, and still is, Óscar Tabárez: *El Maestro*. José Herrera, the physical trainer, is '*El Profe*'. And Mario Rebollo is his assistant, the one who's closest to the players. He's very old school. He is in his sixties and he does things as he has always done them: it's hard work, fitness-based, and tough. It's like a blast from the past for me, eight years after leaving for Europe and encountering different methods. I tell him, 'No one does this any more', but he doesn't care and you have to get on with it. We have the same coaches with the national side we have had since 2006 and they know what a moaner I am so they don't take much notice of me.

El Profe would organise the sessions: not just training, but recovery too. There was an ice bath every day, which is agony, and he would make us take a *siesta* from two to four. We spent a lot of time sleeping. You'd sleep from midnight to nine, train, eat and then you'd be falling asleep again. Or we'd have an *asado*, a Uruguayan barbecue, in the afternoon.

All of that helped immensely, because I was missing Sofi so much; I was so preoccupied with the pregnancy that I needed something to take my mind off it. Some of my team-mates probably didn't even realise how important their company and their support was for me. The time between games is always long anyway; so far away from Sofi, with the birth getting closer, it would have felt like an eternity without them.

I was on the phone constantly. Always calling, sending messages. I kept saying to Sofi: 'Tell Delfi to wait for me – I don't want to miss this for anything in the world.' Not even a World Cup? But the longer we went on, the harder that was. I was getting as edgy as I was getting excited. After the first game, we thought she wouldn't have to wait long, but this was going on and on.

We got through the group, beat South Africa and avoided Argentina. We were starting to play well and in the game against South Korea we also realised that we had another necessary ingredient going for us – luck. They created a lot of chances after I scored on just eight minutes. They were playing better than us and deservedly equalised. The Koreans were running more than us, they were everywhere, all over the pitch, so quick. They hit the post and we hung on. It was raining and we were playing badly, we couldn't keep up. I was unhappy because I felt I was playing particularly poorly; I'd missed quite an easy header. We weren't comfortable and then, with ten minutes to go, as the rain poured down, came probably the best goal of my international career. Just at the point when we were walking the line between going out of the World Cup or reaching the quarter-finals, I received the ball on the left of the area, dropped my shoulder and curled it, right-footed, into the far corner. I watched it all the way, seeing it bend into the net, and then sprinted off in celebration. It was an explosion.

To see the reaction of all my team-mates embracing me – once they had caught me after I hurdled the advertising hoardings, going mad – and the feeling of having put my country in the quarter-finals was one of the greatest moments of my career. Pure ecstasy.

It wasn't until later that it dawned on me: the win meant that the wait would go on. Sofi was back in Barcelona and staying in the tournament kept me away a bit longer. I think I cried half out of joy of making it through and half out of the sadness and fear of missing the birth of our child.

After the game I did what I did after every game: I reached for my phone. I had always called Sofi immediately after every match, but now that was more important than ever. It was hot in Barcelona and she was there, hardly able to move, suffering in the heat, with this huge bump. Sometimes watching me play had made her so nervous she couldn't speak after the games and her mum and dad would tell me: 'It's okay, she had some contractions in injury time but she's fine now, she's lying down.' And of course she was torn between wanting me to win as always, but also knowing that if I lost I would be coming home to be with her. And if she had found the South Korea game too much for her nerves, how was she going to cope with what was coming next?

What came next was Ghana in the quarter-final and a penalty shoot-out to send Uruguay through to the semi-final for the first time in forty years. After the sending off for having 'saved' a goal on the line, I watched Asamoah Gyan miss his penalty from the entrance to the tunnel. I was in tears, heartbroken, but when the ball flew over the bar, I ran off celebrating. Maybe it had been worth it.

By the time we got to the penalty shoot-out, I was in the dressing room, practically having a heart attack. It was a weird feeling being in this quiet room with Guillermo – the drama was unfolding just through the walls, but we were watching it on a television mounted in the corner, the volume muted. We were in a world of our own. So near, so far.

I had called Sofi before the shoot-out started and asked her how she was. I was crying with the tension of everything that I had just done, but at the same time I was saying to her: 'You stay calm! Stay calm! Don't go giving birth!' And then I said: 'Well, sweetheart, I've got to go because the shoot-out is starting.' And I hung up. But I might as well not have done.

Diego Forlán took the first and scored. I sent Sofi a text message: '*Gol!*' And she sent me a message at the same time: '*Gol!*'

Gyan took their first; this time he didn't miss. He takes a great penalty. Victorino . . . '*Gol!*'

Appiah . . . goal. Silence.

Scotti . . . '*Gol!*'

Then Ghana missed. Mensah missed. And I sent Sofi the next text: 'Come on!'

Then 'Mono' Pereira missed. This was agony.

I texted Sofi again: 'Ciao!'

I put the phone down. That was it, no more phones. It obviously wasn't bringing us any luck and the tension was unbearable.

But then Adiyah missed. We were still in front.

People ask me if, down there in the dressing room, I had a sense of who was going to miss and who was going to score, but it was more a case of willing each player from Uruguay to score. And willing the Ghana players to miss. It's hard to explain the desperation you feel. You feel powerless.

By the time *El Loco* scored the winning goal – and with a chip down the middle, a 'Panenka'! – everything had become a blur.

When he stepped up to take his penalty I froze. I'd seen him score a Panenka before and I had a feeling he might try it again. He was the only player who I thought I might be able to second-guess. I said to myself: 'He's going to dink it. No, surely he's not going to dink it . . . is he?'

And Guillermo says to me: 'No, he can't dink it, no way.'

'No, you're right. He can't chip it. Can he? Bloody hell, I think he's going to dink it. No, he won't . . . he can't . . .'

And of course he did.

Guillermo and I were both so nervous that we'd lost count of the score.

It was only when we saw the players running off to celebrate that we leapt into each other's arms. 'We've won!' And then we started running too and we didn't stop until we reached the pitch. It's a big stadium so we basically had to do the hundred metres to get there, and racing along in boots is risky on a hard surface, but I think it was my quickest sprint of the tournament. Dressing room to pitch in a flash, running blind, slipping, head spinning. We were in the semi-final.

Later I got the story from the rest of the players. *Loco* couldn't bear to watch the four previous penalties that we had taken. He's superstitious about watching penalties, but he wants to know what happened too, what the goalkeeper did, because he knows he's up last. So, after every penalty, he asked: 'Did the keeper dive? Which way did he dive?'

'Yes he dived. He dived to his right.'

And with the next penalty the same: 'What did the keeper do? Did he dive?' And the answer came back: 'Yes he dived to his right again.'

Then: 'He dived to the left.'

By the fourth penalty the others had had enough: 'Just chip it, *Loco*! Don't ask us any more!'

And he did.

Loco has scored a lot of Panenka penalties and he'd thought to himself: 'In a World Cup quarter-final the goalkeeper would never expect that.' It would never have entered my head to do such a thing, but that's *Loco*. And when the ball went in all the players ran towards him apart from the defender Mauricio Victorino who just stayed where he was on his knees, praying. Well, not just him: there was so much emotion on our bench that the reserve goalkeeper fainted. Everyone jumped up as one to run on to the pitch but as Juan Castillo got up, his legs gave way and he fell straight back down face-first. He just crumpled in a heap and was out cold for a couple of minutes. We still take the mickey out of Juan for that.

There were people everywhere. I remember seeing Diego Lugano who was out with a knee injury but who jumped off the bench and sprinted out on to the pitch to join the celebrations. Every step must have hurt, but he hardly noticed. Just like Nicolás Lodeiro, who played the second half of extra time with his fifth metatarsal broken. When I came out of the tunnel and ran on to the pitch, a lot of the players ran towards me and embraced me, telling me that if I had not have stopped the goal we would not have gone through. It was very emotional. There were players crying for what we had done, getting a country of just three million people into the last four of the World Cup.

Some of our critics had called us mercenaries earlier in qualifying when things were not going so well. Some people said we were robbing money playing for our country when in fact it's more likely that we lose money when we represent Uruguay. We had played Peru towards the end of the qualifiers and there was almost no one in the stadium – the football association couldn't give away tickets to fill the ground. And all those insults come back to you in that moment as well. Sofi was there in the knockout games in qualifying when people were insulting me. I was the 'donkey' who couldn't score goals. You want to respond but you know the best way to do that is on the pitch, which was what we did.

We had to struggle to get through, but we fought hard in every game. We had gone from donkeys to geniuses in a couple of months, and to reach the last four brought tears to our eyes. We weren't just crying out of happiness, it was pride at everything we had achieved. We were almost out before the tournament started and now we were in the semi-finals. The injuries, the penalty, the poor performances at the start, the time together, the drama, and the handball . . . all that came together in the realisation that we had achieved something incredible.

Then, of course, I remembered the handball and the fact that I wouldn't be able to play in the semi-final. It hit me. And it was an awful feeling.

People talk about me cheating with the handball, but it all started with a Ghana player going down to win a free kick which should never have been awarded. Then, it looked like it might be offside when the first header on goal happened. I don't know if it was offside, all I know is that, first of all, it wasn't a foul before the free kick and, second, I should never have been anywhere near the goal line. I should have been marking a player. But when the ball goes past me my natural reaction is to get back on the line to protect the goal.

I love saving goal-bound shots when we're playing three against three or four against four in training, throwing myself in front of the ball to stop it – usually, though, it's with my foot or head, not with my hand. With the Uruguay squad, in the days leading up to a game we play *picadito*, a kickabout game of 10 vs.10 but with everyone playing everywhere and each team with one player as the designated 'rush' goalkeeper. That's quite often me and some of the national team goalkeepers have been surprised at some of my saves.

It goes back further: at home in Montevideo I have a team picture in a frame. The team is Deportivo Artigas, the side I played for in Salto when I was about six years old. If you look carefully, you'll see that the goalkeeper in the middle of the back row is me.

I have another photograph of me playing in goal, diving to make a save, during a match a couple of years later. I loved playing in goal. If I hadn't been a striker I would have been a goalkeeper – some people might say that explains the diving.

I've yet to be picked to take over from the keeper in a professional game though. There was a chance once when I was at Liverpool. Pepe Reina was sent off with a few minutes to go at Newcastle in April 2012 and we'd aready used our substitutes. I asked Kenny Dalglish to put me in, but he said it had to be José Enrique. He was right, too, because we were losing 2-0 and I was needed at the other end. But if the opportunity comes again in other circumstances I'd like to take the gloves.

So when I saw that the ball had gone past me against Ghana, I automatically went back to the goal line without thinking about it. I could see our goalkeeper Fernando Muslera going out to meet the ball and one of the Ghana players heading the ball. I was on the line and I kept the ball out with my knee. When it came straight back at me I couldn't believe it and I stopped it with my hand.

There was a team-mate right in front of me so I was thinking: 'Nobody saw that.' But the referee blew his whistle. It's not that Jorge Fucile looks that much like me but he has the same dark hair and we were right there together and he already had a yellow card and knew he was missing the next game anyway, so I turned to the referee and signalled that it wasn't me, it was him. I had to try.

The referee wasn't falling for it. Out came the red card.

I walked off the pitch, devastated. I was crying and the only thing going through my head at that point was: 'We're going out of the World Cup, we're going out of the World Cup . . .' I had been sent off and we were going home. Gyan was going to take the penalty and he had already scored a couple from the spot in the tournament and he had hit them brilliantly, so I was convinced he wasn't going to miss. We had no chance. I reached the tunnel and thought, 'Well, I'll watch it anyway.' I had been walking towards the dressing room, but there in the mouth of the tunnel with a FIFA official shadowing me, I stopped and watched the kick. And then I saw the ball go over the bar. He had missed. And one word came out of my mouth: '*Gol!*'

The feeling, the sense of release, was the same as if we'd scored.

Unbelievable.

Sebastián Eguren came off the bench and gave me a huge hug. A massive great bear hug full of gratitude and hope. I'll never forget it. That was when I realised what I'd done; that was when I realised that the sending off had been worth it. I'd stopped a goal, they had missed the penalty, and we were still alive.

There was a paper in South Africa that called it the 'Hand of the Devil' and ran a picture of me with horns, but I still don't think that what I did was so bad. I hadn't scored a goal with my hand like Diego Maradona in 1986. I had prevented a goal and I paid for it. I would rather be guilty of stopping a goal with my hand and be sent off than seriously injuring someone. I didn't harm anyone. I handballed it, I was sent off and they had the chance from the penalty spot to score. It's much worse doing harm to another player and they send you off, but the injury to the player is still there. Gyan is the one who missed the penalty, but everyone said that I had done something terrible. Or that I had been selfish. But I had stopped a goal with my hand because I had no choice. In fact, it wasn't even a case of making a choice: it was a reaction.

The backstreet 'pitch' in Montevideo where I played every day growing up.
Seen here as it is today from the Lemon Tree End to the Women's Prison End.

Urreta FC, the club where I had my first transfer tug of war. I left for
Nacional after a brief dispute over whether I would give my kit back.

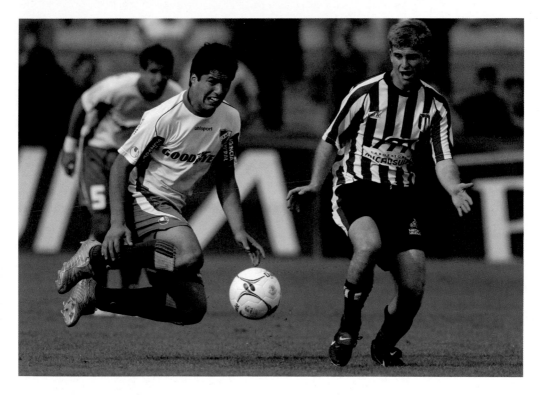

Above and Left: In action for Nacional, the club I had supported all my life; the one that gave me my first professional contract.

Below: My first club in Europe: Holland's FC Groningen. They cheered my goals, then they burned my shirt.

Above: Celebrating a goal against FC Twente.

Below: In the amazing Amsterdam Arena with Sofi and Delfina. The send-off the Ajax fans gave me after I signed for Liverpool, I will never forget.

Going for the spectacular in the famous red and white shirt.

A moment of madness against Eindhoven midfielder Otman
Bakkal that would earn me a seven-game ban.

Winning the Dutch Cup Final against Feyenoord was an Ajax high: one of my famous team-talks delivered in Dutch had worked wonders again.

With my idol and friend Sebastián 'El Loco' Abreu at the 2010 World Cup.

'The Hand of Suarez.' As a kid I had been a decent goalkeeper: the ball came at me on the line, what else was I going to do?

Out comes the red card against Ghana and my World Cup is over. Thanks to the save on the line, Uruguay's tournament can go on.

Receiving my Golden Boot from Martin Jol after scoring 35 goals in 33 games. Few managers have been more influential for me in my career.

Left and Below: Winning the Copa América in 2011 in Argentina was an incredible feeling. It seemed the whole of Uruguay had crossed the River Plate to watch us.

Below: Joining King Kenny at Anfield. With fellow new signing Andy Carroll, standing next to Liverpool's greatest ever number 7.

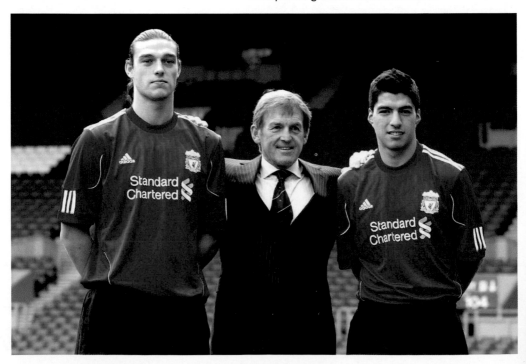

Thanks to the handball Uruguay were in the semi-finals. More than having cheated I felt as if I had made a sacrifice; it certainly wasn't selfish. It was giving everything for my country and for my team. That's the way they saw it in Uruguay. There's a room in my house near Montevideo where some of my trophies and mementos are. One of them, given to me by some fans, is a small replica of a goalkeeper making a brilliant save, with one word scrawled across the bottom: *gracias*.

Sometimes people ask me: 'Would you do it again?' And I come back to the same thing that what I did was nothing compared to injuring another professional. I wouldn't say: 'Yes, I would definitely do it again', but I would say that in that thousandth of a second, pretty much every player in the world would have done the same. It's happened so many times before where the player on the line keeps the ball out with his hand because it's the automatic reaction. He gets sent off, a penalty is given and that is the end of it. But this was the World Cup finals. We were in South Africa. We had already knocked South Africa out and I know the host country was supporting Ghana, Africa's only representative still in the competition. That made it seem worse to people. I wasn't prepared for the repercussions and everything that was said afterwards.

One of Ghana's players, Matthew Amoah, played in Holland for NAC Breda the following season. When we played them, I went to the dressing room beforehand to say hello and to say it was a shame the way the quarter-final had gone, and we wished each other luck for the game ahead. I was sorry for him and for Ghana, but I don't need to feel guilty about what happened. It was no one's fault, really. I would have felt more guilty if I had had to take a penalty and missed it. Or if the referee had not spotted it and not given a penalty and if I had not been sent off. *Then* I would have felt guilty. But I did what I had to do to stop the goal. The referee did what he had to do by sending me off. It was Gyan who didn't do what he had to do.

I sometimes see people from Ghana when I'm in Barcelona and they ask me for photographs. They say to me: 'You are the one who handballed it', and they laugh about it. They don't hold a grudge.

I was going to miss the semi-final but if I hadn't done what I did we wouldn't have been in the semi-final. And of course what nobody really talked about is the enormous responsibility my team-mates had to then score the penalties. Taking penalties in a World Cup finals requires a lot of courage. Our goalkeeper Muslera was incredible. He had studied all of their players and he was in brilliant form at the tournament. He was the hero.

Heading back into the dressing room, knowing that I was going to miss the semi-final, I started thinking about Sofi and Delfi again. I was going to miss our biggest game of the World Cup *and* the birth of my little girl. It was wonderful that Uruguay were in the semi-finals but Delfina was about to be born and I was not going to be there to see it. Sofi was there in Barcelona with the stress of watching me in the World Cup finals, then the red card and penalty shoot-out. And to think that when we said goodbye after the France game we thought it would only be a week until we saw each other again. There were times when Sofi probably half wanted us to get knocked out so I could come home. When we won of course she was really happy, but if we'd lost then it wouldn't have been the worst thing in the world – I suppose she won either way.

The coaching staff helped us focus on what was still to come. 'Enjoy it tonight, but tomorrow we train because in three or four days we have the semi-final.' So there was not much celebration. We knew that there would be time to enjoy ourselves when the World Cup was over, but for now we had to get some sleep. Not that I could sleep much. I spoke to Sofi and tried to unwind, but it didn't help. In those moments, lying awake, I was thinking about the fact that I couldn't play in the semi-final because of the ban and I started to wonder: 'Why did I do that? Why did I handle it? Maybe I could have headed it?'

In fact, when I watched the replay later, I saw that my hands were in front of my face and I thought I really could have headed it clear. If only I had headed it! My arms weren't outstretched. But I had a thousandth of a second to react and I was exhausted from 120 minutes of football.

The semi-final was against Holland, where I was playing my club football. My team-mate from Ajax, goalkeeper Maarten Stekelenburg, had sent me a text when the draw was made. He thought we had a tough group.

'What a shame, you'll be back home early,' he wrote.

'Yes, just like you lot,' I replied.

Now here were our teams facing each other in the semi-final.

I think it was a relief for Holland that I could not play: I was playing well, I knew Dutch football and I knew the players in the Dutch team very well. Or at least I thought I did. I remember telling some of my team-mates that I knew Gio van Bronckhorst, that he was thirty-four or thirty-five and we could let him have the ball because he was getting on a bit. He wasn't what he used to be. So of course he scores an incredible goal from forty metres out. My team-mates said to me afterwards: 'It's a good job Van Bronckhorst is finished.'

As a Uruguayan playing in Holland I would love to have played the semi-final against them. I'm left with that regret, but it's softened by the fact that my team-mates were able to, in part because of the handball. I watched the game from the seats just behind the dugout and it was horrible. I felt impotent. I bit my nails fingernails until they couldn't be bitten any more. It was the feeling of nerves but also of powerlessness. I was so close to the pitch but couldn't do anything to influence what was taking place on it.

I was in the dressing room before and after the game and I was on the pitch before kick-off speaking to some of the Holland players. But I felt removed from it. I watched the game in the stands alongside Fucile, who was also suspended. He had been alongside me on the goal line and now he was beside me in the stands watching the semi-final. That brought back the thoughts of: 'Why didn't the ball go to him on the line? Why didn't *he* handle it?' He could have been the hero and I would have been able to play the semi-final. He was going to miss the next game anyway.

It was even harder because of what was at stake and because Diego Forlán, our best player, was not a hundred per cent fit. I could have helped; they might have needed me. The players who did play were spectacular. Holland were favourites but it was a narrow 3-2 defeat and we fought right to the end as we always do and nearly drew level. It would have been amazing to reach the final but in many ways it was already amazing what we had achieved – getting this far was not something we ever imagined.

We got a sense of how things were back home by talking to our families, through the journalists covering us, and through the media reports. Sofi was telling me how the Uruguayans in Barcelona were celebrating and I thought: 'Well, if it's like that in Spain, imagine what it's like back in Montevideo or Salto.'

Part of me thought: 'Why couldn't they support us like this all the time?' But then I suppose we had not always deserved their support; we hadn't played well in qualifying. Stories reached us of street names that ended in 'Suárez' being changed by supporters during the tournament. They were going round putting a Luis in front of the second name, which made me smile.

The third/fourth-place play-off game probably meant a lot more to us than it did to Germany. It is a strange experience; it's hard but you're playing for the pride of your country. It mattered to me too because I had missed the semi-final and it still felt like a World Cup game to me; I didn't want the handball to be the last thing I did at the World Cup. Uruguay had never finished third before so that gave us something to play for and it had been so long since we had performed this well so we wanted to end the tournament in style. Germany played at half-speed, you could see that their hearts weren't in it, but they were a good side and they still beat us 3-2.

We were playing on Saturday and the World Cup final was on the Sunday. We had to stay until the end of the tournament, in other words. We watched the 2010 World Cup final in the team hotel. You can't help but watch and think: 'That should have been us.' But then you look back on everything we did and it was something to be really proud of. When they named Diego Forlán player of the tournament, it came as a wonderful surprise for us because although he was a star he always behaved like just another player, and we had finished fourth rather than winning the competition. But we were delighted and that award was something that the rest of us shared in. Quite literally: Diego made replicas of the trophy and gave one to everybody in the squad. He had won it thanks to all of us, he said. That trophy was everyone's. It was as if he, and we, had been rewarded for achieving something fantastic and unexpected. Diego deserved it; he worked so hard for all of us.

I didn't really care who won the final. Holland was where I played and I had friends in the team, it was my home at the time, but Spain were playing better football. And Spain was where Sofi was, our second home. I was really pleased for Andrés Iniesta, too – I'd met him through my agent Pere Guardiola, who also represents him, and he's a player I have always admired.

We arrived in Uruguay at night and the next day they'd arranged a parade through the streets of Montevideo on an open-topped bus. From there we had a reception with the president José Mujica, where we were handed medals.

Mujica has always been close to the national team. He's very typical of people from the Uruguayan countryside and his story is fascinating. He's been shot, he's been in prison four times, he's been in hiding. He fought against the dictatorship as a guerrilla and was finally released with the return to democracy in 1985. He told us stories about the time he spent as a political prisoner, about the struggle. That taught him a lot, he said. I could feel my skin prickling as he told the story. I listened to him and it was incredible. Some of the players were really affected by it. He fought and survived during a difficult period in Uruguayan history.

The reception we got back in Uruguay was wonderful and I look back on it very, very fondly. But to tell the truth, at the time I'd reached the point where I couldn't take it any more. Before we travelled to Uruguay, when I was talking about heading straight to Barcelona, lots of my team-mates were saying to me: 'Luis, you've got to be there.' This was a big moment for the country, but I was climbing the walls. The people were really happy and proud of what Uruguay had done and they were grateful to me too because of the handball. My team-mates kept saying to me: 'It won't be right if you're not there.'

They were right of course. And besides, I couldn't have got back sooner. Mostly, I just wanted to get home to see Sofí, but because Spain had reached the final there were no flights left. Loads of people had reserved flights to go to see Spain and then head home again and no matter what I tried, wherever I looked, I just couldn't get a ticket. Sofi was eight months pregnant now, and could give birth any time. That was what I was worried about. Then there were the national team celebrations, so I had to go to Uruguay. I was flying *away* from Sofi.

The parade, with all the people there, old and young, loads of kids, people crying, was just incredible. We then went on the stage and everyone was singing a song inspired by the handball incident:

No es la mano de Dios, es la mano de Suárez,

La puta madre que le parió!

('It's not the hand of God; it's the hand of Suárez, Long live the mother that gave birth to him!')

That was unique, an incredible feeling. But at the same time, I just couldn't take my mind off Sofi. I was thinking: 'I want this to end, get it over with. Quick!'

I finally flew to Spain the next day. I hardly slept and all I could think was 'wait'. When I got to Barcelona and saw Sofi still with her bump, it was such a relief.

There was still time for one more twist. I arrived in Barcelona on 15 July, and on the 28th I had to play in a Champions League qualifier with Ajax against PAOK Saloniki. I'd just got there and now I was supposed to leave again for pre-season training. I phoned the coach, Martin Jol, and said: 'Please, I need some time. Give me ten days here in Barcelona and I can train a couple of days before and play on the 28th. I'm match-fit because of the World Cup.'

He gave me the okay. I spent a few days with Sofi in Barcelona and then went to Amsterdam for the first leg, which we drew 1-1 with me scoring. The return leg was on 4 August in Greece but on 2 August Sofi said to me: 'I've just come back from the doctor and he says that on the 5th I have to be at the hospital at midday. If the baby doesn't come before then they're going to induce.'

I was thinking: 'How am I going to be there by midday on the 5th if I'm playing in Greece on the night of the 4th?'

I went to see the club and told them what was happening. I wasn't playing at the weekend because I had been sent off in the Dutch Super Cup against Twente so I knew that it wouldn't matter if I wasn't in Amsterdam at the weekend. But I still couldn't see a way to be there for the birth because I would be in Greece until late on the evening of the 4th.

That's when Ajax came to my rescue and arranged a private plane to take me straight there after the game. They didn't know if we were even going to qualify for the Champions League, but they set it all up for me and I'll always be grateful to them for that. If I had taken a normal flight, arriving in Barcelona at midday, I would never have made it.

We drew 3-3 and went through on away goals. I scored. I owed them that. And then I made a run for the airport.

I arrived in Barcelona after 2 a.m. I got home around 2.30 and Sofí was there, exhausted. I said to her: 'I can't believe it, tomorrow we're going to have a baby.' We were chatting about it, excited and nervous, and fell asleep at about 3.30 a.m. At 4.30 a.m., Sofi's waters broke.

After all that; after the World Cup, the Champions League qualifiers, the nerves and the worry, the not being there, all the phone calls and messages, the flights and the travelling, the penalty shoot-out, the hand-ball, the parades and the pressure, I'd made it. Just. It had started. Delfina was born at 9.16 in the morning.

She had waited for me.

• • •

Delfi was coming up to a year old when Uruguay went one better and became champions of America — in Argentina.

Uruguay and Argentina are separated by the Río de la Plata, just a couple of hours apart. You can catch a boat from Montevideo to Buenos Aires and that day in July 2011, lots of Uruguayans did. They came across the river in their thousands. It was like an invasion.

A year after the World Cup, we were in the final of the Copa América, up against Paraguay. The match was played at River Plate's Estadio Monumental and it was absolutely packed with Uruguayans. There were more fans from Uruguay than Paraguay, and probably more from Uruguay than Argentina too. They hosted the competition but we had knocked them out in the quarter-finals, 5-4 on penalties.

Uruguay and Argentina don't hate each other but every game between us is a battle on the pitch – very, very tough. I've always had a really good relationship with Argentinians but the rivalry is intense.

We always say to them that all the good things that Argentina boasts about are actually Uruguayan, like the best beef, *dulce de leche*, and even the legendary tango singer Carlos Gardel; they always say that we're just a small town in Argentina.

For the Argentinians, the idea of Uruguay winning another Copa América in Argentina, as we had done in 1916 at the first Copa América which was held on Argentina's centenary, and in 1987, when Enzo Francescoli played up front with Rubén Sosa, was horrible for them. Worse, it took our total to fifteen – one more than theirs. That made the satisfaction even greater for us. The Argentinian media were furious; they thought they would have been favourites. They should have been. But we beat them. And now here we were, taking over *their* stadium and *their* day.

Listening to the fans belting out the Uruguayan national anthem at the Monumental was incredible. It opens with a call to freedom and ends with us singing: 'Heroically, we will fulfil [our duty].' It's a wonderful anthem and not just because I say so: I saw somewhere that it was voted the second best national anthem in the world, after *La Marseillaise*. I get goose bumps when I sing it and when players hear the whole stadium singing, it's very powerful. I think it affects you even more if you live away from home.

Sofi always laughs when I come over all patriotic, but I am very proud of Uruguay. We're a small country, there are very few problems, especially compared to other countries in Latin America. We're a humble country, but a united and very happy one. In 2013, *The Economist* named us Country of the Year. Being away makes me more patriotic and I don't get back there as often as I would like. In truth, I guess I miss things that when I'm there I either don't notice or are not so special as they might then seem from a distance. I remember the good things. And to turn up at the Monumental and see it like that, *hear* it like that, was stunning. Everywhere there were sky-blue shirts. Celebrating in front of the fans was genuinely moving. Some of the banners poked fun at Argentina – one told them the 'right' way to drink *mate*. To win the 2011 Copa América was incredible; to win it in Argentina even more so.

There was a similar feel within the squad as there had been at the World Cup the year before, with the same sense of unity and togetherness. But there were differences: we were in a hotel, not closed off in an isolated training camp, so the families were there with us every day. The time went by faster: there was more going on. All the players' kids would be there together playing. Sofi was there and so was Delfina. I did interviews before the tournament and told people: 'I love the idea of my daughter saying, "My daddy won the Copa América".' And just talking about it made me feel emotional, excited. Motivated too: it became almost like a promise that I had to keep.

We arrived at the tournament in really good shape; confident, fit, ready. We went through the group with draws against Peru and Chile and a win over Mexico. Then it was Argentina, the hosts, and we thought: 'Here we go again.' We'd played South Africa in 2010 and now we faced Argentina at their home. We'd been able to avoid them in 2010 but a year later we couldn't. That's when we felt under pressure; we knew that we would have to suffer and struggle to defeat them.

Uruguay had knocked them out of a Copa América in 1987 and lots of people were reminding us of that, saying it could never happen again. I was determined to prove them wrong. I was really motivated. Maybe too motivated. I was fighting for everything, protesting, sprinting everywhere. Tabárez laid it on the line at half time: 'Luis, either you calm down or I take you off.' I could not carry on playing so crazily, so out of control. By the end of the game I had committed thirteen fouls: I was desperate to win.

In the second half, I was more focused. I played better.

The game finished 1-1, with goals from Diego Pérez and Gonzalo Higuaín, and there had been chances, and disallowed efforts, at both ends, as well as a red card each. Eventually, we went through 5-4 on penalties. Messi, Forlán, Burdisso and I scored. Then Fernando Muslera saved Carlos Tevez's penalty. We went crazy, but we also held our nerve and so did most of their players too. There was a long way to go and the tension grew with each kick. Scotti . . . Pastore . . . Gargano . . . Higuaín – all of them scored. So it was down to Martín Cáceres and he sent us through. Incredibly, we were in the semi-final and that feeling of knocking them out was unreal and the way we had done it summed us up. That was the perfect image of what Uruguay is.

At the same time as we beat Argentina on penalties, Brazil got knocked out by Paraguay and we thought: 'That's it, the Copa América is ours.'

We got Peru in the semi-final. I scored both our goals – two in five minutes – in a 2-0 victory. The first was from a tight angle after a rebound off Diego Forlán's shot; for the second I went round the keeper near the edge of the area, which was an extraordinary feeling – there's a brief moment, before you actually score, when you already know you will; the goal is open and the fans are going mad.

And then came the final. It was the first time the country had got there since 1999, but we were confident that we would win it. Paraguay had played two sets of extra time; unlike the World Cup, the games are every two or three days rather than every four or five; and it was raining. Their legs were heavy and they had played the same players in every match. They were shattered before the final even started and we knew that. We knew we would be better than them physically. As it turned out, we were better than them in every aspect – from the moment we sang the national anthem. They had players going down with cramp, injured, exhausted. They'd made such a huge effort to get to the final. I think they accepted that they couldn't beat us.

I scored the first goal after just eleven minutes, cutting back on my right foot, almost stopping still as the defender went past me, and then finishing with my left. I ran to the other corner, celebrating with the fans at the Monumental. Diego Forlán got two. In twelve months, we had reached the semi-final of the World Cup and now won the Copa América.

You can't help comparing, asking yourself: fourth place at the World Cup or the Copa América? It's hard to decide. The sensations are different. In Argentina, I played really well, scored four, and was voted the player of the tournament. Sofi and Delfi were there too. And we'd won it. Winning the Copa América creates a real sense of history. The World Cup brings you satisfaction too and it may even be a greater achievement, with more international impact, but there's something about that sensation of lifting the trophy and knowing your children can say: 'My dad was champion of América.'

FAME

Sometimes it feels as though I have always been famous. I was the captain of the school team; I was one of the only boys there who was playing Baby Football; I was the one who got chosen to play for Nacional and appear in their centenary celebrations; and when I was eleven years old, I even got to represent the school on a kids' TV show aired on prime-time television. It was presented by Noelia Campo and called Aventujuegos. *And it was a big deal, although I must admit I had no idea that the programme even existed. I was too busy playing football to watch much television, but my classmate Marcos was a fan and he wanted to be on it.*

Marcos was the most intelligent boy in our class and the one who used to watch all these school programmes. He wrote on behalf of the school, applying to be on the show and they wrote back to say he had been successful. The teacher said he would have to represent the class, but the organisers replied that it wasn't quite as straightforward as that. They needed two boys and two girls to go to the studios and take part in what was effectively a trial. There would be a test of the four students and whoever was the best physically would participate in the show.

This meant the teacher had a problem: how to pick the other boy? We had a grand draw. We all had numbers in a big hat and whoever was drawn out would go to the show. My number was picked out – I was the lucky boy. They drew out the two girls and we went along with Marcos for the trial. When we finished the different tests, the organisers said: 'We've decided that physically the one who performed best and who did the tests the quickest, who's best suited to go on the show, is Luis.'

Poor Marcos was devastated. He had been the one who had sent the letter, he was nine years old and he wanted to be on the television. I had robbed him of his moment in the spotlight. He started crying and I felt terrible . . . but not so terrible that I wasn't raring to take my chance to win.

So off I went to the show. One of the games involved a supermarket sweep, where you had to fill a trolley with the things that were on a list given to you beforehand. And whatever you had in your trolley at the end of the game you kept. You could take it all home.

I was thinking: 'This is great, one of those for my brother . . . one of those for my mother . . . one of those for me.' It was brilliant. I ended up with three or four big bags of prizes. And then the teacher delivered the bad news: 'I've decided that all these things should go to Marcos because he was the one who wrote the letter.'

Now I was the one who was devastated.

In the end I understood that I was participating on his behalf and because we had done so well there was a chance I'd be invited back on the show again.

Two days later the programme called to invite us for the next round and

I was determined that the next trolley-load was going to be for me and my family and for no one else. I think I went round even faster the second time than I had the first. I ended up appearing on the show four times. What I grabbed the second time was for me to take home and the next two times what I grabbed went to the school. It was great being on the TV. I told all the family and everyone sat down to watch me. No one was allowed to change the channel. In the overall results at the end of the year we finished seventh out of all the schools that had competed.

That wasn't the last supermarket sweep to end up in the media. There was that photograph of me doing my shopping in Liverpool, coming out of the supermarket with a big trolley full of beer. It was treated like a big deal, like I was living it up, but I wasn't. My family had come over from Uruguay, Sofi's family had come from Barcelona and Lucas Leiva and Philippe Coutinho had their families here too. There were loads of people, forty or so, all coming to our house. Philippe and I had gone out to get the refreshments and, of course, he was behind me with a trolley full of soft drinks and I was in front with the beer. People must have thought: look at the way this guy lives. And I had only just signed a new contract as well.

Not that these pictures always get in the papers straight away: it's not that long since they ran a story about me playing football in my local park with a kid who has Down's Syndrome and presented it as evidence that I had changed, that I was rehabilitated. The kickabout had actually happened almost a year earlier, around the time I was banned for biting Ivanović.

That's the downside of fame: the attention can be overwhelming. You go into the city centre to do some shopping and twenty people come up to you. You prepare yourself psychologically to go to the supermarket: 'Luis, get ready, they're going to be all over you.'

I understand it: I was a kid too and if I had seen a famous footballer I would have done the same. And the good thing in Liverpool was that it's so small that most people had seen me before, so they were kind of used to it. But if I am with my kids and people come over to me, I do feel like I need a little space.

A few weeks before the World Cup, I was at the supermarket for half an hour and twenty-five minutes of that was signing autographs, with Delfi there crying. Sometimes you feel like you can't have a life.

I always told myself that life in another country would be different. Time will tell, but for the first few weeks in Barcelona, there were fans and TV crews outside Sofi's parents' house where we were staying.

Back in Liverpool, it had reached the point where I would go out in a hooded jumper all the time. But sometimes that's even worse. You go into a shopping centre and everyone's dressed normally but then there's this one suspicious-looking guy with his hood up . . .

LET'S GO FOR 7   4

The day I was presented at Liverpool nobody came. I'd just joined the club for £22.8m, the deal had finally been done, and I had started to wonder about the unveiling. I imagined a huge crowd at Anfield, me wearing the red kit out in the middle of the pitch, performing kick-ups.

'I hope I don't make a fool of myself,' I said to Sofi.

I needn't have worried. I was saved the nerves of juggling the ball in front of thousands of fans and all those cameras.

'Come back next week,' they told me. 'There'll be a press conference with Andy Carroll, a couple of questions, a few photos and that's it.'

It would have been nice to have had the full works, but that's not how it is in England. No one gets a full stadium applauding them until they've actually done something. And that's the way it should be.

That's certainly the way it is at Liverpool. There's something about the place. What most struck me about Anfield right from the start is how small and traditional it is. Go into the dressing room and you'll see it. It's not that we didn't have elaborate lockers, it's that we didn't have lockers at all. You'd open the door to the dressing room and find that it's so. . . well, normal. Very basic. There's no luxury. There's a low ceiling, white walls, a long wooden bench that runs round the room painted red, and a Premier League notice by the door about taping up rings and removing jewellery and what time we have to be ready to go out. The physio bench is right in the middle. There is a small television on the wall and a hook for hanging your shirt on. And that's it.

I think it will always be like that. People used to come and visit me and they were always surprised. In there, you're so close together. You're not uncomfortable but you are pretty much on top of your team-mates. I loved that, it motivated me somehow. People might think that they should make it bigger, but you won't find a single player who says that. If you changed it, then it wouldn't be Anfield. It will always be this way.

You go to some stadiums and the dressing rooms are gigantic; you're ten metres from the nearest team-mate and the physio benches are in a different area. At Anfield we were quite literally all in it together. We could all talk to each other and I think that is part of what makes the club special. It immediately felt right to me when I arrived; this was the way I wanted it.

There's no long walk to the pitch either. You're out the door and right there in the tunnel with the opposing team. The visitors' dressing room is even smaller. I've been in there once or twice and I think it's at least a couple of metres smaller. The door is bigger, though. I must admit I hadn't noticed, but apparently the doorframe is deliberately smaller on the home dressing room, which makes the players look bigger and more imposing as they come out. I'm not sure if it works, but it's a nice idea.

There's not much space there to gather before heading down the stairs. The stairs are narrow, barely room for the two teams to go down side-by-side; sometimes you have to let each other pass first. At the end is a door: a plain red door with a little window in it, completely unremarkable except for the fact that one of the most famous grounds in the world is on the other side.

In the dressing room, you couldn't hear the fans because there was usually some music on. The dressing room DJ changed all the time. At first it was Pepe Reina, then it was Dirk Kuyt. Later the idea was that every player picked two songs and it all went on one iPod. The South American players got together and picked a few tunes. I wasn't going to pick too much Uruguayan music, though, because I think they would have chased me out of the dressing room. Then the club signed a new masseur, Pedro Philippou, and he loves music so he took charge.

Sometimes I got annoyed that the music was so loud I couldn't hear myself think when I wanted to focus on the game ahead. Everyone has his own way of preparing for the game and they should be able to follow that without the boom-boom-boom of music.

When we lost or drew then, out of respect, we usually didn't have the same musical accompaniment post-game. Or if we did and I'd rather not be hearing it then I would get up and turn it down or off, much to the amusement of some of the other players. That was the old 'Grumpy' thing coming out, I suppose. But I like to reflect a little after games. If we win and everyone's happy then, okay, put the music on, but even then I would really rather being talking to team-mates about what happened in the game.

Before the match, the sound I loved to hear was the noise of the crowd as the dressing room door opened. It hit you and got louder with every step. And it's not like that just for the big games; it's like that for every game. I always wanted to get out on the pitch as quickly as possible.

It was so exciting to run out in a Liverpool shirt at a full Anfield. To be honest, I suspect it motivated our opponents too, but to do it for Liverpool was something else.

Above the players in the tunnel, of course, is the famous 'This Is Anfield' sign. It was my father-in-law who made me understand just how significant it is when he came to visit and said he wanted to have his picture taken underneath it. He posed under the sign and said: 'This is legendary.'

Sometimes I reached up to touch the sign, sometimes I didn't. When I first joined, I noticed just how many players touched it. With me, it depended what kind of run I was on because I'm superstitious.

So many stadiums are so similar that it's right that things like that should be preserved, that Liverpool should be different. The sense of history at the club is extraordinary. So is the sense of community, the importance of the fans and the idea of togetherness. I don't think there is a club like it. Liverpool is a special city, with a character that makes it different: tough but warm, proud and close-knit. It's especially proud of the Beatles of course: I arrived at Liverpool John Lennon Airport, wondering about the connection. And Sofi will tell you that the Beatles museum is one of the very few museums I've been to. In fact, I enjoyed the exhibition so much I went more than once.

I even got the chance to 'interview' Paul McCartney once. I didn't actually meet him but we did a 'virtual interview' in which we recorded questions and answers for each other. It happened after he had done a concert in Uruguay and mentioned me to the crowd. Before he went to Montevideo a second time, the people organising the tour got in touch and prepared it all. The on-screen 'meeting' starts with us playing at being tour guides.

'Hey, Paul. What things do you recommend for me to do in Liverpool?'

'Hey, Luis. What do you recommend I do in Uruguay?'

I soon found out that he was an Everton fan. Mind you, that didn't stop Liverpool FC – the Uruguayan one, that is – making him an honorary member.

For any player joining Liverpool, it is important to understand the impact that the Hillsborough tragedy had on the club, the fans and the whole local community. That is something that I learned about quickly, although my understanding naturally grew deeper with time. The anniversary came round a couple of months after I arrived and the story was told and videos were shown. The feelings around Anfield and throughout Liverpool in April are powerful and although it is impossible for me to fully appreciate what the families must have gone through, the impact remains huge. The more I learned about what happened the more I could understand why the families feel the way they do and why the fight for justice must go on. The more I admired them, too.

The training ground at Melwood is similar to Anfield. It's much more modern, has recently been redeveloped and the players have everything they need, but there's nothing ostentatious about it. And I can honestly say it's a humble dressing room in every sense of the word: I didn't meet players who believed that they were better than anyone else. I could see it straight away in the way that players spoke to each other, the way they dressed, and the way they treated each other. In part, that comes from people like Steven Gerrard and Jamie Carragher: people who have been at Liverpool all their lives; Scousers who understand what the club is all about. Every club needs people like them. Then there are the staff that have all worked at the club for many, many years. Everyone at Melwood and at the club treats the players so kindly, from Carol and Ann to Ray and Jane. The staff always asked me about the family, about the children: 'When are you going to bring them in?' They made me feel at home, they helped when I was down; it might only be a smile but the value of their emotional support for me and all the players can't be underestimated.

That feeling of community extends to the fans. Sometimes it startled me just how significant the club is in people's lives. That is reflected in the noise they make, the efforts they go to in order to watch the team, the special atmosphere they produce. So special that visiting players know that Anfield is different. Anfield has played a key role in making Liverpool a great and successful club and a collective identity lies at the heart of everything. Reminding the players of that is a way of motivating them daily and trying to ensure that they are genuinely a team.

When you walk through the glass doors into the reception at Melwood, the first thing you see is the European Cup. On the other side is a bust of Bill Shankly, with a quote from him:

Above all, I would like to be remembered as a man who was selfless, who strove and worried so that others could share the glory, and who built up a family of people who could hold their heads up high and say . . .'We are Liverpool'.

Printed all over the walls are photographs and quotes from other players and managers. There are lots of them from opponents too, talking about the atmosphere at Anfield, about how special the fans are there. There are quotes from Steven Gerrard but also from John Terry, Thierry Henry and the following one from Johan Cruyff:

'There's no club in Europe with an anthem like 'You'll Never Walk Alone'. *There's not one club in the world so united with the fans. I sat there watching the Liverpool fans and they sent shivers down my spine. A mass of 40,000 people became one force behind their team. That's something not many teams have. For that I admire Liverpool more than anything.'*

That history is something that people are aware of all around the world. And it is one of the reasons why when they came calling I didn't have to think twice; what I didn't know then but would quickly learn was just how profound the feeling surrounding the club is. Money is always important for any player when he is changing clubs, just as I think it is for anyone changing jobs – you always want to improve your financial situation. But it is never the only factor and it certainly wasn't for me. Aston Villa and Tottenham wanted me too. I think Spurs had doubts about whether I was good enough for them initially, though – I understand that they were leaning towards Rafael Van der Vaart instead – but when Liverpool's interest was confirmed, Spurs got in touch with Ajax and offered the same amount of money. They also told us that they were willing to match the wages Liverpool were offering, but the moment my agent Pere confirmed that Liverpool wanted me, that was that. I wanted to play for them. Financially, I would have been just as well off going to Spurs, but for everything that Liverpool meant in a football sense, for the history, that was where I wanted to go. Time would prove that was the right decision.

The first conversations were with Damien Comolli at Melwood and it was made clear to me that he and manager Kenny Dalglish were both pushing for me and wanted me at the club. Some might have doubted me because I was coming from a league that is considered inferior, but they were not doubts shared by those two and I'll always be grateful to them for the confidence they had in me.

There were people at Ajax who argued that Liverpool was not really a step up at the time: they were not in the Champions League and they weren't in a particularly good position in the league. They knew the ambition I had to be successful at a really big club and they said that this was not that club, even though I was going to be better off financially.

I was aware of the fact that Liverpool had gone a long time without winning the league and that the previous season the club had struggled under Roy Hodgson, but it was not long since they had been in the Champions League final and I also knew about its size and history. And in those first meetings they did not sell me the glorious past; instead, they presented me with the future. I was left in no doubt that the club would be competing to sign top players and that the huge fan base was there to support us as we started challenging for honours. I knew what Liverpool meant and I already wanted to join. Now I was completely sold.

It's always a strange situation when you are waiting for the deal to close. At Groningen I was just about to go back home to Uruguay when it finally happened. This time there was never any doubt in my mind that the deal would go through, but I still had to wait. There were three days of offers and counter-offers. Eventually, I was at home, and Pere called me to say that everything was ready; there were only a few minor details to sort out. It looked like it was done: I was going to be a Liverpool player.

The first thing I thought about was the prospect of playing with Steven Gerrard and with Fernando Torres. All the years playing in Holland and watching those two score goals on television, all the times I had played as Liverpool on the PlayStation, I never really imagined I would be playing alongside those players in real life.

The day I had to travel to Liverpool I wanted Sofi and Delfi to come too, but it didn't quite work out that way. Pere stayed the night with us and we overslept and almost missed the flight. We had to leave Sofi and Delfi at home and go racing to the airport.

It wasn't done yet. There were three or four days when there was no final, official agreement because of differences over the way the money was to be paid but I knew that Kenny wanted me so that made the wait slightly less painful; I never thought there was any chance of things falling through.

I was staying in the Hope Street Hotel and I was basically locked in. Sofi and Delfi had arrived on a later flight. I was there constantly checking the phone for the message that everything was done. I couldn't go out in public or tell the rest of my family what was happening until everything was officially confirmed, but it was a great feeling when on the night of the 30th I finally got the call: I could go and sign. The next day I would have my first training session, and the day after that, make my debut.

When you turn up to your first training session with a new club, it's only natural to be looking at your new team-mates to see what kind of quality there is or isn't in the squad. You're also very conscious of the fact that absolutely everyone is looking at you. You feel like an Egyptian mummy – you only really move your eyes to look left and right! You know that everything you do badly will be seen by everyone. You can sense them saying: 'Uff, look at this one.' In those first few training sessions you feel the eyes of everyone on you. But as soon as you do a few good things, that changes.

At the start, Dalglish presented me to everyone: 'We have a new team-mate. This is Luis.'

I felt a bit embarrassed and even more so when the other players came over and introduced themselves. I think even the biggest names feel that awkwardness on the first day. The welcome was fantastic from everyone, and even if I couldn't actually understand what they were saying to me, the warmth was clear. But it was still a bit strange and I wasn't able to spend any more time with them after the first session, either. That same day I had to go to Dublin to get a work permit. There was no way of getting an appointment that soon in London so we had to travel to Ireland straight after training. The next time I saw my new team-mates was when we were sitting together in the dressing room at Anfield and I was waiting to go down that tunnel and past the 'This Is Anfield' sign for the first time.

● ● ●

Liverpool were going through an upheaval at the time with Fernando Torres leaving and the club negotiating to sign Andy Carroll as well as me. There was a lot of coming and going. I didn't expect the sale of Fernando. The good news was that we were able to move into Fernando's house but the prospect of playing alongside him had excited me, and to never even get to train with him was a real shame. It would have been something to tell my children: 'I played with Fernando Torres.' A lot of supporters have since told me how good it would have been to see us play together. He was a great player, he still is a great player, and he gave a lot to Liverpool.

When I spoke to Fernando, he told me I was moving to a great club and a great city. He told me he was sure I was going to be happy here, but he had made up his mind to leave. I looked at his goalscoring record at Anfield and I remember thinking what a difficult job it would be to follow him. The supporters had loved him; it was going to be hard to prevent people forever comparing me unfavourably to him.

I was lucky. As soon as Fernando was sold, another big signing came. I first met Andy Carroll in the hotel while I was waiting for my deal to go through and although I didn't say it to him, I was thinking: 'I'm glad you're here.' If Liverpool had sold Torres and only signed me, it would have been: 'Suárez comes to replace Torres.' Andy was like a human shield. He cost more than me so all the talk was of him replacing Fernando. I wasn't really talked about that much.

The weather in Liverpool was a little cold and grey, but I was used to that after my time in Holland and the warmth from the people more than made up for it. Liverpudlians were as easy-going and respectful of me and my family as Fernando had told me they would be.

Fernando also introduced me to the neighbours and his friends became mine. When I first moved in Pepe Reina lived at the end of the close and the Argentinian Maxi Rodríguez was nearby too. He had a little girl so that was something we had in common. Fábio Aurélio and Lucas Leiva were nearby too.

Pepe was a big help in those early days. He kept telling me that I had the quality to be a success at Liverpool. I also hit it off with Dirk Kuyt. I understood Dirk on the pitch immediately because we had both come up through the Dutch school. When it came to the typical give-and-go, wall passes and so-on, we were on the same wavelength. He even understood me off the pitch thanks to the Dutch I had learned in Holland.

Another player I really it hit it off with and who impressed me hugely was Glen Johnson. I knew he was a good player because he was an international and Liverpool had paid a lot of money for him. But I was still surprised how good he was. He has a combination of physical strength, power and intelligence that I don't think people in England really appreciate. It's rare to find such athleticism and cleverness in the same player and he has that mix. I tried to build an understanding with him on the pitch. I know as a full-back it's not easy finding a forward who will try to protect you and give you some cover when the team loses possession.

Perhaps he's undervalued because he is not a very English full-back. Technically he's so good that despite being naturally right-footed he actually shoots better with his left.

Glen also speaks a bit of Spanish which helped me. He's different. He's not your typical Englishman. He understands the Spanish and the Latin Americans, the way we are, the jokes we tell, the sense of humour, the character. Eventually all my Liverpool team-mates understood me, but he was like that from the start. He made me feel comfortable, always helped me out, and was very welcoming. He always talked to me face to face, he was very honest and very direct.

I never asked Glen why he speaks Spanish, but he was always looking to improve. If some of us were talking in Spanish, he listened intently, and if there was anything that he didn't understand he asked for a translation. Then, a few days later he'd use the very phrase that he had asked about. I'd think: 'What a memory he's got, he remembers everything!' He'd gone away, looked it up and perfected it.

He showed a real interest and there was something about the way he did that which made me and the other Spanish speakers feel appreciated.

Glen's got three kids and two of them speak Spanish already, even though they're very young. You speak to them in Spanish and they respond. That's because of Glen. He says he's English, but I'm not so sure.

There was a time when Glen's Spanish was better than my English, but not any more. The club arranged for me to have an English teacher and I made slow progress. It was tough because I had a group of friends and their families who spoke Spanish too, and I met up with them a lot, which didn't help me to learn English.

Learning to speak English was the hardest thing for me at first – in fact, it still was by the end of my time at Liverpool. In Holland it was different: they obliged me to speak Dutch and out on the pitch at least Bruno would always try to speak to me in Dutch, translating and explaining things when I didn't understand. Because I was captain at Ajax I had to really force myself to speak Dutch as well, whereas at Liverpool it was easier to get by without speaking great English. Everyone in Holland speaks English and if I had started to learn the language then, I would have probably had an advantage when I came to Liverpool.

I probably speak slightly better English than Dutch now because I have forgotten a lot of my Dutch, but the truth is that I reached a higher level with Dutch than I did with English, although I was improving all the time.

When I first arrived I would speak to Dirk and I would mix my words up; I would be looking at the players and thinking, 'This guy doesn't understand a thing I say.' And it would be because half of the words I was using when I thought I was speaking English were actually Dutch.

I took English classes at home. To start with, it was great but you reach a point when you think that it's better to do fewer classes and speak more to your team-mates. For me it was complicated by the fact that I spoke Dutch and the verbs mixed up in my mind and I made a lot of mistakes. They're not the same but they're similar enough to confuse you. Then there are words in Dutch that are written the same way but they'd be said very differently. In Dutch there's a very throaty 'ghhhh' noise, like you're trying to cough up phlegm, and that doesn't exist in English.

Sometimes gestures are enough and the language of football doesn't really change from one place to the other. You learn that very quickly, although not quite as quickly as you learn the swear words. You always start with them. Always. Dutch, English, Spanish . . . it makes no difference. The first thing I learned in English were the swear words. It's always the insults, and you're not always aware of how strong what you're saying is. The people teaching you think it's hilarious, of course.

That happened in Holland too. I had a Serbian team-mate, Goran Lovre, who spent all day saying one particular phrase which although I never exactly understood, I knew it was an insult and I suspect a pretty nasty one. The Norwegian Erik Nevland would have his favourite Norwegian swear words too. And when these players learned Spanish the first words they learned were, of course, the swear words.

The most important thing we would do in our language lessons would be to go through the kind of questions that I could expect a journalist to ask after a game. I would see foreign team-mates and think: 'How did they reach such an incredible level of English?' The answer is simple: they knew what questions were coming and they prepared. So I did the same. You can prepare for interviews in a way that disguises the flaws in your English. I learned that in interviews you always get asked the same thing so you can give the same answers, which is great because you memorise a phrase, repeat it and you're fine.

I think the first interview I did in English was after a game against Everton at Goodison Park, and the reporter asked me a couple of questions, one of which was *very* familiar. Afterwards, the teacher said: 'See?' It was exactly the question he had told me they would ask, and I had the answer ready. 'Your answer was perfect,' he told me. Of course it was perfect – we'd practised it often enough. 'The most important thing is the three points' . . . 'We knew this would be a hard game and we have been working towards it all week' . . . 'We're happy, but now we have to concentrate on the next game.' It was always the same.

In Holland, it had been similar, but they would sometimes push you on more difficult questions: they'd ask if you were leaving, they'd talk about your own game a bit more directly. By the end, I could give decent responses too.

● ● ●

I looked at the photographs on the walls at Melwood and wondered if one day there would be one up there of me. Kenny Dalglish appeared in a lot of them, but then I wasn't aware just how important he is in Liverpool's history, or of the significance of the shirt he wore. I had always worn number 16 at Ajax – the date of our wedding anniversary – but 16 was already taken when I arrived. Pere told me I could have 7, 11 or 15. 'It's got to be 7 or 11, hasn't it? Let's go for 7,' I said. And that's how it happened. There was nothing more to it.

I had no idea what the number 7 shirt meant, but I soon found out. People kept telling Pere too and he called me: 'Do you realise how big this is?' He told me about Kevin Keegan and Kenny Dalglish and about what they had achieved. He told me about the European Cups and the league titles, about when Liverpool were the best team in the world. I remembered Steve McManaman of course but not them. I didn't really think it would be that important, but people told me about Kenny constantly. I could already feel the pressure building and I could really sense their reverence for him.

In the end though, it was a good decision to choose the 7 shirt. When Suso left on loan, they offered me the chance to take 16 instead, but I stuck with 7. The fact that I had the 7 also encouraged me to look a little closer at the photos and I watched some videos of Kenny too. Now he was my manager.

In a strange way, that actually made me feel better despite the pressure. I thought to myself: 'If someone this adored by the supporters has brought me here and is backing me to succeed, that's got to be a good sign, hasn't it?'

When I arrived, there was a sense that Kenny had come back to save the club. It was a difficult time and he had turned things around in that first season after Hodgson. We were a long way from the European places when I arrived but we went on a long unbeaten run and went into the last game knowing that if we beat Aston Villa, and Tottenham lost, we would reach the Europa League. Unfortunately, we lost 1-0 to Villa, but the result was immaterial because Spurs beat Birmingham 2-1 in their last game to take the Europa League spot anyway.

Kenny's idea of how we were to play was based on the way he had played and the football was good but we never got the good fortune to go with it. I have heard people say that he didn't understand the modern game, but I don't think that is true at all. What is true is that he was not as hands-on as maybe he had been in his first spell, or perhaps that was the way managers, as opposed to coaches, had always traditionally been at Liverpool. Kenny wouldn't talk with the players on a regular basis and that was new and very different for me. I had come from Holland and Uruguay where the coaches would be talking all the time. When he came to tell you something it was because he was upset with you or he wanted you to change something particular. He thought long and hard before saying something to you. Then there was the language barrier. If he had to tell me something in the training sessions then he would say it to Pepe or Lucas and they would translate for me. He would usually observe the training sessions from afar, leaving his coaching staff to take the sessions.

We had Steve Clarke who had been at Chelsea for a long time with José Mourinho and it was strange because sometimes we would train one way, playing one- and two-touch games, or we would play games with a team that you imagined would start at the weekend, but when the match came around there would be two or three different names on the team sheet. Second-guessing the team Kenny was going to put out was difficult.

Steve was good with the tactical side of things. He would do all the set-piece work and he would take the training sessions. His methods were very up-to-date; he did the things that I had always been used to the manager doing. It was striking that Kenny didn't talk as much as I expected, but perhaps he had reached a time in his career when he thought he was not going to be tearing his hair out leading training sessions when he had a very capable coach to do it for him.

I imagine he also wanted his assistants to feel that they were contributing. There are a lot of coaches that behave as if their assistants just don't matter, but Kenny wasn't one of them. He did not have a big ego. He picked the team and we played as he wanted us to play. He decided what we would be doing on the training pitch in the sessions, he just would not be the one driving them – most of the day-to-day work was left to the staff. He did give the pre-match team-talks, though.

To start with, it was one thing for him to speak to me and another thing for me to actually understand what he was saying. There was one game away at Arsenal. I had had a run of games playing from the start and before the team-talk he said to me: 'You today, left out.'

And I said: 'Ah okay, okay.' I thought, 'That's fine, I've played on the left before,' and I went to the team-talk.

I said to José Enrique, the left-back: 'You're going to have someone helping you out today, José.'

Dirk Kuyt overheard and said to me: 'What do you mean?'

'I'm playing on the left today, so I think you're probably playing on the right.'

And then Kenny names the team and I'm on the bench and José Enrique looks at me and Dirk looks at me, confused.

At the end of the team-talk they said to me: 'What did he say to you before?'

'I don't know. "Left out," I think . . . playing out on the left, no?'

They were in hysterics.

Dirk said to me: 'But did he say "left out" or "out on the left" or "outside left"?'

'No, no, definitely "left out". It was very fast but it was definitely "left out".'

And Dirk spelled it out to me: 'Left. Out. Left out of the team. You're not playing.'

Then it all made sense. I understood why Kenny had sought me out before the team-talk to tell me. He probably wondered why I took it so well.

I got a bit wound up once it had sunk in, but it was too late for any reaction.

I got used to the boss's accent in the end but it was tough at the start and the team-talks could be very confusing for me. He wasn't like a lot of the coaches nowadays who usually accompany naming the team with graphics. This idiot-proof technology is great for a player who is yet to grasp the language: the big screen comes out and there you can see the team, with the substitutes underneath the first eleven and then underneath that the players that don't make the squad. But Kenny would just pull out a piece of paper and read the team.

Two days after I signed for the club, he was naming the team and substitutes for the match against Stoke City and I was thinking: 'I didn't hear me in there; what a pity, I'm not in the eighteen.'

I was expecting to be on the bench and to come on and make my debut, but I hadn't even been picked. Maybe the deal had been done that bit too close to the match to risk it. But then on the bus to Anfield Ray Haughton, the player liaison officer, congratulated me and so I asked Pepe Reina: 'Did the manager say Suárez?'

Pepe replied: 'Yes, he said Suárez. Just not the way we say Suárez. He pronounced it in a way it's never been pronounced before but, yes, he said your name. You're on the bench.'

I was delighted. I'd officially signed two days before and now I would be making my debut for Liverpool at Anfield.

I came on as a sub and scored in front of the Kop. I think it was more nerves than anything else that took me round the goalkeeper and every time I watch it on video I expect the man on the line to stop the ball but he never does. This time the stadium was full and everyone was applauding.

● ● ●

Not that it was easy. I remember the first ball I touched at Anfield. I controlled it, looked up, and . . . it had gone.

It was a millisecond, no more.

What happened there? Pff, how quick is this?

I said to myself: 'Luis, you're not going to get a second to think here. You have to do everything fast.' Right from the start I realised that I would have to speed everything up. You have to do it all quicker to get into the game more. And *then* and only then, maybe you can start to slow down again, taking touches, pausing, perhaps even thinking a bit. But to start with it's: *accelerate, accelerate.* That moment was a real 'Welcome to England'. The football there is strong, hard, quick. It was good for that to happen to me at the very start because it meant that there was no doubt in my mind about what was required. That first touch was the first lesson.

I could see it in training too. In the first few sessions, I was wary of Martin Škrtel and Danny Agger because they're very aggressive defenders. Martin can be particularly brutal. Even a couple of seasons later, if he ever wandered over to my side of the pitch then I would wander off to the other side to get away from him. And the same with Danny.

I told them both in the first few sessions: 'Don't worry: I take it easy in training, so you take it easy.' Then I nutmegged one of them without really meaning to and so the gloves came off.

'I thought you were taking it easy? Okay, now we're playing for real.'

I don't think they ever believed me after that.

But our training battles were always in good spirits, as team-mates. The only team-mate it ever got heated with was Jamie Carragher. I think he was frustrated about not playing much and the fact that he was coming towards the end of his career, so there would be a few lively moments but we would always shake hands at the end of the session.

We never fell out on or off the pitch, but I did have to get used to how he was in training. I never train with shin pads and I would say to myself: 'How can a team-mate make a challenge like that in training that could easily have injured me?' Some of the other players said to me: 'That's how Carra is, so make sure you're always on the move or he'll hit you hard.' I expected it from Martin and Danny, but I didn't know Carra so well so I had to learn fast. I'm aggressive in training as well. But not to the point of injuring a team-mate. I appreciate that it's more difficult for a defender – they have to go in hard to show the manager that they should be in the team and it's not always easy to strike that balance.

As they said, that's how Carra was. He was more of a shouter, a complainer, than Stevie Gerrard. He always demanded more: he was the typical tough, aggressive defender. He played the games with an intensity that I don't think I have ever seen from another defender – he *lived* the game.

I loved his commitment. Sometimes he flew in and I thought, 'How can you make a tackle like that?' But I'm not sure if he would have achieved so much, or gone so far, if he had not had that character. That's what drove him on and made him a better player. It was all about personality.

I wouldn't say that during the final season I missed him as such. We never really had a very close relationship; we were team-mates rather than friends. But I did miss the way that he spoke, the way he led, and I admired him. Every time he spoke, I listened.

He was closer to Stevie and the staff at the club than some of his team-mates. He had been there for so long, given this club so much, while other players came and went. Clubs need players like that: people who have been there all their lives, who know the club inside out, who *get it* and can lead others. They're the ones who keep the identity going. People like Jamie Carragher *are* the club.

I think Liverpool have a new Carragher too, and that's Jon Flanagan. He's very, very similar. He has the same personality, he's aggressive on the pitch. He may be limited in technical terms, but he knows that and plays to his strengths. When Carra played as a full-back, if he went up the line he knew what he had to do and what not to do. Flanagan is the same. He knows. He has the spirit and hunger that Carra had, the same ambition to squeeze every last drop of talent out of himself. He's going to go a very long way. Players like that will always go a long way. People may say, 'he hasn't got this, he hasn't got that', but a player like him will succeed. He's not easy to face in training either.

With time, you learn about English football and can take advantage of that acquired knowledge. The speed of the game as it is played in the Premier League actually means that there is more space. The first wave of pressure is incredible but if you can ride that out, everything opens up in front of you. You know that opponents will close you down, but if you can shake them off, if you can turn, you find that there is room to play in. If you get rid of the man on top of you, then you're free.

Speed and aggression sometimes disguises the flaws. There are Premier League teams that, frankly, are not that good tactically. For example, I realised that if I dropped off the front from the centre-forward position into a deeper area, then *both* centre-backs might come with me, which I didn't expect and which means that a team-mate can run into the space and be one-on-one with the goalkeeper. Or I would look at a team's back four and quickly see that one of their full-backs always goes up the pitch and never comes back or maybe that both full-backs go up and you can isolate the two centre-backs. To take advantage of that, though, you have to adapt to the speed of the game and learn how to overcome the first, brutal wave of pressure. I had to adapt to the English mentality and the English way of playing, even if parts of my game will always be the same, and that meant getting used to a game that was harder, where the tackles were flying in.

But it's strange too, difficult to predict: there were times when the referees would give you a free kick for nothing and other times when they don't blow up even though the foul is grotesque. In general, referees let the game flow a lot in England, which I think is good, even if it can be dangerous. Sometimes that worked in my favour. I remember a goal I scored against Cardiff where the defender, Juan Torres Ruiz, claimed a foul. He was right, it was a foul anywhere else in the world, but what I had done is just what players do in England all the time: get my body in there first and use my strength to push him off the ball.

Ruiz is Spanish and he said: 'In Spain, that's a clear foul.'

By then I'd learned so I could respond: 'But this is England.'

Every country has its own interpretation of what is and isn't a foul.

In Premier League games there's so much pushing and pulling in the area that goes unpunished. If you gave a foul every time it happened, there would be hundreds of penalties. It's very physical. That's something that everyone accepts and respects but there are times when defenders go in so hard it's frightening.

Football is different, country to country. And so is 'cheating'. Cheating is cultural and so is the reaction to it. I got a reputation early on for being a diver but in my time in England I got something like twenty yellow cards, of which more than fifteen were for protesting to the referee, for making gestures, saying things I shouldn't or questioning decisions. Not for diving. I only got two yellow cards for diving.

I dive. Yes, I dive. People have seen that in replays. But sometimes I feel like they noticed more when it was me, like they exaggerated how often I dived in England. At times it annoyed me, I admit: why do people talk about me being a diver? What, and others aren't? People said to me: 'How do you know that you only have two yellow cards for diving?' Well, as I was being labelled a diver it was only natural that I should tot it up. And it's not just that I wasn't convinced that I dived any more than anyone else, it's that it was striking to me that they talked so much more about diving than about some of the fouls. I've seen fouls in Premier League matches that are incredible; players getting kicked, hard and deliberately, I've seen players get injured, I've seen them get forced out of action for six months or more. Why doesn't that get criticised? It's true that a player who dives is trying to con the referee but he's not hurting an opponent.

I think I paid for it too. Because I got a reputation it reached the point that things that *were* fouls didn't get given, while some of the 'dives' that people talk about are not simulation at all in my opinion: you go down but you go down because there has been a foul, because you have felt the contact. Why shouldn't you get that penalty? Sometimes there are clear penalties that you don't get if you stay up even though you should. You see the referees in a game a few months later and you might be arguing with him about a foul that he hasn't given and you say: 'This is the second time . . .'

And he'll say: 'When was the first?'

So you tell him. The good thing is that when you tell him he'll normally say, 'Yeah, you're right.' At least he recognises that he has made a mistake. And you admit that you've made mistakes too, that you appealed for things you knew weren't real. Look at defenders: they're forever raising their arms, appealing, even though they know that the forward is not offside.

Everything happens very quickly on a football pitch and often you don't even really have time to think whether you are in the area or outside of it. You just know that you're in a position where you can hurt the opposition. There are times when you can see that the defender is stretching his leg out and you go towards it. Like so much of what you do, it's not always conscious; you just see the chance and reach for it.

The diving incident I remember most was in a frustrating goalless draw at Anfield against Stoke City in October 2012. Sometimes you get so desperate: your team isn't winning, you can see that it's just not working and you end up feeling like you'll try anything. You think: 'A penalty would help.' Then afterwards you think to yourself: 'How could I dive there? The defender wasn't even close to you.' That's how I felt after that one against Stoke — guilty. Afterwards, you sometimes think: 'I'm hurting the other team and they haven't done anything wrong.' The truth is that you do feel bad about that, but on the pitch it all happens so fast, and you feel such a need to do something, *anything*.

After the Stoke game my team-mates didn't say anything, but Stoke manager Tony Pulis did. The truth is he was right: when I saw the footage later I thought: 'Luis, how could you dive there?' The referee didn't get a card out for me, but he should have done. I deserved it.

On the pitch, my Liverpool team-mates would appeal for a penalty too, even if they knew it wasn't one. All players do at every club. And no one ever told me not to dive. Team-mates knew that I was doing it to try to get an advantage and they accepted it. But there were training sessions when I dived for fun and they'd say: 'That's nothing – he's diving as always!' Or another player would dive, or hit the floor, and they'd be shouting: 'Get up! You learned that off Suárez!'

One day Danny Agger came to training with his five-year-old son. I asked his son if he wanted to be a footballer when he grows up and he said yes. We have all our games on DVD in the dressing room at Melwood and so I picked up one of me playing, and I gave it to him, joking: 'Here, you can learn from this.'

Danny said: 'No, no, he wants to be a footballer, not an Olympic diver.'

Lots of players do it, but I think the difference with me is that I got that reputation and then it's hard to get rid of it. There are players who dive much more than me. It's also hard to change the way you are, no matter how much you try. I must admit, I love it when an opposition manager criticises me and then one of his own players goes and does the same. And then does he say anything? Of course not.

It happened with Chelsea: José Mourinho attacked me but he's got four or five players who have picked up cards for simulation. Before a game against Everton, a couple of weeks after the Stoke controversy, David Moyes complained that I was a diver and then his captain, Phil Neville, got a yellow card for diving during the match. I get criticised, fine, but they know that their own players dive too. They know that a player's mind is on trying to do something to help his team win. Then they have to eat their words. I never watched English television and I never looked to see if anyone was having a go at me or not, but of course I read the press once in a while, or people would tell me what had been said, and Moyes's comment struck me. The thing about it was that he said it the day *before* the game . . . so when I scored against them, I dived right in front of him.

I knew I was going to do it if I scored. You can talk after the game, like Pulis did, if I have dived against your team. You're right to. But he complained before the game; he said that he hoped that players like me wouldn't try to trick the referee. That hurt. So I thought: 'You think I dive? I'll show you a dive – close up.'

It didn't come off quite right: the way I fell didn't go the way I wanted it to. But it worked. I enjoyed it. I thought it was a way of saying: 'Sure, talk after the game. But before it, it's better to keep quiet.' No one knew that I was going to do it: none of my team-mates, not even my wife.

The funny thing was that I wasn't even credited with the goal. It ended up being given as an own goal by Leighton Baines because my shot went in off him. Still, I celebrated it as if it was mine (and much worse was that when I got the 'winner' at the end, it was wrongly ruled out for offside). Sofi laughed when she saw it; I think most people did. Even Moyes said afterwards that it was 'great' and that he would have probably done the same. It was just a joke, there was no malice, it wasn't designed to provoke anyone. Moyes came off the bench to say something to me but I couldn't hear him properly because that was just the moment when the players arrived and jumped on top of me. His reaction afterwards was fine, even if he did say that I'd end up diving in front of a lot of managers if everyone who accused me of diving got the same treatment.

He had motivated me. It always motivates me when a manager criticises me or speaks out of turn. I thought: 'How can you say that about a player who is trying to win, just like you are, and *before* the game has even started?'

No one practises diving; it's not something you try to get better at on the training ground. But it is true that sometimes you see it on television and you think: 'How badly did I dive there?! Next time, don't dive like that.'

A forward is always likely to try to get an advantage. I don't like it when defenders come over to reproach you for trying something like that and then in the next move when you jump up for a header with them they throw their arms in the air and tumble to the floor. I think: 'You're doing exactly the same as you just complained about me doing, and I'm not saying anything to you about it.'

People say that diving is a foreign characteristic. I think foreign players are just an easy target; they get focused on more. Imagine what would have happened if instead of Daniel Sturridge it had been me who had dived for a penalty at Old Trafford last season? I'm not really worried about it, but it is a question that's worth asking. Against Sunderland Daniel scored with his hand. Fine, it happens. But if that had been me? The repercussions are different depending on the player. When it is an English player I get the feeling that the media try to justify it, they try to treat it differently. I'm used to that now, I have accepted it. But if an English player was to dive during a World Cup match and win a penalty, are there any English journalists who wouldn't celebrate that? Michael Owen did it in France in 1998. Everyone was happy, weren't they?

They say diving is a South American thing. And, look, it's true that South Americans are more picaresque, more 'alive', looking for any advantage. The South American player is likely to think: 'If I feel any contact, I'm going down.' It comes from South America? Maybe. But the Europeans have learned it too. Even the English. And some of them are quite good at it.

I used to argue much more with defenders than I do now. They'd say: 'Don't dive so much.'

'But it was a foul.'

'Yeah, but you don't need to make such a meal of it.'

Over time I did try to stay on my feet more than I did in those first few months playing in the Premier League, just as I had had to do in Holland. I learned that in England the foul has to be very, very clear for the referee to blow his whistle. There were even times when the referee would say to me: 'Yeah, it was a foul, but it was only a small one, not enough to blow for.' I'd think to myself: 'That's still a foul, then.' But I became accustomed to that and realised that the more I could stay on my feet, the better. The referee will think: 'Wow, he's improved.' And then when you get taken down, he *does* penalise the tackler. He doesn't automatically assume you're trying to con him. That was the theory anyway . . .

I also remember something Damien Comolli said to me in my early days at Liverpool, when people said that I dived a lot, that I was provocative, and I wasn't getting free kicks. He said to me: 'When you have been here for two or three years, when they know you and you have made a name for yourself, they'll respect you a bit more. Watch a video of Didier Drogba, look at the fouls that they give him now compared to what they gave him at first when they wouldn't give a decision in his favour. So, relax, take your time and that will come too. Forget it. In the long run, you will see that they start to give your more free kicks.'

That was another theory. I'm not sure that one was true, either.

● ● ●

In the summer transfer window, at the end of my first season at Liverpool, we signed Stuart Downing, Jordan Henderson and Charlie Adam. I had just come back from winning the Copa América with Uruguay and Sebastián Coates had been signed as well. I came back full of confidence. It felt like the club was backing me as well by signing another Uruguayan and the money they spent showed that Liverpool wanted to progress and to try to win something important. We'd finished the previous season really well under Kenny and there was a sense of us recovering lost identity. Everyone

LET'S GO FOR 7

was optimistic. But the league season unravelled almost from the beginning.

We didn't start well: we didn't win games that we should have won and with each passing week the task before us looked harder. We played quite well but the results just didn't arrive. 'Luck' always seems like a weak excuse but I genuinely thought we were unlucky. I lost count of the number of times we hit the post. I started to wonder: 'Why isn't this happening for us?' We were creating chances but we weren't finishing them off and then our opponents would have one chance and score.

Once you get into that downward spiral, it's hard to break out from it; we felt ourselves sinking, a kind of fatalism seeping in. I knew that the moment we could break that dynamic, we would be okay, but it didn't happen. I was happy with the club, the dressing room was good, the fans . . . everything. But we simply could not get a run of wins going and as time went on the team didn't raise its head. We weren't able to show the fans that Liverpool could be Liverpool again.

The cups were our salvation. They were like a second chance, unburdened by what had happened before. Subconsciously, when you know the league is impossible, it becomes ever harder; the target is taken away from you and you don't have that goal to drive you on. You can't cling on to something that, deep down, you already feel has slipped out of your grasp. But the cups were a new beginning. I remember a team-talk with Kenny and Steve Clarke. They told us that the target for the club was Champions League football but that Liverpool always play to win every competition they are in and that the cups mattered. We knew that, especially as things slipped away from us in the league. We had to win something.

We fielded a strong team in every cup game, really going for it. We had to give a good account of ourselves, portray a better image of the club, after a year in which a lot of money had been invested. It was a question of personal pride. We also knew that a cup could mean European football the following season. As the season progressed, we also knew it might help us to save Kenny from the sack.

We won the Carling Cup, beating Championship side Cardiff City on penalties in the final. The game finished 1-1 after ninety minutes, then Dirk Kuyt put us ahead in extra time, but Cardiff kept battling and equalised with just a couple of minutes remaining. The truth is that on the day we didn't deserve to win. We didn't play well and they played incredibly, they were brilliant. Physically, we were better than them, which is something that I think comes from being the Premier League team, but they played much better football. For them to take us to a penalty shoot-out, with the players we had, was impressive. And once you get to penalties anything can happen. When Cardiff's Anthony Gerrard – who is Steven's cousin – missed the last kick of the shoot-out to hand us victory, we were relieved more than anything else. Proud, too, because it had been a long time since the club won a trophy. And we did feel that we deserved to win the trophy because of how we had got there. The final might not have been impressive, but our journey there had been.

Liverpool came into the competition at the second round stage and after beating Exeter City and Brighton & Hove Albion, we drew Stoke City in the fourth round. We were losing 1-0 at half time but turned it around to win 2-1 and I scored both goals.

People in England talk about a 'wet Wednesday night in Stoke' as if it is the ultimate yardstick. And, yes, it's hard. Bloody hard. It really is true. The fans are very close to you, and Stoke are strong and aggressive. Scoring one of my goals with a header there was incredible for me.

After we went 2-1 up, Stoke were even more direct in their approach than they had been before. It was constant. *Bang, bang, bang.* Our defenders were incredible that day. But it was probably hardest for the midfielders: they hardly touched the ball, spending most of the game watching it fly over their heads. Because I'm a small striker, I prefer the ball on the floor but at least I saw it occasionally. The ball would come flying up the pitch and I had to battle it out with these two giants at the back.

Under Tony Pulis, it was all long balls and throw-ins into the area from practically the middle of the pitch. The first time I had seen Rory Delap take a throw-in, I couldn't believe it. To see that kid there with the towel on the touchline was new. And I was even told that one of his team-mates had a towel stitched inside the bottom of his shirt to dry it for him. I was thinking: 'How can a team train for throw-ins?' But of course they could and it worked for them. And that meant we had to train for them as well. At Melwood, the day before the game, Kenny made us work on defending against long throw-ins from near the halfway line. There was just one difference between our practice and the real thing: the person taking the 'throw-in' had to kick it. We didn't have anyone who could reach the penalty area from there with a throw.

I was surprised when I first experienced Stoke's long-throw bombard-ment, but it was not something I would ever complain about. Every team has its philosophy and Stoke at the time had that philosophy. You have to use all the weapons at your disposal. Delap could deliver incredible throw-ins, so why shouldn't they do it? The play was quite simple: a long throw, a flick-on, and players arriving at the far post. But even if you knew exactly what was coming, it was very hard to stop and they did it so well.

We had to be very strong physically and mentally that night because it was hard to escape the feeling that it was impossible to win there. It was raining, windy and I thought: 'We're going out today.' If we couldn't win there on a sunny afternoon – and we'd lost our previous two league matches at Stoke – how were we going to win there in the wind and the rain?

So when we did fight back to win, we were delighted. We really celebrated the victory because of the way that we did it: we were very proud of that and it gave us a real boost. It was a sign that we wanted to win the cups.

We followed up by beating Chelsea 2-0 at Stamford Bridge, with goals from Martin Kelly and Maxi Rodríguez, and then in the semi-final we knocked out Manchester City, winning 3-2 on aggregate. Before the semi-final, which is played over two legs, we didn't play a single game at home in the tournament.

To win at Chelsea and at City showed that, even if our league form was not very good, we were on the right lines. 'If we can knock them out, why shouldn't we win it?' we thought.

The final was my first game at Wembley. It's incredible, one of the best stadiums I have ever played in. There was something special about the atmosphere that I had never really experienced either: from the sheer numbers of supporters, half of them in red, to the build-up, the pressure and the excitement. Walking in to the dressing room and seeing my locker with a huge photo of me on it; feeling that expectation; picking up the matchday programme and seeing the word 'final' on the cover; going out to warm up and seeing that the stadium is full already; the noise . . . simple things that stay with you. Everything is different. I picked up the programme and kept it. I'll take it out one day and remember that trophy.

After the match, the dressing room was a special place. We had a few new players, there had been a lot of pressure, but it felt like we had done something worthwhile. It was a sign that we wanted to keep on growing.

At the end of the FA Cup final against Chelsea a few months later, it was different. Again, the run had been impressive: Manchester United and Everton, our greatest rivals, had been knocked out en route. But then Didier Drogba beat us on his own. We'd had chances to draw level at 2-1, with Andy Carroll having one cleared off the line, but Drogba was astonishing that day. He would jump between our two centre-backs, all alone, and come down with the ball every time. I knew he was a great player, but that day he still surprised me. I love the attitude Drogba has: I think the striker has to be the first player to try to enthuse the rest of the team with his attitude. His enthusiasm has to be contagious. He has to lead. And Drogba did that. We just couldn't stop him.

Chelsea played well but we felt that we had done enough to have taken the game to penalties. We weren't obliged to win the final for Kenny Dalglish and we wanted to win it for our personal pride, but it is true that we knew that because of our league form he was under pressure and we had seen the cup runs as his salvation as well as our own. We knew that a manager who had given us so much – and who had given me so much personal support – could be helped by winning the cups. And we wanted to save him: we owed him a lot. We left Wembley with our heads held high even though we lost. Neither Kenny nor the players could feel like we had let anyone down.

I left at the end of the season thinking that Kenny was going to continue as manager. I was in Uruguay when I found out that he had been sacked and it really hurt because he had been very close to me, especially after the racism issue (which I will discuss in the next chapter). Then he had told me not to worry about what the press said, not to allow it to bother me, and his support was important for me and for my family during some very difficult weeks. There was a huge amount of respect for Kenny among the players – for everything he represented at the club, for everything he had done, and the affection was genuine. A player always wants to win anyway but it was difficult to see a manager who had pulled us out of trouble in the final four months of the previous season under such pressure. He had helped us then and we wanted to help him now. He transmitted the ambition that we tried to bring to our game.

When he lost his job, it was hard to take. I don't know what kind of relationship Kenny had with the owners and it's not really my business either. He had gone to the United States, where they told him their decision. It felt to us players that it was more an issue between Kenny and the owners than a question of what we had done in that year; a personal question that they discussed among themselves that nobody knows about. The players weren't consulted; in my experience, players never are.

The club had had two or three managers since Rafa Benítez and maybe Kenny had been used to save the club at a specific moment, not as a man to lead a project for the future. They thought there needed to be a change. Football's like that.

Even if it had been the right decision to change the manager, even if we could understand it, even if some players might have welcomed the change, it still hurt. And yet the truth is that footballers can be quite cold too and on one level a change is *always* good. When a new coach comes in there's a kind of renewal, a sense of everyone trying to prove themselves, of everyone getting a second chance. You want to show him your ambition and that of the club. And so does he of course.

The club sent a formal text message out to all the players saying that Kenny was no longer with us, that the club was grateful for everything he had done, and wished him the best, but that it was time to move on. They sent the message out to the players before the press release was issued. It was a very formal message.

Kenny had brought me to Liverpool, he had supported me. I would have liked to have seen him in person and spoken to him under different circumstances, but I sent him a text message to say thank you for giving me a chance, thank you for everything, and wishing him luck. When he replied, the message wished me all the best and told me to always keep the same mentality, the same approach to the game.

'Don't ever change,' he said.

5

'RACIST'

Did I use the Spanish word '*negro*' in an argument that took place, in Spanish, with Patrice Evra on 15 October 2011 in a game between Liverpool and Manchester United?

Yes.

Is the word '*negro*' the same in Spanish as it is in English?

No, absolutely not.

Am I a racist?

No, absolutely not.

I was horrified when I first realised that is what I was being accused of. And I'm still sad and angry to think that this is a stain on my character that will probably be there for ever.

• • •

I knew that Liverpool vs. Manchester United was the biggest game in English football for all the years of rivalry, and maybe even more so since Manchester United surpassed Liverpool in the number of league titles won. It wasn't my first game against them. We had played the season before and there had been no problems; the usual run-ins and clashes but nothing that I remember.

I first became aware that there was a problem when Damien Comolli approached me after the game and asked me if anything had happened between me and Evra. At first I struggled to remember anything specific. There had been an argument with him, but then I had probably had quite a few arguments during the game. Comolli said to me: 'Well, they are complaining about racism'. I was very surprised.

I recalled that the referee had called us over at one point. Evra had come looking for me at a corner asking me why I had kicked him. It is always a bit hypocritical when a defender who spends the whole game kicking you complains of being kicked. He initiated the argument and he chose to do so in Spanish. In the following exchanges between me and him I used the Spanish word 'negro' once.

What some people will never want to accept is that the argument took place in Spanish. I did not use the word 'negro' the way it can be used in English. As I am now fully aware (and I did not even know this at the time), in English there is a word that is spelled the same way but is pronounced differently and it is highly offensive: negro, pronounced nee-gro. Negro (pronounced neh-gro) in Spanish means 'black', nothing more. It is not in itself an insult. Now, people will say: 'Okay, but you said "black" – you shouldn't have.' But Evra had started the argument in Spanish and the Spanish language is full of these ways of addressing someone: *'Guapo'* (handsome), *'Gordo'* (fatty), *'Flaco'* (skinny), 'Rubio' (blond), and so on. Just names based on physical characteristics, nothing more. *Negro* can refer to anyone with dark hair as well as dark skin and I've been used to the word being used in Spanish in this way all my life. My wife sometimes calls me *'Negro'* or (the diminutive version) *'Negrito'*. My grandmother used to call my grandfather *'Negrito'* and she would occasionally call me that too. There are countless South American players who have been known as *'El Negro'*. One of Uruguay's most famous and best-loved players, the legendary Obdulio Varela, was nicknamed *'El Negro Jefe'* ('The Black Chief'). Usually the word is used in a friendly manner and even when it isn't, it does not have racist connotations; it does not imply any kind of rejection or discrimination because someone is black. I'm not trying to pretend it was meant in a friendly way to Evra because clearly we were arguing. But nor was it ever meant as a racist slur.

The second important point is that I said to Evra: *'Por qué, negro?'* *'Por qué'* means: 'Why?' It was me asking him why he was complaining, first about the foul and then about me touching him. I told Comolli this, but by the time my version had been passed down the line to the referee it ended up not as *'Por qué, negro?'*, but as *'Porque eres negro'*, which changes the meaning drastically; *'porque'* doesn't mean 'why?', it means 'because' – the phrase became 'because you are black'. I never said, nor would ever dream of saying, 'because you are black'. And I certainly never said, and never would say, that I would not talk to Evra, or anyone, because they are black.

But nobody had time for these subtleties when I was being condemned for racism. Especially not after the tone had been set by Evra's original accusation that I had called him not '*negro*' but 'nigger', which he later admitted was wrong. Even worse. It would never enter a Spanish speaker's head to use this word; it does not even exist in Spanish. He changed the accusation later but the stigma of me being someone who would use such an abusive term stuck.

According to Evra I had used the N-word – which at first he said was 'nigger' and then changed to 'negro' – five times. But he was the only one that heard it and even he was not sure what he had heard. I had said it once, in the context I have explained above, without intending any racist meaning at all. But on the basis of his accusation I was found guilty. David De Gea was next to both of us in the six-yard box and in his testimony he said he had heard nothing.

I told Comolli what had happened. He then told Kenny Dalglish and they both told the referee and it was that version that went to the hearing. Why did I not go to the referee's room myself? Because nobody told me to and because I did not speak good English. I'm not saying this is Comolli's fault. Absolutely not. He is the one who had to transmit exactly what I had said to the referee and there are intricacies and nuance in the language where you have '*Por qué*' and '*Porque*', and you have the word '*negro*' as it is used in the Spanish language and how it can be used in English.

Regardless of how '*por qué*' became '*porque*' there were about twenty-five cameras focused on the action, and three lip-readers asked to study the footage, and nothing shows me saying what I was accused of repeatedly saying. And no one else heard me say the word despite the fact that according to Evra I had said it five times to him in about ten seconds. Later he told French television channel Canal Plus it had beeen 'ten times'.

Evra doesn't speak Spanish very well. He started the argument in Spanish but it was very basic Spanish – as if I was to say in English: 'Why you hit me?' It was hard for me to understand what he was saying to me. I remember he called me 'Sur Americano' – 'South American' – but I didn't understand much more than that.

If you don't speak Spanish, then don't accuse me of insulting you in that language, let alone insulting you ten times. I can't understand why he didn't confront me in the tunnel. If it had been so offensive wouldn't he have grabbed me and said: 'What did you say to me out there?' And I would have said to him: 'If you really think I said that, then you have not understood me properly.'

If Evra and I had had a conversation after the game then we would have established that I hadn't racially abused him.

You might say: why didn't I initiate that conversation? The answer is obvious: I just had no sense of having said anything wrong, still less racist. I did not think that I had said anything to him that went beyond the ordinary on-field arguments.

It's impossible that I would say the things he accused me of saying with the team-mates that I had at Liverpool and having played in Holland against black players in a country with the highest proportion of players from Curaçao and from Surinam. I had never been involved in anything like this before. And I come to England and with his three words of Spanish, Evra accuses me of racism. I had used the Spanish word for 'black', which for me has no racist overtone, that's all. I was devastated that it was interpreted as racist. There had been no attached insult – 'black this' or 'black that'. If there had been then I would have deserved everything I got and much more. But I used the word 'black' and got an eight-game ban and, much worse, was condemned as a racist.

● ● ●

In the next few days, as I started to realise how serious the situation was, I decided I would not say another word. I could have said a lot of things. Maybe I *should* have said a lot of things. The club told me to stay silent and I was also conscious of the fact that it would be better to say nothing rather than say things when I was angry.

I had not been in England long. My English was still very poor. Language at the time was a far bigger problem for me than it would be now. People will say: 'Well, that's your fault for not learning English.' When I went to Holland I had to make the choice to learn English or Dutch. Out of courtesy to the supporters there I learned Dutch.

Maybe I could have leaned more on my poor English, using that as an excuse or a defence, or even denied having said anything. Maybe someone should have told me: 'Luis, we have every camera angle and none of the footage shows you saying "*negro*"; just deny it.' But I was honest. Some people didn't want to understand that I said '*negro*' in Spanish during an argument in Spanish and in a way that I just didn't understand to be racist and absolutely did not intend to be racist. Maybe I would have avoided all problems if I had just denied ever using the word. Instead I told them what I had said, not least because I did not understand it would be a problem.

In one way it doesn't matter to me because my conscience is clear.

But what hurts is when people say: 'Luis Suárez? – good player, bit crazy sometimes . . . and a racist.' Or worse: 'Luis Suárez: racist.' Nothing else, just that: racist. It's a truly horrible feeling to think that people define me that way. The word hurts, the accusation is painful. It's a terrible thing to be associated with and utterly misrepresents me. I think that is why I reacted the way I did at Fulham when I showed the finger to some abusive supporters and picked up another ban. All I could hear was *that* word.

At the time I tried to avoid the issue. I generally didn't watch English television anyway but I would switch on Spanish television and there would be something about Luis Suárez being accused of racism. My wife would connect to the internet and call me to say: 'Look what they're saying about you.' When my children are older they will do the same. Put 'Luis Suárez' into an internet search engine and up comes the word 'racist'. It's a stain that is there for ever. And it is one that I feel I do not deserve.

It took a while for it to sink in how serious it was. After the match I gave my statement to Comolli and I went home and thought very little of it. 'So what? I said the Spanish word "*negro*" in an argument in Spanish and he's made a fuss about it.' I had said my bit, explained what had happened, and the next day I would go into training and it would all have been forgotten. Even when I put the TV on at home and Spanish television was reporting the incident I never imagined what was heading my way.

The following week it was difficult just going to training. My team-mates were fantastic, as were the coaches. Glen Johnson, who knows how the word can be used in Spanish, was calling me '*negro*' in training for the next few days. 'Let's push up, "*negro*",' he would say. I had used it with him in training before and in the dressing room but by this time I was too scared to use the word in any context.

If I had to go through it all again I would still have the argument but I would be more careful with the words I use. I have learned the hard way. Maybe I should have said from the off: 'Okay, what language are we arguing in here?' Obviously I would never have said 'negro' had we been arguing in English.

Afterwards no opposing defender, black or white, used what had happened against me. There were no provocations along those lines. Black players still came to swap shirts at the end of games. That made me really happy but I was conscious of not wanting to be seen as the guy who goes out of his way to prove he is not a racist. Sometimes I felt I couldn't win. If I swapped shirts with a black player it was because I was a racist trying to hide my racism; and if I didn't swap shirts with a black player it was also because I was a racist.

It was a similar situation when Dani Alves reacted the way he did to having a banana thrown at him by peeling it and eating it and players from all over the world joined him in support with the #somostodos-macacos (#weareallmonkeys) campaign. I wanted to support the campaign and Philippe Coutinho and I had our picture taken but I knew some people would not allow me to stand up against racism without suggesting that me taking an anti-racist stance somehow proved I was a racist.

Sometimes when I'm asked for a photograph with a black fan I'm still conscious of the fact that people will say: 'Look, he stops for this fan because he is black.' But no, I stop because I stop for everyone if I can. It is as if nothing I do is treated as normal any more. That is almost the worst thing of all; it has created an issue for me that never was an issue.

At the time there were countless instances I could have brought up of me having done things that a racist person would never have done, or having friendships that a racist would not have had, but I chose not to.

I thought about showing a video at my hearing that I had posted on my website of me playing football with a young South African boy, helping to make his dream come true of having a kickabout with some players who were playing in the World Cup. But where do you draw the line between trying to show you are not that kind of person and protesting so much that people then believe you have something to hide?

Once the formal letter from the FA had reached the club I don't really think we knew the best way to go about dealing with it. The lawyers took control of the case. They told me throughout the hearing: 'Don't worry, you answered the questions well and things are being said that go in your favour.' They said that it would be two or three games if any, as if the number of games rather than clearing my name was the most important thing. Looking at it now with a cooler head, I don't think we handled it well. We were not able to put across that this word was used in Spanish and that it has nothing to do with the 'negro' word as it is pronounced and used in English; that fact never really got grasped by anyone at the hearing. All that people saw was: 'Suárez said "negro".' And whenever the word appeared in print in the newspapers it was never translated: again it was just 'Suarez said negro', no italics. It was usually the only word not translated – as black – back into English.

People asked why, once I knew how serious all this was, I did not put out a statement. It was because I was furious with the accusation and too proud to make an attempt to publicly explain myself. I felt ganged up on, backed into a corner. The club suggested I write an open letter but I didn't want to. Perhaps that was a mistake, perhaps not. I don't think people were in the mood to hear my side whatever I said. I felt stuck.

The days of the hearing were awful. I got up at 6.30 every morning to be at the hotel where it was held by 7.30. A taxi would come to pick me up and I would go on my own every morning and I would return at eight or nine o'clock at night having spent the whole day in one of the meeting rooms at the hotel waiting to be called. And in the end, amid all the talking, I was only actually asked to give evidence once in the four days: there in my suit with two lawyers in one of four rooms used for the hearing. The panel was in one room, the lawyers representing Evra were in another. And then we were in another room with a fourth room for I don't know what. And that was me for five days.

Every now and then they would bring in sandwiches. I would speak to my wife on the phone and she would ask: 'What are you doing now?'

'Nothing, still just sitting here.'

I didn't understand what I was supposed to be doing there. What was my function locked up in that room?

The lawyers explained to me that there was no proof of any sort that I had done anything wrong, but that I was being accused of having changed my story, that I was now saying I had said one thing but that, via Comolli, I had told the referee I had said something else. Basically, they said my story did not seem credible because of that. There was an interpreter there and she translated everything in the way that I would have said it, but they took more notice of what Damien and Kenny had relayed I said, than what I was now telling them I had said. I would be shown evidence from other players and witnesses and was supposed to verify it but it all needed translating and we all know how big the final report was. I still have it somewhere but I've never read it. I have it in Spanish and it's about 115 pages long. If I read it now I will only get upset all over again.

I was banned for eight games, and, much worse, got labelled a racist, for life.

You can call me 'big-mouth', 'biter', 'diver'. There is proof. But to call me a racist — that hurts a lot. It's a serious accusation. It hurts because of how it affects me, it hurts because my wife had to suffer too through the hearing, watching me getting accused of being someone she knows I'm not, and it hurts because in the future the stain will still be there when my children grow up. It's a slur on my name that no one can take away.

When the ban was announced I did write an open letter to fans, but I never asked for Evra's forgiveness because I felt I had done him no wrong. I had been damaged by this whole case more than anyone. I'm not a racist and at no time did I say anything discriminatory to him. I never said sorry because I had nothing to say sorry for. I felt wronged. I wanted to appeal against the ban but the club felt it best that we just moved on.

If there was ever a chance of reconciliation, what happened pre-match when I next played against Manchester United in February 2012 put paid to it.

I had every intention of shaking Evra's hand in the team line-up before the match. I had spoken to my wife about it before the game and said that I would.

Kenny had also called me the day before.

'Luis, are you going to give him your hand?'

'Yes, yes, I don't have a problem with it.'

As I was walking down the line, Evra was shaking everybody's hand, but he lowered his hand when I reached him. He shook Jordan Henderson's hand before me, and his hand moved downwards, away from mine. The images are there for everyone to see. My hand stayed outstretched at the same level but once he'd lowered his, I thought: 'Okay, he's not going shake my hand', and I continued along the line.

I had every intention of shaking his hand.

Pepe Reina was behind me in the line and he said to me afterwards: 'I saw what he did – he lowered his hand so you couldn't shake it.'

Once I had passed him he started with the show of grabbing my arm and protesting that I hadn't shaken his hand. And he looked towards Sir Alex Ferguson to see if Daddy was watching. If it was a trap, I fell into it.

Glen said to me: 'He would have been up all night before the game thinking about what to do at the handshake. He had it planned.'

For the stain that he had put on my character I was probably wrong in trying to shake his hand in the first place.

My wife was watching in the stands and before I could speak to her she had texted me to say: 'He didn't give you his hand. He lowered it as you walked past.'

He then grabbed my arm after I had walked past so it looked like he wanted to shake hands and I didn't. The headlines were written: 'Unrepentant Suárez refuses to shake hands.'

The word 'unrepentant' is used a lot about me when it comes to what happened with Evra. I think it misses the point entirely. You cannot believe in your innocence and be repentant at the same time.

Had I let Kenny down? No, because I said I would offer him my hand and I did. Kenny was too worried about the game to worry about whether we had shaken hands or not anyway. He defended me throughout. He said to me: 'Every time I go into a press conference I have to take a shield to bat off all the Luis questions: "Luis this; Luis that".' He reached the point where he had to say: 'Are we here to talk about football or Luis?' It was difficult for him. But he knows how grateful I am for all that he did for me.

The players were fantastic too and Kenny backed them in their idea of wearing T-shirts in support of me. Glen Johnson supported me brilliantly throughout everything. For him to do that even though I had not been at the club very long made no difference to the verdict, but it meant a huge amount to me. Steven Gerrard was also fantastic. He came up to me in that first Manchester United game after the ban when I was being abused by everyone and said to me: 'Today you are going to show that you are one of the best players in the world.'

People have asked me since if there is a part of me that sees Evra's side – if he thought I had abused him then isn't his reaction understandable? But why didn't he come to me with the accusation? Why didn't he acccuse me on the pitch or afterwards? Come to me after the game with a Spanish team-mate and he can tell me what he thinks I said and what he thinks it means, or we could have met later. Why didn't he ever confront me? The head of the PFA proposed a meeting between Evra and me a few days after the incident and I said to Comolli that if I had to explain

the situation then, fine, I would do. I don't know why the meeting never
happened. It certainly was not because I had said no to it. Perhaps it was
because the investigation started and we were hardly going to be sat
down together with the PFA if at the same time Evra was going to be
accusing me of racism at an FA hearing.

The hearing left me with a stain on my character. Evra came out of it
as the innocent victim and I came out of it with my reputation tarnished
for ever, labelled as a racist.

I will always be grateful for the way Liverpool defended me. People at
the time said: 'They are defending him because he is a good player and
they can't afford not to.' No. They defended me because they knew me.
They knew what kind of person I was inside the dressing room. They knew
how I was with my family. They knew what I'm like off the pitch.

They know me. They know I'm not a racist.

FORTUNE

When I was at Ajax a Dutch magazine published an article saying that I was the best-paid player in Holland. Not only was the story untrue, but they claimed that I was earning twice as much as I actually was. I denied it, but you can't deny every story that comes out in the media because you'd be responding permanently and it would end up driving you crazy.

When I was at Liverpool, there was another story claiming that I was entitled to a huge bonus when I passed the twenty-goal mark in a season for the club. Wrong again. I got on to the club this time so they could officially deny it because I didn't want Liverpool fans thinking: 'Ah, now he's scored his twenty goals he won't be too fussed if he doesn't score any more.'

The exaggeration isn't really necessary because the truth about the money in football is staggering enough. The marketing that has developed around the game has taken it to another level, generating huge amounts of money. The interest is colossal. You ask yourself: 'How can a country pay a team €3 million to play one friendly game?' But they get their money back from what they make from the match and all that goes on around the match; it is worth it for them. Top players now earn more in a week than

Pelé and Maradona would have earned in a year because football now generates so much money.

And wherever there are people ready to give money to players, there are other people ready to take it off them.

The cash runs right the way down to the young kid coming through into the first team at the top clubs, and even the not-so-big clubs. A teenager suddenly on relatively big money is a magnet for the wrong kind of friends and associates. There is never any shortage of people who want to help you spend your wages when you are young, naive and flush.

There are leeches that see players as an easy target; they've got money and often they haven't got the education to know how best to use it. The leeches also think that a footballer doesn't care how much he spends or what he spends it on and sometimes they're right. They think to themselves: 'It's tough to sell a scam to a businessman, a doctor or a lawyer but I can sell it to a naive young footballer with my eyes shut.' There are offers to invest in all manner of things. Players are asked to buy plots of land that will then have properties built on them. Once you have handed over the money it turns out that getting building permission is impossible and your money is lost.

There are people who try to get close to you and you don't know why they're trying to get close to you. You think 'He thinks I'm a good guy', but then you wonder. You start to become disillusioned. Some people are attracted by the fame and the money not because they want to be your friend. That hurts. I hate that. They see you as an opportunity. You realise 'He came to me because I'm a footballer so that he could make this or that proposal or take advantage.' You get used to it but at first you don't realise;

at that stage you're an easy target. That's part of the world that swirls around you in football.

I was fortunate that when I was young people approached me in that way and I learned. The hard way, but I learned. And I acted. And then word gets round: 'Don't approach that guy: he's not going to get involved.' I think people see me now as someone who shuts the door. They say: 'It's hard to get close to him.' People don't approach me now because they know what I'm like. I don't know if they've been warned but there seems to be a sense now that I'm not easy prey and that has been good for me. There are a lot of team-mates who still have people approaching them, trying to get close to them, at the age of thirty. And if it's still happening with them, maybe it's just because they're more approachable or maybe it's because people have heard that they're easy; people think they can find a way to get to them and take advantage. They know that they can't do that to me.

I think that comes from coming to Europe so young and seeing the way things were. I wouldn't want seventeen- or eighteen-year-old kids to live through what I lived through. I've invested money that I have never seen again. Someone comes to you at twenty-one and they say: 'If you invest in this now, in three or four years it'll really pay off.' You might have team-mates who have invested there too, and that's part of it: get a player on board and they think they'll get others. Or they show you a video and you think: 'Oh, this is spectacular, wonderful.' In this case, it was property. So I invested. And seven years later I'm still waiting . . .

In Latin America as a young player your biggest dilemma is whether or not to sell your registration rights to an agent. It's the ultimate get-rich-

quick scheme, but in the long term you have waived your rights to unilaterally decide your destiny or profit solely from future moves.

Almost overnight, as a young player, your problem can go from having no money to having more than you have the sense or experience to deal with.

When I was twelve I had agents from Defensor and Danubio, two of the other big sides in Montevideo, knocking on my door and offering me money. I told them I didn't want to sign a contract with anyone at the time. Wilson Pirez and José Luis Esposito, two Nacional directors, helped me so much when I was a young teenager who had started to catch people's attention. They knew all the problems my family had. They knew that my parents had separated and they made sure I was okay financially. It wasn't easy to turn down the money that was being offered to me by other clubs, but Wilson and José Luis gave me a strong foundation that meant I could say no. I was lucky to have such good people around me.

There was even more pressure by the time I was seventeen, eighteen, and was earning a bit more money after making the first team at Nacional. Then the vultures really started to circle. An agent came and offered my dad, who I was living with at the time, $25,000 for me to give up twenty per cent of my registration, handing it over to them. I already had an informal agreement with Daniel Fonseca, but we had nothing signed.

It was hard to turn all that money down. At Nacional I was earning around 4,000 pesos a month. That's about £100.

I remember thinking: 'Wow, 25,000 dollars! I'm going to be rich. I should sign.'

Dad said: 'It's a lot of money, Luis, take it.'

But Sofi said: 'No, no, no. If you never signed anything with Fonseca, why are you going to sign now? And if you trust Fonseca, why are you going to betray him?'

And so I let the opportunity pass me by. Again I was blessed with sound advice from Sofi, but it wasn't easy to say no.

In my head, I was already dividing up the cash, thinking what part I could give to my mum and what part I could give to my sister; I knew it could change our lives. Or at least that's what I thought at the time.

Ultimately you have to put your faith in someone and when two former players that you grew up idolising come to you then you are more likely to put your trust in them. Fonseca and Carlos 'El Pato' Aguilera had taken me under their wing at Nacional. They were partners. Aguilera and Fonseca had been Uruguayan internationals and both had played in Serie A, which I grew up watching on the television as a kid. I was ready for a move away from Uruguay and with Sofi in Europe there was even more urgency.

When they took me on, they told me that I would get private Italian lessons, receive a food basket once a month for my mother, earn 100 dollars a month and then whatever I earned from Nacional, which I didn't count on because there was never any guarantee that they would pay us every month.

Fonseca and Aguilera later ended their partnership and I had to choose between them. I had one telling me one thing and the other telling me something else. I decided to put my trust in Fonseca. I felt that I had his full backing, not that I had ever had a problem with El Pato, and I still say hello to him whenever I see him. He knows I simply had to choose between the two. I never actually signed an agreement with Fonseca. I'm not really sure why. I think I said to him a couple of times: 'If I give you my word then I give you my word.'

I soon realised that of all the players Fonseca had, I was the one that he paid the least. I was the one who would be the last in line to receive new boots. What I did receive I shared with the family and I was able to support my dad a little bit because he was going through a difficult time.

There were lots of promises about the future. Every time he saw me he talked about how this was going to happen and that was going to happen and he was impressive. He had a big car and he had lived in Italy. Everything seemed good. I used to talk with the other young players he looked after and we would talk about his car and the house he had. It's not that you think: 'That's going to be me one day', so much as you believe that if he has those things then he's successful, he must have something. He is some-thing. And you could be too.

When I stepped up from the Nacional youth team I was owned 100 per cent by Nacional; but in Uruguay, if you move, 20 per cent of any transfer fee goes to the player. So if Fonseca was going to buy me from Nacional then he would pay a million dollars to Nacional for me and $200,000 of that would go to me. Fonseca said I should reject the $200,000 and that he would pay only $800,000 to Nacional. Because that would save him money he would then include an extra $200,000 in my first big contract in Europe. At the time I was desperate to get to Europe and my attitude was: 'Okay, whatever it takes. I just want to go.' If you are going to put that in my contract, then perfect. I don't need it right now. For once in my life I was too trusting and when I realised the mistake it was too late.

The whole issue of agents is tough. Parents try to do the best by their sons by grabbing the money when they can, but they are often actually doing a lot more damage to their child's ability to earn more in the future. I dodged most of the potentially damaging deals. I had spent a lot of time on the street and I was alive to most of the tricks and traps that lie in wait.

Sometimes the pressure can come from your own family too. I love my parents and my brothers and sisters and want to help them, but I make a rule that if they are not going to help themselves then there is no deal. We have all come from the same world; we've all lived lives where the opportunities are limited and you have to struggle to keep going. Nothing has been gifted to me. I fell out with my dad for a while because he thought that he didn't need to work any more because he was the father of Luis Suárez. I told him: 'Who is the one who plays football, me or you?'

Of course I'm going to help him because he is my dad, but he has to do his part. We were fighting over this for a while and it was terrible, but I managed to find him a job. He's now been in that job for over a year and he is happy. My mother has a bakery, selling bread from her own house. I have six siblings and lots of nieces and nephews and I just want them to see me as their brother or uncle and not a famous footballer.

With a big family like mine there is always someone with a problem, but most family issues cannot be solved by money. You have the money and you still have the problem or you solve the problem for them and then they come back with their uncle and their uncle's brother who also has a problem. I've had the 'My brother plays football and he never helps me' accusation levelled at me, but I'm not going to help anyone who is not helping themselves.

They can accuse me of being tight-fisted but they know deep down that it is about putting a proper value on things. I'll help people if they are willing to appreciate and value what they have. It's about self-respect. I have a strong work ethic: maybe it comes from having struggled so hard to get here; the endless buses and long walks, scraping money together for the things some people take for granted. I will be the same with my own children. They will have everything that I can give them, but they have to know how to appreciate the value of things in life.

I wouldn't go and buy a mansion for my brothers or sisters. They're not going to leap from a rented house to a massive palace because that's not the way we are; it's not who we are. They wouldn't be happy, they wouldn't be comfortable. They're from a different kind of neighbourhood. My family accepts that and they accept me the way I am but there are people who attach themselves to football families who don't understand that. If a family stops working because the son or the brother is earning a lot of money and playing in Europe, I don't respect that.

I told my dad when I was coming to Europe that he should stop working. That was a mistake that I regretted later on. Initially I thought: 'He's going to be comfortable.' Later I thought: 'Why did I say that to him?' He felt valued through his work, he'd been working for years, it was part of who he was. It gave him his self-esteem, his identity. If your father doesn't want to work, it's a problem. And people around him would be saying: 'It's Luis Suárez's dad.' But he has his own life, he has to have his own value and worth. I had to say to him: 'I'm not going to help you any more until you value what you've got, who you are, what you do.' It was hard to convince him of that but we got there in the end. Actually, the problem was often not them but the people around them, people saying: 'You are Suárez's dad, you should this or that.' Your son can help you, he can facilitate things for you, but not sort out your whole life. You have to value yourself, you have a life of your own to lead. Because if not, everyone will look at you differently too. They'll say: 'Ah, that guy's loaded because his son is a foot-baller. What an easy life.' Your self-esteem, your self-respect, should mean you don't accept that.

You should never lose that sense of valuing what you have and appreci-ating how you have worked for it. I remember when I was ten or eleven and a team-mate of my older brother came to the house and brought us some second-hand clothes. I can still picture the joy on my younger brother's face. My family and friends are never going to say that I've changed with success because I haven't. You'll never see me buying lots of flash cars. I'm not against it if that is what you want to do, but I have never really understood it. It's not me.

THE RODGERS REVOLUTION

6

There was a moment during the first real, in-depth conversation that I had with Brendan Rodgers when I looked at him and it hit me: 'He's right.' We had been talking for a little while, he was explaining the way that he wanted the team to play, and everything was falling into place. Everything he said made perfect sense. I was completely convinced.

When Kenny left, the rumours about who would replace him started. That can be unsettling for a player because you don't always know any more about what's going on than anyone else does: you're not so different from the fans, reading about it in the papers. Soon Brendan Rodgers emerged as the favourite. He wasn't a 'big-name' manager and I didn't know much about him, but Swansea City were a team that stood out because of their attractive style of play; they were different and especially impressive for a team that had only been promoted to the Premier League the season before.

One of our last games of the 2011/12 season had been away at Swansea. I'd bumped into Brendan in a corridor afterwards and he said in Spanish: 'You're an excellent player, congratulations.'

I remember thinking: 'That's interesting, the Swansea manager speaks Spanish.'

The first chat I had with him was at Melwood, just after he was confirmed as Liverpool's new manager. It wasn't a long conversation, just the typical welcome-to-the-club stuff. But he also wanted to talk to me because there had been suggestions that there was a chance of me going to Juventus. I had only been playing in the Premier League for a season and a half and I wasn't keen to move. When a new manager comes in you always feel like you want to see how things will turn out and I told him that, yes, of course I would stay at Liverpool.

Brendan spoke to me in Spanish and he told me to give him time, to give him a chance, and that I would like the way we were going to play. It would suit me. He said we would bring the ball out on the floor, keep possession and play attacking football. I remember him saying: 'It's not so hard to bring the ball out from the back on the floor, you know.'

When he later explained what he meant in detail, I started to see that things were going to be different. In a nutshell, his philosophy was this:

You've got four players in the defensive line and you've got the goalkeeper, who at the time was Pepe Reina, who is good with the ball at his feet. You've got the two central defenders outside the area and you've got one of the central midfielders who can come for the ball. And if he's marked, the other one can come for it. If you have thirty metres from your goalkeeper to the midfield, if the players are good with the ball at their feet, at most the opposition are going to pressure you with two men. No one else is going to come. If you can pass it well, if your positioning is good, it is *impossible* for them to take the ball off you. Why? Because you outnumber them and you will always have a line of pass open which allows you to progress up the pitch.

A midfielder drops into the space which the central defenders open out, the goalkeeper becomes an 'outfield' player and you carry the ball forward that way.

I listened and I was sold. It seemed so simple but no one had walked me through it like that before. I thought: 'He's right, it *is* impossible in a thirty-metre space, with the players Liverpool have got, with the ability that Pepe Reina has with the ball at his feet, for them to get the ball off us.' Unless we made a simple mistake, of course.

Over the first few weeks, that idea was the basis of the work we did with Brendan, the first of the building blocks in constructing a new approach. From the start, it convinced me. It made sense. And although the results weren't good, I could see that we were playing better. I was excited. Brendan's philosophy was to play on the floor, keep possession of the ball and, if we lost it, to pressure to get it back. Don't panic, don't play so fast as we had the previous season, look for the spaces at the right time.

If I was excited, others were worried. And, no, not because of the famous envelopes that appeared during a TV documentary about the club. Mostly, we just joked about that particular episode, but the manager's methods really worked for us.

For those who didn't see the documentary, Brendan had got the entire squad together during pre-season soon after he had taken over and showed us three envelopes. He told us that inside each envelope was a piece of paper on which he had written the name of someone who would let the team down during the coming season. It was our duty, he said, to make sure that it wasn't our name in there. At the end of the year, he would open the envelopes and reveal the names inside. I hadn't seen a manager do that before and of course afterwards lots of the players were talking about it.

There was a group of us sitting there and Glen Johnson came over and said: 'I know who's in the envelopes. I know what's written on all three pieces of paper.'

'Who? What?'

'"Number 3" . . . "José" . . . and "Enrique".'

We fell about.

José Enrique protested: 'No, no, no, no, *inglés* – I'm not there, you are!'

'Yeah, I saw you.'

We never did find out what was written in those envelopes. It was unusual and I must admit that for a moment I did think: 'How can you think before the season has even started that there are three people who are going to let you down? And if there is a name in there and he plays well, and you doubted him, what are you going to do then?'

But it was clear to me that, actually, he didn't think that at all. I'm sure there were no names, it was just a way of motivating us; a tactic to make sure we gave everything. And in truth it got forgotten pretty quickly.

I was much more interested in the way we were going to play. Others were interested for different reasons. It can be frightening to play like that; it takes nerve. Some centre-backs prefer not to have the ball that often. They prefer not to risk being caught with it. You could see that sometimes the central defenders felt under pressure and wanted to hit it long, but Brendan kept insisting and, gradually, they got used to it. Slowly they became more comfortable bringing the ball out. We adapted. Danny Agger and Martin Škrtel improved a lot. Technically, they're fine and they've gained more confidence in their ability. They've become better players. Before it might be two passes and then hit it long but Brendan has changed that. For that to work, the goalkeeper has to act like another outfield player and right from the start they began to be coached differently too. Confidence came through repetition.

We also worked on the coordination of the pressure to get the ball back. Chasing a player down is pretty pointless if you do it on your own; done collectively, it can be very effective.

The new style suited me. Playing in England where all the centre-backs are tall and strong, the long punt up the pitch is no good to me, but a quick ball to release me either side of them works well. Mostly, I need the ball on the floor and Brendan knew that and he also worked with me on the movements I could make to isolate defenders. He was confident that if I could take them on one-on-one, I would be likely to beat them. He was keen to play to my strengths and my style suited his.

He knew that I'm a very instinctive player, who plays on intuition. He knew that if he put me in as a static number nine, waiting for the wingers to put crosses in, I'd be no good. Not no good, in fact, but worse than that – I'm not there. He knew that I'm a mobile striker and that a lot of the time you'll find me outside the area, looking for space, moving. I won't be there as a target for two wide men to aim crosses at.

Andy Carroll would be, of course. Every coach has his taste in players and given the type of game that Andy offered, it was natural that Brendan didn't include him in his plans.

Andy is tall, strong, good in the air. But I think people were wrong about him: he was also technically very good indeed. He can strike a ball very cleanly with his left foot and with so much power. The power he was able to produce always stood out to me in training sessions. It was a shame that injuries reduced the number of times we could play together in our first season at Liverpool.

Yet for a short passing game in which you're looking to release people into space with a lot of pace, he doesn't fit. He wanted to play for England so it was important for him to get games, which meant looking for a way to move on and eventually he joined West Ham on loan. The coach was honest with him, which is always the best way: if you're not going to select a player, tell him.

Something similar happened with Charlie Adam. Charlie's passing was good, but it was suited to a longer passing type of game and Brendan wanted shorter, sharper passing and quicker movement. That shift in style was symbolised by the arrival of Joe Allen from Swansea.

Brendan described Joe as the 'Welsh Xavi'; it didn't quite work that way, and that's some tag to have, but Joe was especially brilliant the first ten games or so and I thought he was an excellent signing. Brendan knew him really well from their time at Swansea and Joe's first few games were fantastic. He was very good with the ball, he fitted the philosophy perfectly and defensively he was exceptional; above all, he understood the movements Brendan wanted straight away, while Stevie and Jordan Henderson began a process of adapting to his style.

With time, they adapted too. In Jordan's case, the proof came last season. Jordan had changed so much. To start with, maybe he wanted to do too much at once, but he is intelligent and he learned with Brendan in the first year even if he didn't play much. You watched him the following season and he was playing the passes when he saw them. He was taking his time, he was calmer, cleverer. He learned to understand the movements of Daniel and me more too, while the shift to a one-touch game suited him. He also rebelled against the critics; maybe they brought out a part of his character that we didn't know he had.

Brendan changed him; he changed us all.

I remembered Rafa Benítez's Liverpool, which was a team based on being very defensively strong and looking to break, so I didn't necessarily see the new Liverpool as the recovery of historic values, but soon people were talking about that. I heard fans talking about 'pass and move', the way the great Liverpool sides of the Seventies and Eighties had played. From my point of view, there was something in that idea of Joe as the Welsh Xavi. I wouldn't say that we played like Barcelona because it was impossible to emulate the speed, touch and technique of their passing game at the time. But you could see a Spanish influence in the way that Brendan worked. He was interested in Spain, he had studied there, and what he'd learned there was at the heart of our style of play: passing, pressuring high, quick movement, arriving into the area rather than standing there waiting for it, coming inside from wide positions.

It's not quite that simple, of course. You always have to adapt to your environment. For example, Barcelona wouldn't be the same in the English league. In Spain they let you play more. The defenders and the midfielders can play but that's partly because they're allowed to play. The opponents will come and pressure in the middle of the pitch, but no higher. In England, they pressure you more aggressively, they're much more on top of you. Barcelona would have to adapt to that. Equally, if you put Liverpool in the Spanish league they would not be the same. When you see a Spanish team play against an English team, you get a glimpse of that: the Spanish team pressures, sure, but it's different. The English team runs much more, but they often run less intelligently. Generally, English teams are less well ordered. Brendan stood out: his tactical work was exceptional while some opponents seemed to do little in this area.

Brendan quickly showed that he was adaptable too. Changes were made depending on the opposition. Sometimes, if they only had one up front he would leave three back rather than four and use the full-back to give width and depth to the attack. He also knows that he has to listen to the player, to know what he is comfortable doing, and he's exceptional at that.

Liverpool are in very good hands with Brendan Rodgers. The way he coached us during my time there was impressive and I am sure that the methods I enjoyed and found so effective will continue to be employed. Everything Brendan does is built towards perfecting the mechanics of football and making adjustments for the next game or to fulfil a particular objective. Although there weren't any specific instructions to begin with, I knew that as soon as I got into training on Tuesday all the exercises were conditioned by the game the following weekend. It might be a small exercise where we couldn't yet see what he was working towards, but it was always building towards the match. If we did a drill in which the cones had been placed in wider positions, we had a good idea that at the weekend he was going to ask us to open the pitch out. Another example: there was a drill in which four big poles were lined up and we did a three- or four-touch move in which the final pass left a man running beyond the poles: it'd be two forwards and two midfielders and the passes would go *one, two, three, through* . . . Again, it was not said explicitly, but repeating a drill like that would usually be because we were about to face a defence that steps out together in a line. Get the move right and you were one-on-one.

He doesn't explicitly tell players the plans for the game all week long because that would just wear you down and you'd end up switching off. If you came into training on Tuesday and he was already telling us how the opposition's left back was going to play then by the Friday we'd all be going mad. So we worked slowly towards the game and then on the Thursday or the Friday, he might say, 'they're weak here' or 'they're vulner-able in this space'. The instructions became more explicit: 'Look, if they step up here, you're faster than them cutting inside'; 'They always hold the line and you can run past them'; or 'Watch the left back – he's the one who reacts slowly and doesn't step up, playing you onside. He stands watching and doesn't respond as quickly as the other defenders.'

Sometimes what we worked towards was even more explicitly focused on the opposition. When we faced Andy Carroll again, Brendan had seen that West Ham played the ball to the full-backs who then lofted diagonal balls looking for him. So in training we had Martin Kelly pretending to be

Andy, playing like him. We were working against movements that were designed to mimic the way the opposition play. Brendan didn't obsess about telling us about opponents constantly, but through working on certain exercises the message seeped into our minds.

It was the same at the other end of the pitch: depending on the opponents, you would see me make different runs. So, that same week when we were preparing to play West Ham, we knew that their two defenders to the right – our left – were slower. One of the moves we worked on then was receiving the ball on that side and clipping it inside between the two players, knowing that I'm faster and that it would be hard for them to turn quickly enough. You might have seen me turn outside from the middle, because I knew the central defenders didn't want to follow me, but that they would probably feel forced to. It might not be that Brendan said specifically, 'they're slow', it would more be that we'd work on that movement: *arc towards a wide position, receive, turn, clip, run.*

There was always a video session the day before the game. It showed us how the opposition played and where their weaknesses were. The videos were ten or fifteen minutes long – much longer would be counterproductive, I think – and showed us when the defence held the line, when they marked zonally or man to man, or which full-back was the slowest to come out. Then Brendan would say: 'Okay, this guy holds his ground, the winger can go round *here* and the striker makes *this* run . . .'

We'd always practise dead-ball scenarios the day before the game as well. A lot of Premier League teams seemed unprepared for them. Yes, they were ready for a set-play delivered into the area, but they didn't seem ready for the quick free-kick that puts a player in or starts off a new move. There are a lot of coaches who, like Brendan, have studied in Spain and they are bringing that to England, so it is changing. But cleverly prepared movement still catches teams out in England when it might not elsewhere. For example, one of the first games we played under Brendan was against Manchester City at home. City were in a zone, with just two or three players marking man-to-man. At the far post was the then Manchester City defender Kolo Touré. Sebastián Coates was in the area and he made a movement towards the ball and then stopped, so that Touré got blocked off, and Martin Škrtel arrived unmarked at the far post to score.

For the striker there is another element: the goalkeeper. Some stand their ground, others will come out for the ball and you know that too. At Liverpool, I watched videos or the coaching staff would tell me what to expect. Hugo Lloris always comes out: he's very, very quick off his line. You know that you have to react fast or he will smother you but you also know you have the chance to lob him, because you can be confident he's coming off his line. He's very good indeed; sometimes he's over-confident but he has rare agility and speed of reaction. He's one example; then you get goalkeepers who always come out and spread themselves with their legs open, so you know that you can put the ball under them.

I always watch goalkeepers closely and talk to my team-mates about them. I'll usually know if he favours a particular side, if he is quick or slow, if I can finish close to his body or have to put the ball away from him. You know there are some goalkeepers that if you feint to shoot, he'll dive;

with others you can feint all you like but he's just not going to go down, so you have to finish. Goalkeepers will watch me too of course but that doesn't really cross your mind during the game. It's not like you're bluffing and double-bluffing; where that can happen is with penalties. The truth is that you can think about how you're going to finish during a match again and again, you can analyse the goalkeeper endlessly, but when it comes to it you might not do it anyway. Intuition takes over. What you can do, though, is condition your thought-process so that your intuition is informed, at a subconscious level, by what you have studied and what you know about the goalkeeper in front of you.

● ● ●

If the work with Brendan was good, the results were not. We lost 3-0 to West Brom on the first day, with mistakes costing us despite actually starting the game pretty well, and we didn't win any of our first five matches. When we lost the opening game, we were already thinking: 'This is going to be a struggle'. Then there was a 2-2 draw with Manchester City; we were 1-0 and 2-1 up but we conceded a Carlos Tevez goal ten minutes from the end. We were winning 2-1 when Martin made a mistake and they equalised. After that we were beaten 2-0 at home by Arsenal and then Manchester United beat us 2-1 at Anfield. Jonjo Shelvey was sent off shortly before half time against United. Until then, I thought we were the better team: we were more aggressive, we were attacking.

Despite being down to ten men, Stevie did score to put us in the lead a minute after the interval. It was an especially emotional moment for him. Ninety-six balloons had been released by Bobby Charlton and Ian Rush before the game to commemorate Hillsborough – a sign that beyond the footballing rivalry there is a fight for justice which brings people together – and when Stevie scored he celebrated by pointing to the heavens, remembering his cousin who died in the tragedy at the age of just ten. With only ten men on the pitch, it was hard to maintain our superiority, though. Rafael equalised and when Robin Van Persie scored a penalty near the end it felt like a sign that they were going to be ahead of all of us that year. The season was only five weeks old, so emotionally that was hard to take. It brought home that we were set for a difficult campaign; that early optimism was shaken.

At times luck plays a part and it felt like we just didn't have it. It can be hard to convince the players that it's a good idea to go for a new style and that task becomes even more difficult when the results aren't good. After the United game we were eighteenth. We hadn't won and people started comparing the team's record to that under Roy Hodgson. We were playing well, the style was good, but the results were awful and your faith in a new approach is tested by that. I was convinced that in the long run we were going to get it right, that the style, the analysis and the hard work would pay off, but it's inevitable that doubts creep in. You think: 'Pff, this is going to be *hard*.' Our aim was to get into the Champions League, but that was slipping away from us already, and the season had barely started.

Then the fixture list came to our rescue. Next up, Norwich. We won 5-2 at Carrow Road and I scored a hat-trick. It was the second, con-secutive hat-trick I had scored there. People say I must have something against them and sometimes you ask yourself: 'Why do I keep scoring such lovely goals against Norwich and not against City or Chelsea or United?' That year, I'd watched a brilliant shot against Arsenal come back off the post – something that would become a recurring theme – and I immediately thought: 'That would have gone in against Norwich.' Norwich goalkeeper John Ruddy probably thought, 'Yeah, you'd have scored that against me', too.

One of Norwich's players did say something to me the last time we played that made me laugh: 'You're up against your friend today,' he said.

But Ruddy's a good goalkeeper, it's not his fault. I'm lucky against him. He said to me himself: 'Always you! Hey, next time, don't worry about turning up, alright?'

When I left for Barcelona, he joked on Twitter that he surely deserved a cut of the transfer fee.

It really is luck. I scored in the second minute of that game and, suddenly, I thought: 'Okay, this is different. Everything's going to go well today.' When I scored the first against Norwich that day I didn't even hit the ball that well, but right there everything changed, the confidence flowed through me. I thought: 'Well, if that's gone in, everything will go in.'

Sometimes it works against you, but it can take only the smallest thing to get you going. The following season against Norwich, in December 2013, I was awful for the first ten or fifteen minutes; I lost every ball. At one point I was running at a defender and I was tripping up, stumbling, and I lost it again. I said to myself: 'Luis, you're in for a long night if you can't get past a Norwich defender.' It's not that I think they're not good players, it's that they're supposed to be *my* team.

I started to get desperate. I was so annoyed with myself. Then I scored from a long way out, then from the corner, then another one, then another. Four goals! Inexplicable. I wasn't even playing well, but suddenly the luck was on my side. Suddenly I was unstoppable.

There are times when every shot seems to be going in, but when things aren't going well, strikers go mad desperately trying to score, determined to break the run. You reach the point where you think: 'What the hell is happening to me?' You start looking for solutions. You change things in your routine. You change boots. You go out on to the pitch in a different order. You train differently. And yet you learn that training isn't really the issue: you can get to the game after a week of great sessions thinking, 'I'm on form', but you're not. I'd rather not be scoring all week; I'd rather save my goals until the game. It's true that almost straight away in a game you know if you're going to play well or not, although there have been times when it has taken the manager to pull me aside at half time, saying something to change my focus or the way I'm playing, or just delivering a wake-up call, to get me to perform better: 'What's the matter with you?'

And then, almost by chance, a bad run can suddenly end. I've come to realise that the best thing to do is not to look for it, that the bad run will end naturally. I'm gradually learning that I have to be calmer. Sometimes my intuition tells me that I'm going to have a bad patch, even before people really realise: sometimes I just know. It's helpful to recognise that, rather than desperately chasing the goal. It's better to forget it and play, enjoy the game, not the goals. When I'm confident I'll take on a shot from a position that I would never normally shoot from; when I'm struggling to score goals and I have a half-chance, I'll look for the pass instead. That's better than obsessing about scoring. And sometimes it'll come and I'll think: 'Luis, you're so lucky.'

The Norwich game was something of a turning point for us, proof that we were improving, and from that moment our expectations grew. It's true that we only won one of the next five but we didn't lose either and we drew with Everton (2-2) and Chelsea (1-1) along the way.

I probably enjoyed Everton-Liverpool more than Liverpool-Everton derby games; the atmosphere at Goodison got me going. The fans were close to the pitch, noisy, and I liked feeling that they were against us. I scored that day – the one which I celebrated by diving in front of David Moyes – and Stevie thought he'd set me up for an injury-time winner. His free-kick was headed down by Sebastián Coates and I knocked the ball into the net. It took the linesman a long time to raise his flag for offside and by the time any of us realised, Stevie had run eighty yards towards the Liverpool fans to celebrate. He had his back to the linesman, so he had no idea the goal had been ruled out. We were furious, but couldn't help but laugh a bit too.

● ● ●

Things were looking up, but we needed something more. The squad was short, despite signing Fabio Borini from Roma. I knew that if I got injured or suspended we didn't really have anyone to replace me and the same was true if anything happened to Joe Allen. We had Suso and Raheem Sterling but they were still both very young and the manager didn't really have much more. We knew that if a game got complicated we didn't have substitutes to bring on to change things either; there just weren't enough players. We talked about it among ourselves, but we didn't need to tell the manager. He knew it. In fact, he said so. He told us that there would be players arriving in January. What we didn't know was who.

When Daniel Sturridge and Philippe Coutinho signed we were delighted. It wasn't just that they are good players, it was also that they both came with an attitude that said: 'We're here to help.' Things had not been going that well for either of them at their previous clubs, so they were determined to really make it work at Liverpool, to prove themselves. They also had the faith and the trust of the manager. Brendan put them straight in.

Daniel's first game was an FA Cup tie at Mansfield Town in January and he scored. We won 2-1 and I scored too – with my hand. It was entirely accidental but that was at a time when whatever went wrong seemed to have huge repercussions if I was involved. The ball hit me on the hand. It wasn't deliberate. When I scored, I assumed that it had been disallowed. It wasn't until I looked at the referee and saw that he was heading back to the halfway line that I realised it was a goal. And, honestly, I thought straight away: 'Here we go again.' I was already anticipating people attacking me.

Their manager Paul Cox understood; he described the handball as 'instinctive'. He knew I hadn't done it deliberately and he said that he would have celebrated if one of his players had scored like that. He admitted that it wasn't my job to disallow the goal. It was the referee's job.

Some people said I was celebrating the handball by kissing my hand, adding insult to injury But that was the same way I always celebrate. I remember when I was a kid watching players with trademark celebrations: Claudio 'Piojo' López, Marcelo Salas, Ronaldo, or Bebeto. And you would say to yourself: 'I'd love to have a celebration of my own one day.' I was in Holland at the time, bored in the Ajax team hotel, and I was speaking to Sofi on the phone and I said to her: 'You know what? I've been thinking and I reckon I need a celebration of my own.' My own copyright. When I was a kid I wanted to celebrate like Marcelo Salas, but I didn't want to copy anyone. I was standing there in front of the mirror thinking: 'What can I do?' And I started waggling my fingers up and down, and I thought, 'Yeah, that's not so bad . . .' It wasn't a gunslinger thing, I wasn't trying to be El Pistolero or anything, it was just the fingers. More of a dance than a shooting gesture. And Sofi said, 'Yeah, that's okay, I suppose.'

Later came the gesture of kissing my wedding ring finger, which was for Sofi. Then Delfina was born and it became: kiss the ring finger and then the wrist, where I had Delfina's name tattooed. Some Liverpool fans worked out that Delfina was an anagram of Anfield and so that went down pretty well, although I had no idea: it was pure chance.

When Benjamin was born I didn't really want to have another tattoo in a line on the same wrist, but I had to do something for him, so I was going to put it on the other wrist. Then I realised that if I tattooed his name on the other wrist I'd need five minutes to celebrate every goal. So I got his name tattooed on the same wrist as Delfi. I swear that in the end I did it that way because of my celebration: I couldn't kiss my ring, then one wrist, then the other. It was getting out of hand already.

But that's why I celebrated like that against Mansfield; not because I'd just scored with my hand.

Above: Clashing with Patrice Evra.
I didn't start the argument; little
did I know what was to follow.

Below: The handshake that never was. I
had every intention of shaking his hand,
but I ended up the bad guy once again.

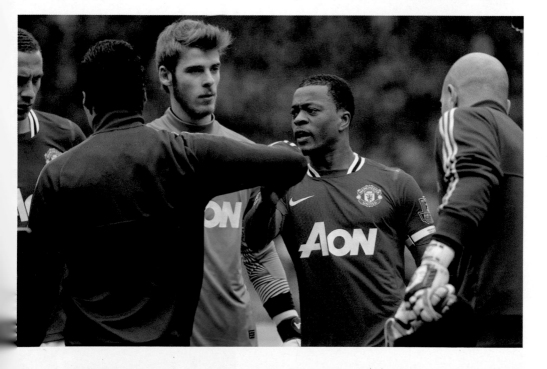

In the aftermath of the Evra incident my team-mates' support was fantastic.

Captaining Liverpool was a great honour for me.

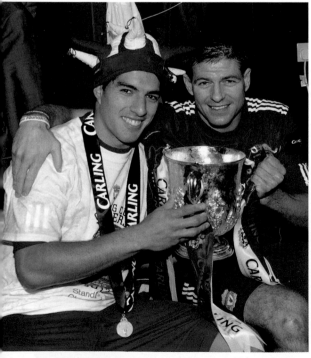

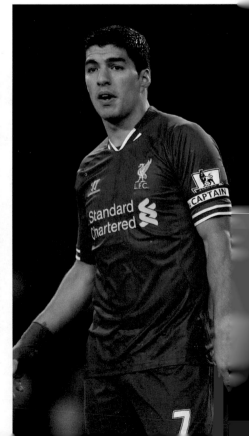

Captain Fantastic. Celebrating our Carling Cup win with Stevie. I idolised him as a teenager and now I have a signed shirt of his on my wall.

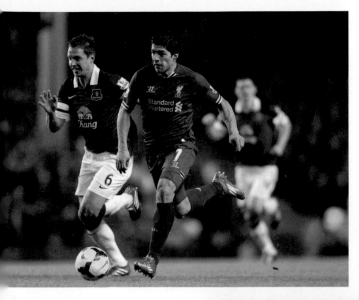

Left: I loved playing in the derby against Everton. Here I am against Phil Jagielka who I would face again at the 2014 World Cup.

Below: I always seemed to do well against Norwich. This volley in December 2013 was my first of four in a 5-1 win.

Below: This one's definitely a dive. I throw myself down in front of David Moyes after his comments before the Merseyside derby.

With the love of my life, my wife Sofi.

Above and Below: My two beautiful children – Delfina and Benjamin.

When the final whistle went at Selhurst Park, I just wanted to disappear. Kolo Touré led me from the pitch.

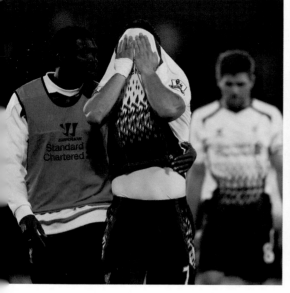

Proud to win the PFA Player of the Year award. But it was the ceremony none of us wanted to go to, coming just hours after defeat to Chelsea.

Showing off my Golden Samba award to Delfina and Benjamin at Anfield.

When I scored the first goal against England I embraced Walter Ferreira, who had worked tirelessly to get me fit for the game.

The second goal against England. 'When you hit it you were falling, you couldn't stand anymore', Walter told me afterwards.

Moments after biting Italian defender Giorgio Chiellini. Diego Godin scored shortly after and we were through...but I was going home.

The incredible Uruguayan fans supporting me in Brazil even after I had been sent home.

Struggling to reach the Court of Arbitration. It was worth it: they lifted my ban from all football activity.

Finally presented as a Barcelona player.

For one night only. My Barcelona debut against Mexican side Club León.

With my new team-mates.

After beating Mansfield we drew Oldham Athletic away. For the first time, I was made Liverpool's captain. The truth is, I was surprised. As I didn't speak much English, I didn't see myself as the ideal candidate. When Brendan said I was going to be captain I went to see him and said that I preferred him to give the armband to someone else. I thought it was better for Martin Škrtel to be captain but Brendan told me that the staff had decided that I would be captain so I gratefully accepted it. My first job as captain was to go to see Martin and explain to him what had happened because I didn't want him to feel usurped and because, honestly, I thought he was a better candidate for the captaincy than me. He said he didn't mind. It wasn't that I didn't want to be the captain of Liverpool, it was that I didn't want to disrespect team-mates who deserved it more. It was an honour.

On the pitch, being captain didn't change anything very much, but there were some jobs that I had to do and some things I had to change. When I was at Ajax, I used to play with my socks rolled down and my shirt hanging out, but that changed as soon as they made me captain; I tucked my shirt in and pulled my socks up, literally.

At Liverpool that continued and now, of course, I also had to lead the team out. Which is a bit of a problem for someone who's superstitious and always goes out last.

There were other jobs to do too which I wasn't aware of. I was sitting there in the away dressing room at Oldham, listening to music with my headphones in and the assistant coach Colin Pascoe came over and said: 'Luis, we've got to go and see the referee.' You go in to talk to the other captain, the referee tells you about what time you have to be ready in the tunnel and asks you to make sure your team-mates have taken off their jewellery and covered their rings with tape.

Unlike in Holland, I didn't have to do a team-talk or anything like that. I would have died of embarrassment. I didn't even know how to say 'heads' or 'tails'. Luckily, the referee had brought a coin of his own which had a picture of the sun on one side and I knew that, so I just said: 'Sun'. I couldn't really say much else and if they had started to talk to me about anything else I would have been sunk. I didn't have the English for it. I was nervous.

And then when it came to it, the game was terrible; not exactly the way I dreamed of captaining Liverpool. When you play a lower division team in the Cup, there's always a risk. It's hard to stop yourself just assuming you're going to win. But then the game was slower than normal, I felt myself getting cold, and all the while our opponents were growing in confidence. We lost 3-2. It was horrible to get knocked out of the Cup by Oldham. I had started the game as captain and I finished it a failure.

We were improving overall, though. And the new boys, Daniel Sturridge and Philippe Coutinho, were making a huge difference.

Philippe was incredible. He changed us completely. He's the one that gave us faith in having the ball because his technical ability is so good. You knew that he wouldn't lose it, you knew that he would produce something special with it, that he would always choose the right pass. He got tired very quickly in his first games for the club and had to be substituted because he had come from a league that is not as physical and he was not playing that often, but you could see straight away that he was different. We were all hugely impressed with him from day one.

Meanwhile, Daniel was about to become the best partner I'd had in my career. I had seen Daniel play at Chelsea, although truth be told I didn't even know that he had been at Manchester City. I also had no idea that his dad had been a player. But I had watched him play and I liked him a lot. I could see that he could make a difference. When I watched him in training, my appreciation for his ability grew. I knew that he was quick but the way that he could finish really struck me. Every shot went in. Every time. He had the talent and Liverpool offered him the opportunity and continuity that he hadn't had at Chelsea. He had the ambition to make sure that if he was given that, he would perform.

The first time I spoke to Daniel at Melwood, he surprised me because he said to me: 'Together, you and I can do something big here.' It's natural that players can feel that a new signing is coming to compete with them for a place and I'm no different. Nor, I assumed, was Daniel.

It's not normal for a new player to be quite so bold as Daniel was that day, and I did momentarily think, 'What's this guy saying that to me for?' But right from the start, he saw it as the two of us going out there together. Daniel would have been entitled to be worried, to think to himself: 'Luis is the number 9, I'm not going to get many chances here either, just like at Chelsea.' He probably thought that, initially, he would have to wait for his chance, rather than necessarily to play with me all the time. And to start with we didn't always play together. But Brendan wanted us both to be in the team and Daniel knew that we needed that help. We knew it too.

Playing us both did involve making changes, though, and I was not entirely sure about it to begin with. Brendan asked if I could play some games on the right or the left, or even as a number 10. I think I played as a number 10 more often than not and that was essentially to make it possible for us both to play at the same time. When Brendan first asked, there was a bit of me that thought: 'Hang on, I'm the number 9.' But he was intelligent in the way he presented it to me, saying: 'Luis, we need another striker so that we don't rely solely on you and also to try to open space up for you.' I accepted his reasoning and I soon saw that it would help me and the team too.

It wasn't always a smooth process. And when I said, 'I'm the number 9', well, part of the problem was that I'm not really. At first, Brendan wanted me to spend more time in the area and it didn't really work the way that he would have liked, mainly because I wouldn't always get into the box in time or I didn't always limit my movements to the areas he wanted me to occupy. I'm not a static player. He would give me videos and explain to me the kind of movements that he wanted me to make and I understood what he wanted; the problem was that it just didn't come naturally to me to play like that. I can't be in there waiting for the ball. To begin with, we were creating chances but I wasn't in the area to finish them off.

We didn't really talk about it that much. In truth, I suspect Brendan got a bit tired of telling me what kind of movements he wanted, where he wanted me to be positioned, only to see that I just wasn't going to change. Not because I was being stubborn or ignoring him, not because I thought I knew better – although players do have a tendency to think that – but just because my game is my game and my nature took over. I might be in the position that he wanted me to be in, inside the area, for ten or fifteen minutes, thinking carefully about his instructions, but then the next twenty-five I'd be drifting back out to my old position, as my instincts kicked in. He kept saying to me not to drop so deep, or not to pull so wide, because he wanted me in the area and because if you lose the ball so deep it puts the team in trouble. But it was hard for me.

When Daniel came and he played in the middle and I played a few games wider, I saw that I could help the team and that it suited me. But I couldn't play as a winger; I still had that tendency to come inside. I can play two or three games on the wing for you, but by the fourth game, I'll be annoyed. I won't play all season there because it's just not my position. Brendan's style evolved because of the players he had and one of those players was me. He wants the players to feel comfortable on the pitch and when he saw that I am most comfortable moving from the middle to the left and then coming inside, he looked for a way to take advantage of that and get the best out of me.

Brendan also realised that there would come a time that I might not track the full-back, that I might not react quickly enough in defensive areas, so he looked for a formula by which he could play me and Daniel in a way that meant we were both comfortable. At times decisions are made to keep good players happy as much as they are to create a particular tactical structure. It's not easy for managers.

Brendan found a way. Some of the mechanisms were learned of course but we naturally made different runs and we found ourselves in different positions. As it turned out we complemented each other very well. It's hard for defenders when there are two players who are mobile. If you have someone like Daniel who moves well, who's quick, who finishes chances well, then that makes space for me and vice versa. Opposition managers thought: 'You've got to mark Suárez', but that left space for Daniel; it wasn't so obvious to them what to do.

I suspect people doubted that it could work, that they thought: 'Sure, they'll pass the ball to each other sometimes but ultimately they're selfish.' I'll tell you something: *all* strikers are selfish. Every striker is an egotist. Every one. I don't know of any that aren't. But that's not a bad thing and it's not a problem either; the team benefits from that. When I say strikers are selfish, that's the way it should be. There are times when attackers who are generous waste chances precisely because they want to pass the ball when they shouldn't; it's about wanting to win games.

Of course, you have times when you argue on the pitch, but that's often a product of the way you see things in the heat of the moment and you're not always right. Sometimes, you make a run and you start shouting for it and you're convinced you're free. Meanwhile, your team-mate with the ball is looking at you and thinking: 'He's got two men on him.' You say something to him and people think you're arguing, or that you don't get on, but that's not true – it's just that you thought you could see the chance to shoot and he couldn't see it. You watch it back on the television later and he's right. Or he may say sorry that he made the wrong decision and explain that he thought you were marked when he looked up.

Then maybe three or four games later he passes it to you every time and you think: '*Today* he's passing to me?' Of course: because every game is different, the circumstances change, the spaces you have are different. He can be wrong, but he is taking a decision for the right reason every time. You can be wrong too. This time he saw that passing to you was a good option, the time before he didn't. That's all. People might see you talking or calling for the ball, even arguing, and they assume there is a problem between you, but that's not the case.

By the end of the 2012/13 season, I had scored 23 league goals, despite missing the final five games because of the ban for biting Branislav Ivanović; at that point I was ahead of Robin van Persie. Daniel had scored eleven and he had only been with us for half the season.

Daniel and I never talked about who had scored more goals. Not even as a joke. We both like to score goals, but neither of us is obsessed by being the star or the top scorer. The selfishness is a footballing one. It is about the drive for goals within the game, about trying to win. It is not about, in either of our cases, wanting to be bigger than anyone else. It's about the way we play, that sense of helping the team, not about racking up goals for the sake of statistics.

The only time I remember even being aware of statistics while I was at Liverpool was during the final Premier League game of last season against Newcastle, the game that would turn out to be my last for the club. I knew that I would win the European Golden Shoe if I scored a goal or two. I wasn't obsessed by scoring and I never put individual awards ahead of team ones, but it is true that that day I thought about it. I knew that it would be an important award for me and for Liverpool. I told Stevie I would like to take the penalty if there was one. When we were winning and players were gesturing for us just to keep the ball, I was saying the opposite. I wanted us to attack, to go forward. I got wound up. I was shouting, 'No, no, attack!' I wanted to score for me, but I also wanted the team to go for it. I thought about myself that time, it's true. But that was the only time and only on the final day; my personal goal tally was never the driving force during the season.

If I just wanted goals for goals' sake, I would have asked Stevie to let me take the penalties a long time before, to chase the record. But that never occurred to me before and it didn't occur to Daniel either. In February of that season, we were beating Swansea 4-0 and we got a penalty. Daniel asked Stevie if he could take it – not because he wanted the goal in itself, but because it was a good way of breaking a bad run and getting back on track. Stevie gave it to him and he scored; just another understated indication of the kind of captain he is.

As for Daniel and me, the partnership turned out so well that people started to call us the 'SAS'. Mind you, I have a confession to make: I knew that SAS stood for 'Sturridge and Suárez' but I had no idea what the actual SAS was.

MATCH DAY

By the end of my time at Liverpool, the ritual was well established. At the end of every game, the physios would come round the dressing room and hand out the smoothies.

'Luis, what flavour do you want? Chocolate or fruit?'

They always asked and sometimes I'd even answer.

One day it would be, 'Chocolate'; another, 'Fruit'.

But it made no difference and it became a bit of a game: they knew that whatever flavour I said, it would end up in the bin. At Liverpool the smoothies are specially prepared, just like they are at other clubs too, and I know that Barcelona use them as well. They're designed to help our recovery and the staff at Liverpool tried, and tried, to make me drink them but in the end they just gave up. Virtually all I drink is water – lots and lots of water.

It started when I was in Holland and I haven't stopped since.

In part it's nerves. In the build-up to the game, I'm constantly sipping water. I have always got a bottle in my hand. The physios can't believe how much I drink. Before a game, I can easily get through four or five litres of water. And with that and the mate, I take on loads of fluid. During the game, you forget about everything but afterwards it hits me and I am in and out of the toilet constantly. I'll meet my wife afterwards and almost as soon as I'm there with her, it will be: 'Hang on, I've just got to go the toilet.'

Then twenty minutes later it's: 'Won't be a minute, I'm just going to the toilet.'

It's handy when it comes to the drug testing after the game. Most players take ages to give a sample, but I'm in and out in no time.

It drives Sofi mad and my team-mates are always laughing at me – if we're on the bus or catching a flight, I'm always dashing off. They're looking at me, thinking: 'What? Again?'

I hardly eat anything either. Liverpool's physios, and the staff with the Uruguay team, have said to me before: 'How can you drink so much water, never want to eat anything and then run about the way you do during games?'

If we're playing at 3 p.m., I'll get up at nine-thirty or ten and I'll have my mate which has a litre and a half of water in. Then I'm on to the little bottles of water all the way up to the game: I'll get through five or six of those, all in about two-and-a-half, three hours. The last thing I want is a big plate of pasta on top of that.

When we play at lunchtime, I'll have a bit of toast with my mate at breakfast, but nothing else. I sit there and watch players tuck into huge bowls of pasta at ten in the morning and I don't know how they do it. At one or two o'clock in the afternoon, fine, but this is at ten in the morning. I won't touch it. And even at lunchtime, I barely eat anything: no pasta, no shakes, just water and a bit of salad.

Physios, nutritionists, managers and coaches have all tried to encourage me to eat more, but it's pointless now. They don't understand why I hardly ever get muscular injuries. It defies the science, but it seems to work for me. I'm not against the idea that you have a nutritional smoothie after games if it helps your recovery from the match, but whenever I've taken them I've felt ill.

For me, it's water: water before the game, water at half time and water at full time too. It became a routine. They'd come round and ask: 'Chocolate or fruit?' They never knew what I was going to say. But they did know where it was going to end up. Barcelona's physios have been warned . . .

7

Even before Steven Gerrard started talking we could see the tears welling up in his eyes. We saw then what it meant, we could feel what a huge moment this was. This was real and it was raw. He hadn't done it for show. In fact, when he saw the TV cameras, he tried to hide his face. It was 13 April 2014. We had just beaten Manchester City 3-2 and now we really did believe that we could win the league. Stevie pulled the players in a huddle. We stood there on the pitch at Anfield, arms round each other, exhausted and elated, a tiny circle in the middle of a deafening noise, people celebrating all around us. And there he delivered an incredible speech that still sends a shiver down my back when I think about it.

It wasn't the first time his words had moved me. The previous summer, I had virtually made up my mind that I had to leave Liverpool. Stevie's intervention helped changed my mind.

On a personal level, 2012/13 had been a very good season until *that* moment against Chelsea. I don't know what was going through my mind at the time; afterwards, everything went through my mind.

The season ended five games early for me because of the ban, and I felt like my time in England had to end too. Politicians, who should have more important things to worry about, had joined the queue to condemn me and I had had enough. David Cameron said I set 'the most appalling example'. When even the Prime Minister is passing comment on your behaviour, it's probably time to think about leaving the country.

I felt like I was stuck in the middle while all around me people took aim. Everyone had their say and no one was saying anything good. I felt suffocated. I wanted to leave.

The desire to get away in the summer of 2013 was the accumulation of various things. The previous season had seen us fail to get into the Champions League; I had been given a ten-game ban for biting Ivanović and was back to being Public Enemy Number One. I was unable even to take my little girl to the park in peace and I felt under siege with the paparazzi following me and my family wherever we went. I think most people would struggle to cope with that level of negative attention. It was getting to me and upsetting the lives of the people I love most. I'm not a robot, I have feelings. And I was mostly feeling miserable at the time.

I was tired of seeing myself in the papers all the time. I was tired of: 'Suárez is this' and 'Suárez is that'. I was tired of everybody pontificating about me and my actions. If it wasn't the Prime Minister then it was the manager of this team or that team and I just thought: 'I can't stand this any more. I want out.' I just wanted to leave England. I thought Sofi and the children and I would all be better off elsewhere.

I was conscious of the fact that I had done something wrong on the pitch. I had accepted my punishment, apologised, and still the critics kept on. I couldn't see a way out and I thought it was going to be virtually impossible to come back and start playing again in England. In my confused state, getting out of the country seemed like the only solution.

I was also still not playing in the Champions League. I was approaching my twenty-seventh birthday and I was looking at another season outside of Europe's top competition. I was aware of a clause in my contract that meant that if Liverpool finished outside the Champions League I could negotiate a move away provided a buying club offered over £40 million for me. So I had the reasons to leave; I had the contractual right to do so; and if the rumours were to be believed I had clubs who were interested in me too. It was down to my representative, Pere Guardiola, to find out what the options were. He didn't have it easy. I was the guy who had just been banned for ten games for biting someone and a year earlier had been accused of being a racist. I think there were big clubs who thought I'd bring problems and damage their image. Part of me thought: 'Judge me on what I do on the pitch' – but then again, the biting incidents happened on the pitch.

There were clubs that showed an interest, but only one officially made a bid that went over the £40m threshold: Arsenal.

This was not going to get any less complicated and the deeper in I got, the more torn I became, the more confused and unsure, but one idea kept resurfacing: I have to go. I wanted out because I wanted out of England, but there was also my frustration at not being able to play in the Champions League. Now here was a club that was in the Champions

League, but was still in England. My head was all over the place. Would this move be the answer or would it create even more problems? I didn't know what to do. I was not training well; emotionally, I was not right. I wanted people to understand why I wanted to leave but I was just being seen as the greedy player with no loyalty, something that is very far from the truth.

Because Arsenal had emerged as the club most interested in signing me, I started to wonder whether a change of city might have the same effect as a change of country. I told myself that it's easier for players to become anonymous in London and that was what I wanted. I couldn't walk down the street or go to a supermarket in peace any more. My family felt under pressure too. I had told Pere that I couldn't go to another club in England. There had been too much abuse and too much attention; there were the three cars of photographers following me and my family out of our house and the four cars that would follow us home. If you can't walk down to the end of the street in peace, it's time to go. But maybe, I now told myself, London was an option. A big city; a chance to get lost and to play Champions League football. Deep down, it wasn't what I really wanted, but I began to tell myself that this might work. The doubts surfaced quickly, though. Going to Arsenal had the potential to be even worse. I would still be in the same country only I would have Liverpool fans against me as well as everybody else. I was about to alienate the only people who had really stood by me, people whose support I had been so grateful for.

I've never really thought about what would have happened if Liverpool had accepted Arsenal's bid. Would I have become an Arsenal player? I would have regretted it and I'm not just saying that because of the way things turned out for the team – I don't know what position Liverpool would have finished in in 2013/14 without me or in what position Arsenal would have finished with me – but the regret would have eaten away at me when I saw the Liverpool supporters and when they saw me in the shirt of one of their rivals.

There was one reason for going to Arsenal and that was the European football they offered. I had tried to convince myself that it was the key when really the key was getting away from it all; it was as if I was on the rebound. I was grasping for a way out, telling myself that anything would be better. I just needed to do something, I didn't know what, but *something*.

That was where Steven Gerrard came in. He assured me that if I stayed at Liverpool we would be back in the Champions League in just one season. If I was going to leave Liverpool, he said, I should only do it for one of the giant clubs abroad. I shouldn't take a move that did not entirely convince. If I was going to go it had to be the right move and for the right reasons. We exchanged text messages while I was in Japan with Uruguay, then spoke at Melwood. I had been training apart from the Liverpool team before the trip, but I did have a knock, otherwise I think I would have been with the group. This wasn't an attempt to force my way out – Stevie knew that. He understood.

He told me to wait. There was no point missing what could be a big season for Liverpool and the chance to make it up to the fans after the ban, and no point in leaving unless it was for a huge new football challenge. Something clicked inside my head after speaking with him. I came away thinking: 'I've fought so hard to get where I am today as a player, I'm not going to ruin it all for something stupid, an ill-thought-out and wrong turn in my career. I had thought that moving on was the answer; now I was convinced that it wasn't.

Footballers understand how it is. If a player leaves for a better situation the other players usually congratulate him because they know he has done it to improve himself. Stevie knew that I had not wanted to show a lack of respect to my team-mates. But he also told me that I hadn't been the same in the training sessions. I accepted that, I thought he was right. I made my mind up that from that point on I was going to train harder than ever.

There was another massive factor too, one I would eventually be grateful for even if I did not see it that way at the time As determined as Stevie was that I stayed, Liverpool were determined to keep me. Right from the start they were adamant that I was going nowhere. The club never wavered. Even when the private, informal offers were higher than the Arsenal one, they were publicly making it clear that whatever the money was on the table, they were going to turn it down.

I'd previously had a text message conversation with club chairman Tom Werner. I had been prepared to go the United States and explain my situation to the owners of the club, but they said to me: 'Luis, you are staying. Our position is as Brendan and Ian Ayre have said it is: you're not leaving. We don't want to sell you.'

Once I had said I wanted to go and then it had become clear that I would be staying, I was in a potentially difficult situation and I knew there was only one solution: be brave and stick my chest out to meet the bullets. Work hard on the training ground and run until I dropped on the pitch. I had never had a problem with Liverpool. I never had anything against the fans or against my team-mates. I just wanted my life to change, to escape the pressure and tension.

The months went by and I was scoring goals again, but it still bothered me that I had said what I said in the summer. I still felt bad. I didn't talk a great deal with the manager – in fact, during September and October I hardly spoke to Brendan at all. Conversation was at a minimum and strictly about football. I felt bad about everything that had happened between us. I had reached a point of desperation. When I did move the following summer, it was totally different.

Brendan had said that I had shown a lack of respect to the players by speaking out publicly of my desire to leave. I think if he had said that to my face it would have felt totally different. But he had said it publicly. We weren't talking a lot at the time and for him to address me through the media upset me. Why had he not just come to me and said those things? He would argue: 'Why did you say in the media what you could have said to me face to face?' The difference to me was that he and the club knew how I felt before I had gone public. He was the first to be told. I did not make a public statement until, desperate, confused and feeling stuck, I thought I had to.

Brendan knows what it's like to be a player. He had done the same as a coach, looking to improve and grow. He had gone from Swansea to Liverpool.

Before what had happened with Ivanović, the conversations with him had been more general – 'How is the family?', 'How are things away from football?' But during those first couple of months of the season it was strictly football. Gradually the relationship thawed. In October we had a conversation that more or less drew a line under the whole affair; it was time to forget it and play. There was a sense of forgetting everything that had happened and concentrating on working together for the good of Liverpool. It was a relief. That was underlined by signing a new contract with the club. I was happy; I did not want any confrontation. If I was going to go, it was going to be done in the right way and for the right price; it would be good for everyone.

The players were happy that things had been sorted and that I was staying. Martin Škrtel kept winding me up, telling me: 'I'm still waiting for you to say you are sorry in front of the entire dressing room.'

The club was showing me more than ever that they valued the work that I was doing on the pitch. There was a moment when the owner John Henry put a private plane at my disposal so that I could return quickly from international duty with Uruguay to play the derby against Everton, which showed that there was still a lot of affection towards me. They had never done that for a player before and it showed me that they really valued me and valued my ability to bounce back as well. I think they recognised that after all that had happened – the suspension, the wanting to leave, doing an interview to say as much, and all the problems that those things had caused – I was still capable of working hard, playing well and scoring goals. I think they appreciated that. I also think they had always known that. It was one of the reasons they were so convinced that it was right to fight to keep hold of me: they knew I was never going to sulk or not give a hundred per cent. They knew that once I crossed that line, I would do everything I could to win for them.

It isn't in my character to stop running or down tools. I remember when I said to Brendan that I was not comfortable and that if I stayed I was not going to be happy. He said to me: 'Yeah, but I know what you are like. I know how you live.'

A bit later I was in my hotel room going over his words in my head and I realised what he had meant. He knew that for all that I wanted to go, if I stayed, I would never create the slightest problem for him.

That is why it hurt me at the time to hear certain ex-Liverpool players come out and say that I lacked loyalty. They ought to know better. They know how much you have to take your family's well-being into consideration and they also knew how I had come to feel so worn down. If I tried to force a move by refusing to play, by feigning injury or by not giving my all for the team, then – and only then – could they say I lacked loyalty. The players who don't run for their team-mates and for their club are the ones who lack loyalty. That's something that you could never accuse me of.

I had been so confused; hurt, under pressure, a little desperate, unsure of where to turn, with contradictory thoughts swirling round my head.

I'm certain now that it would have been wrong to go to one of Liverpool's direct rivals. I would have lost the happiness I recovered over the course of the season and it would have been the wrong move. I would have missed out on the pride of having a son born in Liverpool, I would have let down the people who looked after me, who defended me and understood me, who knew me best. I would not have had the satisfaction of working through that, of proving to myself and to others that I could overcome it, of helping to fulfil the promise of bringing Liverpool back to the Champions League. The following season, I was happy on and off the pitch and that is largely because I stayed. I was fortunate: I could have ruined that. When I spoke to Tom Werner he always said thank you for all that I was doing for the club and that meant a lot to me. He had understood too, and I understood his position. Ultimately, I was grateful for it. He and others had stopped me from making a mistake. The words of my captain, the determination of the club not to let me leave, and my own change of heart had meant that in the end I stayed. And, as Brendan knew, I would be doing so with all my heart; no half-measures. The overriding sensation as the 2013/14 season progressed was one of relief. I was so glad I stayed. I was so glad that the relationship with the supporters survived too. Even with the fans who are most difficult to convince, goals tend to cure all ills. I think they knew I had been unhappy and that now I wanted to make it up to them. Now we were on the verge.

● ● ●

This was how we dreamt it; we had known for a long time that it could be a huge day.

I remember waking up that Sunday morning in April and looking at the clock. *Not long now.*

That day something was moving in Liverpool. You could see it and hear it, *feel* it. Everything had been building towards this moment for weeks and now it felt as if this was the moment that would define our season. More than our season – some supporters told us Liverpool had waited more than twenty years for this. As for me, I'd almost walked away and now look. Now we were close to glory. We'd kept on winning and winning and winning, the momentum growing. We had won nine Premier League games in a row and with every victory it became more real. Win one more today and, never mind finishing in the top four like Steven Gerrard had promised, we might actually win the title.

That's how the fans felt. I'd heard it thousands of times over the previous few weeks: 'Luis, we *have* to win the league.' Supporters had started lining the road outside the team hotel and outside Anfield ever since the Sunderland game at the end of March. I'd never seen that in England before and in the days before we played Manchester City whenever I came across fans they were even more insistent: 'We've got to win on Sunday.'

I was thinking: 'Calm down, there are still four or five games to go.'

The fans chanted: 'We're going to win the league! We're going to win the league! And now you're going to believe us, we're going to win the league!'

No, don't sing that. Not yet. Sing something else. *Please.*

But we all understood the excitement. I was a fan; I watched Nacional matches like they watch Liverpool matches, with real passion. I would go mad when we won (and mad when we lost). Besides, it was not just that we understood the excitement; it was that we had started to share it. It was inescapable. *And now you're going to believe us?* We had started to. Maybe, just maybe, we really could win the league. And when we beat Manchester City with four games to go, I really did believe.

The Premier League title was within touching distance. We had taken a giant step. I tried not to think about it, and superstition meant that virtually nobody dared say so, at least not openly, but we could not help it. We knew that the City game was big.

As the bus got closer to Anfield on the morning of the match, it slowed to a crawl. There were thousands of fans lining the route, singing and waving flags and scarves. There were Uruguayan flags among them. Some let off fireworks. It took the bus ages to nudge its way through.

On board, we all tried to stick to our normal pre-match routines, like any other game. I always took a little speaker so that four or five of us could listen to a bit of Spanish music or even Uruguayan music. I wouldn't put it on too loud because not everyone liked it. There would be a table of four with Iago Aspas, Coutinho, Lucas and Luis Alberto around it. Danny Agger listening in and laughing. Steven Gerrard further back. Glen Johnson with his headphones on, Daniel Sturridge too. On another table nearer the front would be Jon Flanagan, Joe Allen, Martin Kelly and Jordan Henderson, talking among themselves. At the very front was the boss. Sometimes one of his assistants would pass through to show us videos on an iPad. Maybe he'd show me some set-pieces or show Stevie some footage of their keeper facing penalties.

That day, though, was different, even though we tried to keep the routine. It was impossible not to be drawn to what was happening outside. Players had their phones out and were recording the scenes through the windows. For most footballers, seeing that support, what it means to people, is a source of motivation. For others, it can be frightening: some fear they will make a mistake. But we were ready: we were calm.

Eventually, we pulled up outside the ground. Through the main doors and along the narrow corridor, the dressing room is more or less organised according to the players' positions on the pitch. Bill Shankly wanted it that way as a way of bringing players together who would be close during the game. As you went through the small door, to your left was the goal-keeper Simon Mignolet, then Johnson, Agger, Škrtel, Kolo . . . Gerrard, Henderson, Allen . . . Moses, Sturridge. Defence, midfield, attack. We were all in our usual spots, but it felt different that day.

I had Philippe Coutinho alongside me and I was talking to him. He's only twenty-one and he's a phenomenal player – he picks a pass in a split-second before a defender has had the time to think – but he gets frustrated if he's not on the ball. I told him he didn't need to worry or get wound up. I'm a good friend of his, but we'd argued in the past out on the pitch. That afternoon, I told him he didn't need to prove anything because he was one of the best players in his position in the world. Don't get distracted: relax, just play.

I spoke to Raheem Sterling too. If he wants to, Raheem can be the best in the world one-on-one. He's just nineteen. Sometimes he uses his speed and his ability in one-on-ones to the detriment of the team and he just has to learn when to use a one-two instead of dribbling. As quick as he is, it is sometimes quicker to use a wall pass than a solo run. He's improving all the time; games like this one would help him. Stevie has talked with him a lot too and he really listens.

I don't really know why I decided to speak to them on that day. I don't see myself as a leader in the dressing room, but I have been around a long time now; playing very important games for Ajax when I was only twenty-one and playing in the World Cup and the Copa América with Uruguay. I remember what it was like as a young player when an older player came and said something to me; it put me at ease, particularly before a game where there was a lot at stake. And now I wanted to put them at ease. I suppose I could feel that this was not an ordinary match. The players around me know that if I lose my temper with them on the pitch, they should ignore me because I'm on their side and I'll go on supporting them. I had that support and I wanted them to have it too.

I spoke to them just before we went out into the tunnel for the kick-off. You never want to get a pep talk before the warm-up or you'll go out fired up too early and you'll use up too much energy too soon. I'm not saying they went out on to the pitch especially motivated because of what I said – and Stevie was talking to them as well – but the timing is important. Say it just before you leave the dressing room to start the game and that is what is in the player's mind. I'd been through the same thing many times with Uruguay as a young player – I'd get a word in the ear from Diego Forlán or from 'Loco' Abreu and go out on to the pitch with their words in my head, believing I could take on the world.

For the previous three months or so, Brendan Rodgers had been deliv-ering very special team-talks. He had contacted our mothers, one by one, and asked them to write something about their son. Before every game as we went on the run that saw us come close to winning the title, he would spend the final few minutes before we went out reading what one of them had said in front of the whole team. The final word came not from the manager but a player's mum.

He never told us whose mum's message he was reading out. He'd read it all and then go back to one phrase, picking out a line that he felt would really touch us.

One mother might say: 'It was the dream of my son to play for Liverpool

211

since he was nine years old and now look at him.' Or: 'Whenever I'm in Liverpool I can sense the affection the people have for my son.'

Sometimes it ended up almost like a quiz: *whose mum is it this week?* Other times the big clue dropped straight away and you knew immediately. If the note began with 'My son started playing on the streets of Brazil when he was . . .', or, 'My son wanted to be a goalkeeper from the time he learned to walk', that pretty much gave the game away. The day he used my mum's words he started by saying: 'I'm going to talk in Spanish today', so I had a good idea that it might be my turn. He read my mum's message in Spanish and then in English. It was genuinely moving to hear what she had written. At the end, he went back to the phrase: 'You can now find Liverpool shirts in every house in Uruguay.'

Brendan had tried this 'mum motivation' tactic one week and we'd won so he kept doing it. That day against City was no exception as he read out a message from Philippe's mother.

When we went out on to the pitch, there was a tribute to the victims of Hillsborough, a quarter of a century on. To be stood still around the centre circle as the mosaic spread across the Kop saying '96, 25 years', and the stadium fell silent – not quiet but *silent* – had an impact that is hard to explain. I've stood there for many a minute's silence before but never anything like that; there was something powerful about finding myself in the middle of it. There was a stillness and my thoughts took over. I thought about how so many people lost their lives, but, above all, I thought about those they left behind and the dignity with which they have kept their loved ones' memories alive and fought for justice. I thought about how this was something that everyone in English football respects and supports; I'm not sure if that would be the same elsewhere.

After the silence came the roar. We were ready to start the game and that day it felt like we were saying to ourselves: 'Now we have to show what Liverpool really is by winning the game for the ninety-six and for their families here. We have to win the title for them.' It was such a powerful mix of emotions from the silence to the noise of the crowd and the feeling of responsibility. Some people say it is harder to start a game after a moment like that, that it loads the pressure on or takes your focus from the task in hand, but I feel like it concentrates your mind.

I had spoken to Philippe before the game, but when it came to the moment that really mattered, he didn't hear me. Luckily. When the ball ran to him from Vincent Kompany's sliced clearance in the second half, he was facing backwards towards the edge of the area rather than the goal and the first thing I thought was that he could lay it back to me. But by the time I had shouted his name the ball was already in the net. There was a moment's pause, as if he didn't really know how to celebrate, and then he disappeared under a pile of bodies.

The goal had come when we weren't playing well and the game was slipping away from us a little. City had drawn level at 2-2 after we'd taken a 2-0 lead, and they looked more likely to score than we did. Our third goal was a huge blow for them and they couldn't really respond. If the game had stayed 2-2 with them dominating possession as they were doing, playing as well as they were, the final result might have been different; I think they would have probably won it.

They were flying and Philippe's goal took the wind out of them. You could see them physically fold a little. They started playing longer passes and we closed up well at the back. That was the only thing they could do.

We weren't going to hurry either. I ended up arguing with Sami Nasri and David Silva at one point because they wanted me to get on and take a free kick quickly, but if we're winning 3-2 or 2-1 and the clock is ticking away I'm not in any hurry. And if the opposition get wound up, fine. I could see that they thought they might wind me up, maybe get me sent off, but I was just saying: 'No, I'll take the free kick when I want to, not when you tell me to.'

I'd been booked after just five minutes. Once, that might have been cause for concern but I'd reached a point where I was responding better in those kind of situations. I know when I am on a yellow card: in fact, sometimes I *need* that card to calm me down, to focus my energies. This time, I felt in control.

For me, Philippe's goal was the Goal of the Season. He was looking away from the goal, his eyeline was at a right-angle with the goal and the way he hit it was just perfect. Perhaps for a fan or journalist watching the game it was not a great goal, but if you look at the technique – which is far from easy – and you put it into the context of that game then it was the best for me. It was the best because of what it meant, because of the result and because of the goal itself. It took us so close.

At the time we thought that game showed that we had the luck of the champions. We thought: 'If we've won this, suffering like that, there's a reason. There's something there.' We'd benefited too from Vincent Kompany getting injured in midweek and Yaya Touré going off after picking up a knock. Kompany is probably the hardest defender I faced in the

Premier League – he organises City, and is one of the best in the world in his position. Players who say they want the opposition's best footballers to be on the pitch are not telling the truth; I wanted him to miss out, of course I did. As it turned out, he played despite the injury but we profited from his mistake.

After the game, Brendan's talk was brief and low-key. He congratulated us for the work we had done not just in that game, but in the three previous games too. He told us that the way we had played showed why we were where we were; despite the increased pressure, we had stuck together and shown our quality.

Some people look back on the aftermath to that game, on the way that Steven Gerrard gathered us together, and they say that we celebrated the title too soon; that the huddle was us thinking we'd done it, that we were complacent. Rubbish. I'm amazed people say that when the TV microphones actually caught Stevie's words: 'We go again.'

This wasn't a team that thought it had won the league; it was, though, a team that thought it had taken a huge step. And we *had* taken a huge step. We had made it possible; we had beaten our nearest rivals for the title. It was in our hands now. But there was more to do.

It was a very clear message from our captain. We had done an incredible job but the game was gone and it was on to the next one. It was a moment to enjoy, but we then had to start concentrating on the Norwich game.

Not 'we're there', but 'we go again'.

We had to go again but we knew we were close. That was the moment we thought we could win the league. And then the following week we beat Norwich, despite struggling. We were on edge, we almost threw it away. And it was as if there was a kind of destiny guiding us. I just didn't yet know how cruel it would be.

●　●　●

From where I was on the pitch, I saw it unfold clearly. The moment that it all started to slip away. I saw the ball go under Stevie's foot and Demba Ba running through, all on his own. All I could do was pray that Simon would stop him somehow. Unfortunately, he couldn't.

If I had been in Stevie's shoes, I don't know if I would have been able to carry on playing. Emotionally, it must have been very, very hard. In the previous weeks, so much had been said about him, the expectation had built so much, the talk had been about him leading Liverpool, his club, to a first title in over twenty years, on the twenty-fifth anniversary of the Hillsborough disaster, in which his cousin had died, and then that happens. The captain, the former youth-teamer, the one-club man, a Scouser born and bred, and he was the unlucky one to make a crucial mistake.

Right from the start at Liverpool, there was something about Steven Gerrard that struck me and that's the enormous respect everyone has for him, all the way to the trainees who occasionally join in the passing drills in training. Whoever loses possession of the ball has to go in the middle. I always tried to hit my passes to Stevie that little bit harder so that he was the player who had to go in the middle. But what happened? I played the pass to him, he miscontrolled it because I'd hit it so hard, and I waited for him to go in the middle and he waited for me to go in the middle because of the pass. He'd never get upset with me, just smile and calmly say to one of the trainees: 'Okay, you decide – who has to go in the middle?' And every time, without fail, they pointed to me. That's respect.

Stevie is a quiet captain. If I ever saw him shouting, then I knew he was furious about something and that he was in the right. He doesn't raise his voice for the sake of it. He doesn't like being that sort of captain and I love the way he is, as do all the players. He is not a captain who is going to rollick you in front of everyone on the pitch, but if he says something to you in the dressing room at half time or after the game then you listen because you know he's thought about what he is going to say to you. He has a cool head and I respect that. He's an extremely intelligent player too. He had played so well in a role that was not his own last season, but it didn't surprise me: no one reads the game better.

But he still hadn't won the league title. He deserved to. Stevie had started to believe, we all had. And now it had been virtually taken away from him and like *that*, with him slipping against Chelsea. It's cruel, very hard to take. A huge part of what we were achieving was down to him; he was the spirit of that side, the standard-bearer.

I'm convinced that if Chelsea had not scored like that, they would not have scored at all. And once you are a goal down against them, it's virtually impossible.

At half time, it was hard to talk to Stevie and there was nothing we could say anyway. We were conscious of the fact that we had to overcome his mistake and go out in the second half and win the game for him. We really did think like that. He had done so much for us all. In the second half we did everything we could to try to win it and so did he. He had taken few shots over the course of the season but in that second half everything changed; he was shooting a lot, trying to get us back in it. I don't think it was about anxiety, as some people have said. It was more a tactical thing, logical. Chelsea played so deep and it was so hard to find a way through them, the only way to score was from outside the area and lots of opportunities opened up for him to shoot.

We didn't play that well, but I honestly think that there was nothing we could have done differently. We had ten players in front of us, almost all of them in the penalty area. We could try a one-two, or move the ball quickly from player to player to try to pull them out of position, seeking to create some space, but then there would always be another defender in front of us. It's very hard when you see that there is no space to move into.

Meanwhile, every time we looked up at the clock, time was running out.

We had gone into the game knowing that a draw was good for us. With the atmosphere at Anfield, with the fact that we had just beaten City, our attitude remained the same: we wanted to win. But we were conscious of the fact that with a draw we were still ahead of everyone. What I didn't expect was for them to play for the draw. It's true that they won the game but I am convinced that without that stroke of luck, they would not have scored. We never fell into the trap of thinking that they didn't care. José Mourinho had been saying that the priority was the Champions League, that the game at Anfield virtually didn't matter. We listened to him talking about playing with subs and read the newspapers saying 'it'll be a team full of kids' or 'they're going to let Liverpool win', but we never believed that. No chance. Stevie had talked about going again against Norwich and we also knew we would have to play well against Chelsea. We never believed they would hand us the title. We knew that some of the normal starters weren't going to play, but we also knew that if they wanted to win the league – and people forget that they still had a chance to do that – they would have to play to win. For them to try to waste time when the draw was no good to them was something that I didn't understand. The draw was fine by me. It suited us. It didn't suit them.

It was an ugly game, hard to play. No player enjoys playing like that, when the other team sits so deep. Still less to be the team sitting deep. Every coach plays the way that suits him, so I don't mind that. The only thing I didn't like was the way that they wasted time from the very start. I was asking myself: 'Why are they doing this from the first minute?'

I even asked one of their players.

'What do you want me to do? If he makes us play like this, I have to play like this,' he replied. 'What else can I do? If I don't, I won't play. What would you do?'

Strategically, there are lots of teams that play defensively and then try to come and attack you on the break, if at all. That's normal, no problem. But the way that they seemed to be playing with the clock frustrated us. They tried to wind us up, I think, and we were drawn into that. 'Come on, hurry up.' We should not have been dragged in. Mourinho knew: if you waste time, if you break it up from the very start, they're going to get frustrated, they're going to play a bit more crazily, they'll do anything.

They pulled us out of our normal routine. And of course we never imagined the slip and that was what truly made it hard for us. Nor did they. You can't plan for a player to slip.

Previously, as the wins had racked up, people would talk about winning the league and I always said: 'Shh, don't even mention it. You'll jinx it.' The truth is that I never heard any of the English players talking about the celebrations or anything like that, but within the Spanish-speaking group there were players imagining what it would be like if we won the league. And I kept telling them to be quiet.

I'm very superstitious like that. When I was a kid in Uruguay, probably aged eight or nine, I went to the shop on the way to a game. I had a fifty cent coin as change and I shoved it down my sock. It made its way down my leg and I could feel it by my foot. The game started and, although I could feel it, I scored six or seven goals. We won 9-1. So the coin went down the sock the next week and the week after that and the week after that, until one week I didn't score and the coin didn't go in the sock again.

Another one is my obsession with being last out on to the pitch. It affects me to the point where I'm already wound-up and angry before the game has even started if I haven't been the last on to the pitch. It was a problem when I first turned up at Liverpool because Pepe Reina had the same superstition so I had to be the second to last out.

We'd find ourselves both hanging back by the door of the dressing room saying:

'After you.'

'No, after you.'

He rumbled me pretty quickly: 'Hey, mate, you like to be last out, don't you?'

When we had gone two or three games without a win I negotiated a change. I would go out last to see if that changed our luck. And if we won and I scored I'd be sure to tell Pepe it was because I'd been last out that our luck had turned.

I can't even stand to get good luck messages before a game. My family know not to send me messages or call me. If someone says: 'Good luck, Luis' before a game in which I can't shoot straight to save my life then, in my mind, that person is clearly the curse. I tell them afterwards never to contact me on match day again.

But one day after the Norwich game, I – me, of all people – had blown it when I'd asked Ray Haughton what was going to happen at the end of the season. Would we have to stay for some kind of event, would there be receptions, that sort of thing?

I never said *when* we won the league; it was always *if* we won the league. And it was a question of getting organised, that's all – we would head to Barcelona to see Sofi's family and then on to Uruguay and I needed to look at flights. He said that, yes, there were plans just in case anything happened, just in case we won the league. As far as I know, no one else had asked him. But I had.

Immediately, I was kicking myself for even asking – 'Why the hell did I ask? *Why?*' All I had wanted to do was work out which flights to catch, but I was furious with myself. What had I done? The Chelsea game brought that moment, when I had asked, back into my mind.

After the Chelsea game, the title was out of our hands, because if we won our last two games, and Manchester City won theirs, they were probably going to beat us on goal difference. But we still thought we had a very good chance; we felt like it depended on us.

The 3-3 draw against Crystal Palace in the next match hurt much more than losing to Chelsea. Partly because it now felt definitive, partly because of the way it happened.

A team like Liverpool, playing like that, with no problems, leading 3-0, shouldn't let that happen. You can lose a three-goal lead against Chelsea, Arsenal, Manchester City, but not Crystal Palace, not at that moment with the way we were playing, when we were so far ahead of them in the table and they had nothing to play for. And that was our fault. All of our faults.

At 3-0, we kept pouring forward, looking for more goals. When I scored the third goal, I ran into the net to get the ball, to get us going again. Out on the pitch, we got caught up in the moment and we started to think that there were more goals to be had, loads of them. Somehow, that idea of chasing down Manchester City's superior goal difference seemed possible and that was the only thing in our heads: *goals, goals, goals.* There was a contagiousness about the atmosphere: the fans were screaming for us to go forward and we were aware of that. We could feel it. For a moment, we actually thought we could do it.

When I thought about it coldly a few days later, I realised we had been so stupid. We had a chance of beating them on goal difference but we needed a miracle. At 3-0 up, our goal difference was +53, compared to +59 for City. Even if we'd scored three more goals in that last ten minutes ourselves, we'd have been three behind them and we only had one game to play to their two. It was an impossible task. And by drawing, we gave up the title.

We knew that if we beat Palace, City were *obliged* to win and that meant a huge amount of pressure would be on them. The Chelsea loss was a bad one, probably fatal, because if we had drawn or won there we thought we would probably win the league: we expected to beat Palace and then the final day at home against Newcastle we would have a great chance. But even though we lost to Chelsea, we were still in there and we thought that City could easily drop points in their final three games with all the pressure on them. When we drew to Palace we knew it was over: not just because of the points but because the pressure on City was no longer the same. City could draw a game and it wouldn't matter — they'd still win the league.

That's why it hurt more. Although, in a way, I think that I would rather lose the league on points than on goal difference. If you finish level, it seems wrong not to win the league. There should be a play-off, a final for the title. Why are they champions? Because of a few more goals? No. Let's play a final. If we had lost the title on goal difference, that sense of impotence would have been even greater.

We lost really going for it and, although that cost us, that's something to be proud of. It is the way that we played all season: we attacked teams. But that doesn't diminish the pain. When Crystal Palace made it 3-2 I still thought it was impossible that they would equalise but when they scored the third, I wanted to die.

At the final whistle, I couldn't control the tears. I pulled my shirt over my head and just wanted to disappear. I knew that Stevie had been over to me and Glen too. I knew because I had felt them and heard them. But I hadn't seen them. I knew that it was Kolo who came over and led me off the pitch as well. He guided me, talking to me all the way. At Selhurst Park the tunnel is in one corner of the pitch; I was right at the other end. It seemed to take an eternity to get there; I was being led almost as if I was a blind man. I didn't take my head out from inside my shirt the entire way. Kolo walked me all the way, talking: 'Okay, okay, we're nearly there.' I didn't want anyone to take a picture of me crying; the tears were streaming down my face and I didn't want people to see that.

I wanted to lift my head out and to pull the shirt back down, I wanted to say: 'That's it, I'm not crying.' But I couldn't. It was pride. I live football very differently to most players. Most people won't have realised but when I scored against Manchester United during our 3-0 win in March I had cried too. I cried with the emotion of it; if you look at photos from that game, you'll see my eyes are red.

I tried to hide how much it hurt, but everybody could imagine that I was crying under the shirt. They could see my body heaving.

If I hadn't cried at Palace, maybe I would have been so wound up that the emotion would have come out a different way. Maybe I would have done something I would have regretted later, lost my head and broken something in the dressing room. I have never broken anything, although I have kicked a few things. Hard, too.

In the dressing room, there was absolute silence. No one said a word. Not one word for twenty minutes, at least. No one moved, no one talked, no one did anything. We just sat there.

Kolo was the person who broke the silence. That's the way he is; it's his personality. In truth, there might have been players thinking: 'Kolo, shut up.' But he wanted to support us and I really appreciate what he did for me, leading me off the pitch. It's rarer than you might think to find a player who supports you like he did that night. And the important thing for me is that he didn't just do it there, as we went off the pitch, in front of everyone. No. He stood by me in the dressing room, when I still felt awful, and on the team bus afterwards he came over and sat with me for a bit. He came to see how I was, to try to comfort me.

But there was no comfort. Not really.

The following Sunday there was theoretically a chance of winning the league. We didn't make the assumption that City would win, we hadn't given it up entirely, but deep down we knew it wasn't going to happen.

It had been so many years and we never imagined that we would be in that situation, with a chance to win the league. I didn't know it yet, but it would be my last chance too. We had been so close, only to lose it in the most painful way. It had been a unique opportunity and when it slipped through our fingers at Palace I felt lost. Powerless and lost.

FRIENDS & HEROES

There is a signed Steven Gerrard shirt that proudly hangs in my home in Uruguay among the newspaper cuttings and old photos. In black pen, he has dedicated it to 'the best I've played with'. For one of the most important players in Liverpool's history to say that about me feels incredible, especially when I remember having chosen him in my Liverpool team on the PlayStation when I was a teenager at Nacional and watching him scoring goals on the television when I was at Groningen and Ajax.

Stevie's not the first idol of mine to become a team-mate. The best example would have to be Sebastián 'El Loco' Abreu, who I looked up to at Nacional and then ended up standing alongside in the tunnel once I had made it to the first team. It was a great feeling as a young player, desperate to make it but still unsure of myself, for my hero to tell me that I had a great attitude on the pitch and the right personality to be a success.

El Loco is a footballing father to me. A Nacional legend and a Uruguayan international. He was my idol and my role model. He filled me with so much confidence as a kid. He was a real joker too. I played once very early in my career against the Uruguayan international Alvaro 'Tata' González, who was a good friend of Loco's. I had one of my best games against him, scoring a goal that still ranks as one of my favourites. It was a long ball forward, I turned inside one player and Tata came across to stop me, but I cut back past him to the left and scored. After the game, I went to Loco's house and he wanted to congratulate me. He had already moved to play for a club in Mexico by this point. Tata González turned up. I didn't know him; I only knew him from the game.

When he came in, he looked at me as if to say: 'What's he doing here?'

Loco said to him: 'I brought him here so that you could see his face. All you saw during the game was his back.'

For a young player to suddenly be with Sebastián Abreu was incredible. I supported Nacional when I was little so to then be able to share a dressing room with one of its greatest players was something I would never have dared dream about. In the early days I just used to sit there with my mouth shut, unable to say anything. He 'adopted' me. I had a very good relationship with him, even though I am much more shy than he is, and I'm now the godfather to one of his children. He showed me how to be with people. He gave me social skills that I had maybe not learned. He's a very sociable person and everyone adores him. He was just a real hero at Nacional and to have become his good friend is one of the gifts that football has given me.

It just makes a huge difference when the players you most admire, the leaders of the team, make you feel welcome. I remember when I first played alongside Diego Forlán for Uruguay and him asking me how things were going in Holland. Here was one of the most important players in the history of Uruguayan football and he was asking me how my career was going.

Both Diego and Loco were examples for me in my career in terms of how to behave towards team-mates. I really don't like to see established players badly treating young players coming through from the youth team. I saw a lot of it in Uruguay and Holland – players who because of their name thought they were above others. I can get annoyed with a seventeen-year-old kid when I'm training, of course I can, but never because I feel I can pick on him. You are not superior to anyone else out on the pitch. If a kid comes up to train with the first-team squad and he's treated badly then I'd like to think I'd always defend him. Not to be the good guy but just because I believe that is the way it should be. I've got no time for players who believe they can abuse their seniority. I didn't put up with it in Uruguay and I never will.

It didn't happen that much to me and when it did I never used to respond. That's a difference that I see today. The teenagers do talk back; they've got their answers ready. Then you get the older players who don't like the answers and they'll start giving them a kicking in training. I've seen it happen. And answering back is not the solution either. It's best to get on with it in silence, but make sure it doesn't happen again.

Coming up through the ranks at Nacional the older players would play practical jokes like cutting your trousers up or throwing your clothes out. I had my clothes thrown out and the first mobile phone I ever had was in one of the pockets. Having a phone was something incredible for me and they threw it out. There would be some players who would get your hat and put it on the heater so it burnt.

I'm pretty sure most of these things don't happen any more and maybe it's because the young players coming up started answering back. When it's a joke that's fine. You make first-team training and they shave your head – okay, it's part of football, but when it goes beyond that to bullying I can't abide it.

I have tried to help some players out along the way. I tried to give new signing Nicolás Lodeiro a leg-up at Ajax. He was on the bench every week and I said to Martin Jol, our coach at the time: 'Give him a little bit of game time.' And Martin said: 'Of course, no problem.' I knew if he could just play fifteen or twenty minutes he was going to be happy. He had come from Uruguay and he wasn't playing. I could understand what he was going through. The team was playing well and he needed to feel part of that. And he had the quality to be playing at Ajax. I helped him the way Bruno Silva had helped me at Groningen.

The first player I met when I signed for Liverpool was Lucas Leiva and he is a genuine friend. We had a group of Spanish speakers at Liverpool and we would meet with the wives and girlfriends away from the pitch. Just to have something to eat and to talk and sometimes play Monopoly. Did I cheat? When I could, not that it did me much good – the wives were tough negotiators and I don't remember winning many times.

But that sort of social life away from the game is often the exception. It's difficult to explain exactly why it's hard to make friends in football, but I think it's in the nature of the game itself. Your team-mates can also be your rivals at times so it can be a lonely existence. I can count my real, close friends in football on the fingers of my hands. I have a lot of team-mates past and present, and good ones too, but to a find a real friend is tough. It's easy to find someone who is your best mate when things are going well for you and then as soon as things turn, suddenly they're as keen to celebrate your misfortune as they were to celebrate your success.

Football can make relationships harder: we are all in competition with each other up to a point so rivalry and then jealousy can play a part, although I don't think envy is one of my faults and I would never let a personal friendship, or the lack of one, damage my relationship with a team-mate. Friendships can change the way you interact though, as well as the way you analyse the game, even if only subconsciously. Imagine three players on the pitch: you, your friend and another team-mate. Your friend is the player who misses a good chance and you think to yourself: 'Ah, what a shame, he deserved to score that.' But if your other team-mate misses a chance, you might not feel the same way. That's natural. Sometimes you can't help but take the friendships you build off the pitch out on to the pitch and it shows in those small details.

My experience of Holland and England suggests that Dutch or English players are less likely to come together in a group than Argentinians or Uruguayans. Naturally, groups tend to develop based on language and culture but I don't think it's a problem in terms of creating groups or cliques. The reality is that, like it or not, in every team there are groups of players that you get on with better or worse and if that's not based on language it will be based on something else.

Your team-mates are not always your friends but when you make a friend in the game then it's a friend for life. And if he's a hero of yours too, then even better.

THAT WAS ANFIELD

8

Nothing sums up the bittersweet feeling from my last season at Liverpool like the night of the 2-0 defeat to Chelsea. I was off to the Grosvenor House Hotel to pick up an award, when the only award I had really wanted had just slipped from my grasp.

It should have been one of the proudest nights of my career. And I should have been there with my captain Steven Gerrard but I had to go alone.

The previous summer when I said I wanted to leave the club, when my head was all over the place and I didn't know which way to turn, no one gave me better guidance than Stevie. More than anyone else, he was the one who made me change my mind and stay for another season. Now I was off to collect the Player of the Year award from the PFA. He should have been there with me, but he couldn't face it. And I completely understood why.

We were in the Anfield dressing room with the ramifications of the defeat by Chelsea still sinking in. It was a sad day but it was also the day

231

of the ceremony. I said to him: 'Do we change into our suits now or do we go in normal clothes?'

Stevie said: 'I'm not going.'

We had lost a game that we only needed to draw, and *that* slip had happened to him. I didn't blame him at all; I didn't blame him for the slip and I didn't blame him for not wanting to go. I understood because I didn't feel like going either.

Everything had been prepared. Our things had been placed on the bus that was waiting to take us to the airport. The shoes were shined and the suits were hanging up on board. They had to send someone out to go and bring them all back in. We were all supposed to go together: Stevie, Raheem, Daniel, me and the manager, but I was the only player who ended up on the plane.

I felt I had to show up out of respect for the players who had voted for me. I am glad I did. I didn't know it then but this was my last season in the Premier League and for all the controversies along the way I can honestly say that, for the most part, I had absolutely loved it. It is a wonderful league with a style of football that suits me perfectly. To be voted best player is something I will always be immensely proud of.

It was a grim journey with Brendan, a few directors, and Sofi. There was silence for most of the way. We had had such high expectations at the start of the day but now we were just feeling numb.

But when I reached the hotel and began looking through the programme that listed players who had won the award before, it began to sink in just how privileged I was. The feeling of 'what am I doing here?' began to subside. Now I was proud to be there; proud to be listed with those players, men who had made history in England.

Sofi said to me: 'Think about why you are here. This is an important achievement and lots of players would love to be in your position.' And I thought: 'She's right.' Lots of players would love to win this award. I had voted for Yaya Touré in my category, and for Luke Shaw, who came second to Eden Hazard, as best young player – both would have been worthy winners. I thought about all those players looking back on the season and deciding that I had been the best in the Premier League, and I felt honoured.

Players always thank their team-mates at these awards but my gratitude was especially genuine. My mind went back to that conversation with Stevie before the season started and how he made me believe we could end up back in the Champions League. Tottenham had lost Gareth Bale and we knew that he had been the linchpin of their team. They had brought in other players but it was always going to take time for them all to get used to the Premier League. We knew that if Arsenal didn't sign players they would continue along the same lines and we could compete with them. Manchester United had a new coach. We were sure that Manchester City and Chelsea would be at the top but the other contenders were now within our reach.

Of course even Stevie couldn't have imagined just how good the season was going to be. The objective was to get ourselves into the top four yet there we were, the team who had finished seventh the previous season, competing for the title, losing only one of our last nineteen games. On the twenty-fifth anniversary of Hillsborough, we had so nearly won the league.

I ended the season with the feeling that we could go again. For the club to be back in the Champions League after so many years is wonderful. I know some of the players were a bit unhappy because they had not played a great deal and some were even thinking that it was time to move on. I had conversations with some of them and tried to tell them it was the worst time for them to leave, especially those who had spent a long time at Liverpool during the difficult years when we were finishing seventh or eighth and not really fighting for anything. Back in the Champions League, there would be more squad rotation; there would be more games and the same players couldn't play every week. What I wasn't contemplating then was that it would be me that would go.

I hope the great players that I have left behind can continue to take the club forward. Coming so close to winning the league last season should serve as a springboard to push on. Despite their great history Liverpool have had difficulty attracting players recently when they've not qualififed for the Champions League. That season we'd lost out on Mohamed Salah and on Willian, both to Chelsea. But now with the prospect of Champions League football back again, added to the great history, the club's pulling power should be stronger than ever.

It should be a time for the club to look forward and there is nothing to be gained from over-analysis of last season. Losing the league title by such a fine margin hurts but it is torturous to think, 'if only we'd won here' or 'if only I'd scored that goal there'. It makes no sense because if you do that for some games, you have to do it for *every* game. You go back to the very first match of the season and think that if Simon Mignolet hadn't saved that penalty against Stoke City, we might never have been in contention eight months later. Or if Sunderland hadn't beaten Chelsea and drawn with Manchester City, then maybe we wouldn't have been fighting for the league at all. But we did. We fought all the way to the finish.

When people say to me, 'What if you had played every game?', I usually reply, 'We'd have won it on goal difference.' In our first three games we beat Stoke, Aston Villa and Manchester United but all three 1-0. I'm joking, of course. All the 'ifs' and 'buts' get you nowhere. It was hard to watch those games at the start of the season when I was suspended but we won most of them and the team played very well. I don't think things would have changed much. A player can win a game or a few matches, but a team wins the league. Liverpool are a team. My team-mates won those games and picked up those very important points. And they can continue to do so without me now.

At the end of the season there was a team meal after the final game with the wives and families of all the staff invited. Brendan gave a speech in which he congratulated us for a great campaign. We should be proud of what we had done, he told us. And for all the hurt, we were. In sport you're taught that first is best and second is nowhere. But when you come from nowhere to finish second it's different.

As my Uruguay coach Óscar *'El Maestro'* Tabárez has told me many times: 'Victories are not always about trophies. The journey is the goal.' Besides, we had started the season with a target and we had reached it. We were conscious of what we had achieved. Liverpool were back in the Champions League. In that sense the season had been a huge success.

I flew off to the World Cup knowing that Raheem Sterling and Jordan Henderson would be there too. Their seasons had been another major plus, a sign of how well we had played. Some people had said they weren't good enough a year earlier but they both ended up in the England team going to Brazil. I made sure I called them both to congratulate them when they made the squad. They deserved it not just as players but because they are good people and I was enormously happy for them.

Glen Johnson and Daniel Sturridge would be waiting for me in São Paulo too with England drawn in the same group as Uruguay. And that would give me the chance to swap shirts with Stevie who had played a big part in me staying at the club by promising that we would get back into the Champions League. He had been as good as his word. So good, in fact, that we almost won the league.

Brendan's team-talk before the last match of the season focused on the fact that we wanted to say farewell to the fans in the right way. We did that with a 2-1 win over Newcastle at Anfield and then went back out on to the pitch after the game. It was an emotional lap of honour but not as emotional as it might have been had I known it was my last for the club.

I had finished the season with 31 goals, enough to win the Golden Boot. And the Liverpool supporters presented me with a boot that is just as special – the Kop's annual player of the season award, the Golden Samba. I had won it for the second year running. Their support had always been incredible. I will miss hearing the 'Luis Suárez – I just can't get enough' song and, most of all, the feeling I used to get when leaving the tiny dressing room and taking my place in the narrow tunnel beneath the 'This Is Anfield' sign, knowing that any minute I would be hearing one of football's greatest anthems: 'You'll Never Walk Alone'. Those supporters made sure that I never did, and I only wish I could have left them with the league title they deserved.

MANAGEMENT

I understand managers.

Sometimes.

Their job must be very difficult. You work all week to prepare for a game, you lose and you don't even have time to get bitter about it, to lick your wounds or digest it, or to escape the defeat, seeking shelter in your family. And if you win, you have no time to enjoy it. You're immediately preparing for the next match. Straight away you're watching videos again, planning, trying to work out the best way to win.

A player has three or four days between matches to be relaxed, calm, disconnected . . . or to moan about the manager. Players talk about coaches a great deal and we say a lot of things. But then later on, you think: 'No, no, why did I say that about him? It's not even true.' We can be difficult and sometimes even nasty about managers, that's the truth. Normally it's when you're wound up about something and you really slag him off. Then you think about it later and you wonder: 'Why would I say that?' Other times, we can be cold. A manager gets sacked and we just carry on.

Managers have to deal with that. There are times when they take decisions to keep players happy as well as to improve the team. As players you watch and you think: 'Why's he putting him in the team?' You wouldn't ever say that to the manager but you do think it. Imagine you're the manager: if you have two players who like to play in the same position, they both score goals, one is injured and the one who takes over from him scores goals, then when the other one comes back to fitness, what are you going to do? He only missed out because of injury, it wasn't his fault, and he had been scoring goals. But now you have two of them. You have to find a way of putting them both in. You might have to change the whole team to fit them in. A manager must think: 'I'm going to have to take someone else out to fit him in . . . and then he is going to be angry.'

It's not easy, no. And one thing I am absolutely clear about is that I'm not going to be a manager. I think the time will come when I'd prefer just to get out. The atmosphere, the environment in which footballers live is very complicated. If you come out of that at the end of your career, I think it's very hard to go back into it again. If you carry on in football, you continue to be surrounded by the game, by agents, who can be difficult, by the constant competition, internally as well as externally, by the pressure and the interests. Worse, as a manager, you're the one that has to handle all of that and strike a balance. When I retire, I think I would like to get away from it, at least to start with. I already am someone who prefers to be at home. The concentraciones kill me. I'd rather be with my family. After so many years of travel, hotels, games, I wouldn't want to get back into that again. If a friend becomes a coach and wants me to be an assistant or something, then maybe. And people do say the assistant is the brains . . .

ENGLAND, *MY* ENGLAND

9

Walter Ferreira was diagnosed with cancer in January 2014, aged sixty-two. He suffered Hodgkin's lymphoma, and was forced to give up the work he loved to fight it. The chemotherapy left him exhausted and made his hair fall out; he was still battling against it in the summer of 2014 when he flew to Brazil for the World Cup. We travelled on 9 June, only two weeks after his last chemotherapy session, and the doctors didn't finally agree to let him go until just six days before we boarded the plane. He still hadn't been given the all-clear and had to continue his treatment there: in fact, the day before our first game a blood test showed that his red blood cell count was low. They were difficult days. But there he was. And instead of worrying about himself, he was worrying about me.

Walter had been the physiotherapist at Nacional for as long as anyone could remember. It was there that I had first met him, ten years earlier.

Every player did their rehabilitation with him and there was no one else like him. His nickname was 'Holy Hands'. Walter had been with the Uruguayan national team for a quarter of a century. Because of the cancer, he wasn't officially part of the set-up any more but he boarded the plane with us and everyone was delighted to see him. He was there for me and I was there because of him.

When I was diagnosed with an injury to a meniscus in my knee at the end of the league season, I knew one thing: I wanted Walter on my side. I couldn't bear the thought of missing the World Cup and he wouldn't let me. He had looked after my treatment from the start and one day, as the tournament approached, I said to him: 'Walter, are you coming with me? Because if you're not coming, I don't want to go. I believe in you. Without you, I'm not sure that I can do this.'

He thought about it and eventually he said yes.

The day I was operated on had been incredible. Purely by coincidence, the surgeon that operated on me was the brother of Enzo Francescoli, one of the greatest players in Uruguay's history. The operation had been a success, he said, but there were still doubts and fears. There was less than a month to go until the World Cup. I was wheeled out of the hospital in a chair and there were so many people there: we had to push our way through a crowd to the ambulance that took me home. There were people there when I reached my house outside Montevideo too – fans, well-wishers and journalists. They waited and waited with their cameras in the cold. I'm not sure if they thought that I was going to come out and give them an interview.

The affection and the concern was astonishing and reinforced just how big the 2014 World Cup was for Uruguay. I'd flown in from Liverpool and the World Cup seemed to me to be more of a presence than it was in England, eclipsing everything. There were flags and banners everywhere. Every TV programme had a World Cup theme. Every advertisement did too. People were talking about destiny. The World Cup was an obsession. We were heading back to Brazil, where our country had enjoyed its greatest moment, beating the hosts in the final in 1950. Everyone was dreaming of doing it again. The memory never goes away, even for those who are too young to remember it at all. It's as if we're born with it. And we knew that Brazil didn't want to face us: there was something about us that worried them, like the memory had never left them either. On Avenida Brasil in Montevideo, they had changed the street numbers so that every building was now number 1950.

Uruguay had waited over fifty years for this. No one was talking about anything else and everyone seemed to be talking about my injury. It felt like I was at the heart of this moment; there were stories every day. I seemed to be listening to meniscus tales constantly. Since I got injured, everyone was a doctor or a physiotherapist. Everyone seemed to be offering up a diagnosis and a prognosis. There were stories saying that my entire knee was destroyed, the cruciate too. It was silly, really. The expectation was huge and the media were desperate to know what was going on. We had to work away from the cameras because we knew that one day they'd say: 'Today he's jogging but he doesn't look quite right.' Then the next it would be: 'Suárez runs!' That can load pressure on and also create a false impression.

I saw reports saying that I had told some of the Liverpool players that

I would make it for the game against England for sure, when I hadn't said that. All I'd said was 'See you there'. But there seemed to be an obsession with interpreting every move I made.

One day I went to the Complejo Celeste, Uruguay's training camp in the countryside outside Montevideo, to meet the rest of the players for lunch. I hadn't been able to train with them yet, but I wanted to be part of the group. I had felt isolated and I wanted to spend time with them, to put my mind at rest and theirs too. The following day there was a photograph in the papers of me arriving there, 'walking normally'. But the photo was from two years earlier. They hadn't seen me. If they had, they would have seen that, actually, I *was* limping.

Everyone was asking the same question: 'Will Suárez make it?' And I was asking myself the same thing. At the time I probably didn't realise it, and on the surface I was strong and confident, but the pressure was building.

The expectations were huge and the responsibility was loading up – the players knew that our supporters thought we could win the competition. And while we were determined to go into the competition quietly, humbly, we were convinced that we could have a great World Cup. We'd come close in South Africa in 2010 and we were a better team four years on; we didn't want to be remembered for that, we wanted to be remembered for this. Our generation could leave a real mark. It felt like a unique opportunity. The unity of four years before was still there in the squad and it was unlike anything I had ever experienced before. We felt like genuine contenders. This was *the* World Cup. We had a team that could do damage to the rest. Everything felt right, except my knee.

After years of international underachievement, Óscar Tabárez had changed everything. The *Maestro* arrived to lead the national team in 2006. He wrote a report on the state of football in Uruguay and that became a road map for us, followed religiously by the football association and the players. He changed absolutely everything, from the youth team all the way to the top. He deserves an entire chapter to be dedicated to him in the history of Uruguayan football because he is the one that put everything into place, all the way through the system, coordinating everything with the coaches and laying down a path to follow. It's not just the senior team: you can see his hand in the success of the Under-17s and Under 20's too, both of whom reached the World Cup finals in 2009 and 2013 respectively. This was more than a footballing plan; it was a philosophy, a way of being.

He had led us to a World Cup semi-final in 2010 and a historic Copa América victory in Argentina the following year. Brazil 2014 felt like the culmination of his work.

The *Maestro* doesn't like ill discipline. He has always been very strict about the way we should behave and the way we should play. One of the things he changed was exactly that. He did not want us to lose the fighting spirit that sets us apart, but he did want us to channel it, to use it well. He kept insisting on the need for control. Over the years, Uruguay had suffered because of players getting sent off for aggression and he didn't like it – and when he does not like something, he says so. He is direct, honest, and to the point.

With time we learned to understand him and we learned how to behave and play. He has always been fantastic with us; he knows what we need and he has supported us always. His work has been reflected in my career:

he's very, very important to me; he has guided me and fought for me. That made it even harder to take when I let him down.

This felt like our time and it felt like my time too. I knew that it was my World Cup because of my age, because of the expectations, because of how I had played during the season for Liverpool. That was one of the things that was most painful in the aftermath of the Italy game: that this had been our moment. But then what happened, happened. When the ban was handed down after I had bitten Giorgio Chiellini, you could see that emotionally the team died. They were sunk. No one wanted to say so, but you could see it. We were all hurt by it, all damaged, not just me. If it had been a ban for five or ten games, then fine. But because of the way that it happened, because of the impact, because of the repercussions, because of the way I was marched out of the team hotel and out of the World Cup, it hurt them. And that hurt me. I was forced to leave them, alone. They still had a World Cup to play for, but all anyone talked about was me.

I was in Montevideo, having been sent home from the World Cup, and I was watching the press conference on the television when Tabárez announced that he was resigning his post on the FIFA Strategic Committee, in support of me. Ever since the Italy game I had felt depressed. I was in shock, numb. The sadness overwhelmed me. I watched him and the tears started rolling down my face again. I couldn't believe what he was doing for me. It was the press conference *before a game* and just about the only thing he was talking about was me. And he was there defending me. That broke my heart. To see how much he loved me, to see what was happening, what the consequences of what I had done were, was soul-destroying. I felt indebted to him, I felt so grateful to have his support and so upset at what I had done.

My team-mates had supported me too. I wrote to them all and thanked them for their support but there was nothing I could say really. I came out on to the balcony of my house to thank the people who had gathered there to support me too. Some people thought it wasn't the right thing to do, that it made me the centre of attention, but my intention was the complete opposite. It was cold, winter, and they had been there a long time. I wanted to thank them, but what I really wanted was for them to forget me and to back the national team: to cheer them on, not lament me not being there. I went out there to ask them to go home and forget about me. Uruguay had a vital knockout game against Colombia to come and Brazil awaited after that. Brazil in Brazil again, sixty-four years later. But it was over for me. I regretted it so much.

None of my team-mates blamed me but I am sure they must have asked: 'Why?' Virtually everyone in Uruguay supported me, but some people did blame me for us getting knocked out and that cut deep. I was devastated. It wasn't fair on my team-mates to say that and everyone who knows me understands what I did to be there. I was desperate to be at the World Cup. I love Uruguay. I risked my career. I might have made my knee worse; I could have been out for four or five months. If it had gone wrong, who knows what might have happened. Even when my knee seemed to be progressing well, I never knew what the next day might bring. If it had swollen up, it would have been all over.

On the outside, I had been positive as I prepared for the World Cup. I never cried once after the operation. I said I was sure I would get there and, with Walter's help, I convinced myself that I really would get there. I pushed the fear down, away from the surface. My wife said she couldn't believe how strong I was being. I had told myself that was the way it had to be. Injuries in your knee are not only a physical question, although that's the most important thing, but also a question of your mind. If you're thinking: 'Oh no, I'm not going to make it', 'I can't cope with this', 'This hurts', 'It's never going to get better', then it's harder. Right from the start my objective was clear: be strong emotionally and physically.

When I was a kid, aged twelve or thirteen, a car ran over my foot. I had broken my fifth metatarsal and I didn't realise. They put a plaster cast on, but I carried on playing in the schoolyard. When they eventually took the plaster off, the heel had been totally worn away from playing in the cast and the doctor was furious. A week later, I went to play a proper competitive match. I would get a lot of injuries, cuts and scrapes but I would keep playing, even if I was in agony. Pain rarely got in the way of playing. I was indestructible; I wouldn't stop for anyone. I was desperate to play football, no matter what. Walter said that I wasn't normal. The doctors who carried out my operation and the doctors at Barcelona that I've spoken to since say that the injury I endured normally means two months out. But I played against England exactly four weeks after the operation.

For the first few days, I was sitting at home, not putting any weight on my knee. I couldn't even pick the kids up or play with them. Everyone fussed around me. I had to sit with my leg up on a cushion. It felt ridiculous. But soon we got to work and then it was relentless. The goal was the World Cup and England. It meant everything to me.

The key was to strengthen the quadriceps and quickly, and that meant pushing myself to the limit. Some of the equipment was set up at home; rehabilitation was twenty-four hours a day. Walter gave me confidence and took away my fears. I was anxious about taking the next step, but he forced me. I would be saying that I was scared to do things and he would be saying: 'Throw away the crutches . . . Walk!'

'No, Walter . . .'

'Let go of them!'

He would insult me, goading me. He'd force me to take the next step. He got me off the crutches quickly and with each step he'd make me realise that it was okay.

He'd say: 'No, no, your quadriceps are fine . . . it's better than yesterday. You can do this.'

And then a few days later he would admit: 'To tell the truth, your quadriceps were in a bad way last week. They were fucked.'

'But, you said . . . '

'I said that to motivate you, to get you going. Your quads were in a terrible state. But now they really are fine.'

Every day, morning and afternoon, Sofi and I went from our house outside Montevideo to Prado where he lived. Walter was too ill to leave home. And Walter and I worked and worked. Three sessions a day, every day. Every day started and ended in the same way: with a huge pack of ice wrapped around my knee.

Liverpool's doctors were saying: 'Don't push it, be careful, take it easy . . . you could risk having problems in the future.'

Walter was saying: 'Keep working.'

And when Liverpool's doctors came out to visit me at the World Cup, they were amazed at how good a condition my knee was in, the range of movement, the fact that it had not swollen up. They thought it was incredible how much work we were doing already, the amount of weight we were putting through it. They had been kept up to date with everything we did, sent the X-rays and the training plan, but of course they had been concerned and had never expected the progress to be so swift. The work Walter did was incredible, a miracle.

Every day Sofi spent hours with Carmen, Walter's wife. Carmen always said that it was doing Walter good too: he had a purpose, a target, something to take his mind off his own battle. He was getting better; we fought together. 'He's stronger now with Luis,' Carmen said.

Walter and I would talk. I'd ask how he was. He used to have long hair, he used to eat everything. Now, he hardly ate anything and most of his hair had fallen out. But he was getting better and he never wavered. He is a tough character, determined and single-minded. Getting people better is what he does best and it helped him get better too. And when the time came, he came to Brazil. I kept thinking to myself: 'Luis, all the effort that Walter's making, his fight, his illness. He's fighting for his health, but he's in Brazil and he's here for you.'

He was always positive.

Every day I'd ask: 'Walter, will I make it to the World Cup?'

'Yes, you'll make it. You'll see.'

●　●　●

It was late in Uruguay's first game. The omens had not been good from the moment customs officers had confiscated the squad's supply of our beloved sweet toffee, *dulce de leche* – 120 kilos of the stuff – on arrival in Brazil. Now we were losing to Costa Rica and I was getting more and more wound up. I was a second away from marching up to the fourth official and making the substitution myself. It was hard to watch. I felt our World Cup slipping away already and this was the game people said would be 'easy'. I'd always insisted that there was no way it was going to be easy, but I hadn't expected things to be so hard: if we didn't win this, we would have to beat England and Italy. It was looking like sudden death already, and against two gigantic teams. We had to avoid that. I had gone out to warm up on my own and I was itching to dash back to the bench and say: '*Maestro*, I'm going on.' I wanted to play, desperately. The *Maestro* had other ideas.

I always knew that. For a moment, I was furious. But I also knew that I wasn't ever going to go on. Tabárez had no intention of me even being on the bench and he had told me that. He had only included me in the match-day squad in the end because he thought that I might as well be on the bench to frighten Costa Rica. It would also allow me to feel part of the group after a month in which I'd been almost entirely isolated. But I wasn't ready. In truth, I wasn't ready to play five minutes, let alone make an impact on the game. I knew he was doing me a favour not putting me on. The knee had responded well and I had strengthened my quadriceps, but not enough. I had trained with my team-mates a few times, briefly, but it had been little more than a kickabout. I'm sure that if I had played against Costa Rica I'd have made things worse. I might have done myself some damage. I wasn't fit enough. Never mind Costa Rica, I wasn't really fit enough to play England.

But it was England. For me this was *the* game. The biggest match of the whole World Cup. And now there was no other way out: we had to win. I'd watched us lose 1-0 to Costa Rica and now it was England, *my* England. I had dreamed of this; it had been on my mind for so long. I needed it. I knew England's players and they knew me. The front page of one newspaper said 'Get Well *Slowly*, Luis.' I knew they respected me; I felt like they were frightened of me. I hadn't played a competitive match for over a month, not since the final day against Newcastle, and now here I was. And just in case I wasn't motivated enough, Roy Hodgson had said something before the game about me not being world class unless I did it on this stage, as if I hadn't proved anything in the Premier League. As if I hadn't been at the World Cup in 2010. As if he hadn't seen the 2011 Copa América.

I wouldn't call it 'revenge' but his comments did sting and made me more determined. I had a point to prove; afterwards I said: 'That's for those who doubted me.' I never felt like I had to be the saviour. But I did think about our situation: on edge and against England. And I thought: 'I'll have to take that all on now.'

Two days before the game, my knee started hurting again. I could feel a pain inside. It wasn't on the same side as the meniscus but on the other side, where the 'goose foot' tendons are. I could feel it in training, but I was desperate to play and I worked through it. I had problems and the fear returned. I was scared that it might have all been for nothing. I tried to forget it and sleep. The following day I could feel it again, though. I was talking to my wife on the phone in the hotel and as I sat down in the bathroom I felt it pull again.

'I'll speak to you later,' I said and hung up.

I went straight down the hall to Walter.

'Do something, Walter. It hurts, and I need to play tomorrow.'

He gave me a painkiller and said: 'It's nothing. Tomorrow you're going to be fine.'

But the next day it still hurt. He gave me another injection. But during the warm-up it still hurt.

'Walter . . .'

He couldn't give me another injection, not now. He rubbed a cream into my knee, hard.

'It's gone, it's gone,' he said, passing his hand over my knee.

But it hadn't gone.

I was scared and I was in pain. Scared of the meniscus on one side and aware of the pain in the tendon on the other. But it was England, the game I'd been so determined not to miss, and I trusted Walter.

When the game started it was strange. I'd always felt that there were weaknesses in the English defence that we could exploit, but I hadn't expected this. I had played against Gary Cahill and Phil Jagielka lots of times and usually played well. I was confident that I could cause them problems. But I had never felt the kind of respect that I felt that day. Maybe they thought I wasn't really fit, but to me it felt more like respect. In a Premier League game, they wouldn't have let me receive the ball and turn like they did in Brazil. It was as if they were being extra cautious. In other games they had been right up behind me. I kept thinking: 'This is weird, they're giving me so much space.' I felt like they were worried and as time went on the better I felt.

We were playing well, the confidence grew and then the goal came; as the ball came over from the right, I pulled away slightly and then headed it back in the same direction past Joe Hart. When it hit the net, I set off for the bench. I hadn't planned it, I hadn't even thought about it. But in that surge of adrenaline, everything that Walter and I had been through came flooding back. He'd left the bench to hand some water to the defenders and didn't see me arrive to embrace him. He had given me everything, through his own illness, and I grabbed him and held him, pointing at him.

The second goal was strange. England had equalised in the seventieth minute and I thought our chances of winning had vanished. I was struggling badly. I couldn't run. Cramp had shot up both calves. I glanced across at the bench and the idea of asking to be taken off kept returning to my mind, but something stopped me. Physically, I was dead; emotionally, I couldn't take any more. I was in an offside position, tired, and thinking: 'We're going to lose, that's it.' We weren't creating chances. And then, suddenly, the ball came past and into the space in front of me, off the head of Steven Gerrard.

I couldn't run, but I was running after it. All I could do was close my eyes and whack it. I was surprised that it went in. I just hit it, I didn't think at all. Genuinely, I couldn't believe it when it went in. Everything was a blur, impossible to describe. I've got a photograph that a journalist gave me. It's me on my knees, my arms out, this huge stadium around me. I couldn't believe it. I had spotted my family high in the stand during the second half and now I looked up again. Everyone was going mad. Sofi later told me that Delfi, who'd spent the season watching Jordan, Glen, Raheem, Daniel and Stevie, had turned to her and said: 'Why are you happy that Liverpool are losing, Mummy?'

'No, no,' Sofi said. 'Daddy won. Uruguay won.'

I felt for Stevie. The ball through to me had come off him and it was quite hard talking to him and Glen afterwards. We'd just been through something similar together with Liverpool and Stevie knew it was his last World Cup. It wasn't a nice way for it to end; it was cruel that it had happened to him at all, but for it to happen to him twice was even worse. He didn't deserve it. I had swapped shirts with Glen after the first half but after the game I didn't swap with anyone. I later gave shirts to Jordan Henderson and to Stevie, but it didn't feel like the right time amidst their disappointment. I didn't talk to them much; I embraced them but that was it. I had enjoyed beating England, of course. And for me it was extra special after everything that had happened. But I did feel for them.

I genuinely love English football but England had gone out of another World Cup and another debate was about to start; the post-mortems began. When people talk about a lack of resources, it makes me laugh. If England, over there in the 'first world', don't have the resources, with the quality and quantity of players there are, with the facilities that they have to train, with the economic muscle the game has there, with the millions of players there are, where does that leave the rest of us? Where does that leave Uruguay?

I think the reasons lie elsewhere. I can't claim to have the answer, but coming from the outside, looking upon the game with different eyes, you do see some things that others perhaps don't and I do think that English football is affected by the lack of a winter break. I understand the Christmas and New Year programme is special but to have a fifteen- or twenty-day break after that in January so that players can stop both physically and mentally could have enormous benefits. Instead, there's an extra cup competition squeezed into the fixture list.

The other thing to take into consideration is that it's not just the number of games in England, it is the intensity of each game. If you compare the intensity of the Bundesliga, La Liga and the Premier League, you can see that the English league's harder. The players who come from abroad notice the intensity even more. That lies at the root of the problem for English teams in Europe. You see this not just with the national team but with the Champions League too, in my opinion.

I watched the way Bayern won the Champions League and then the way that Real Madrid did, and I think you could see the impact of that month's break. They have fifteen days off and then come back to fifteen days' preparation for the second half of the season. It's a chance for players to relax, to see their families: the legs get a break, the brain gets a break and when you come back you can't wait to play. You could also see it with us last season: Liverpool's title bid was probably strengthened by not playing in Europe. We didn't have a winter break, but we did have time to get off the conveyor belt and feel more refreshed. If English teams stopped for fifteen days – and I realise this will never happen, but if it did – I think you'd see the difference in the way English teams were able to compete in European competition and with the national team.

Players in England just don't have a rest as things stand. Footballers love to play and love to compete and we don't always appreciate how much it would help to stop; while from the outside, fans don't always appreciate the pressure that players are under too. It's draining when you are in competition without any sort of break: you find yourself just wanting two or three days to get away from the tension and the effort. By the time they get to the World Cup, England's players are shattered.

For me, the reasons were different of course, but I was shattered too. I could hardly move and emotionally I was in pieces: I was exhausted and elated at the same time. I'd never had an experience like that victory against England. I was so grateful to Walter. He was fighting for his life, for his health, against a terrible illness. He has now overcome the cancer, thank God, but he was not yet entirely in the clear at that time. He had needed an injection the day before the game. In the dressing room, I hugged Walter. And hugged him and hugged him. I wouldn't let go. 'It was you Walter, it was you . . .' It was the first time I ever saw him cry.

There are people in the Federation who have known him for twenty-five years or more. It was the first time they had seen him cry too. He's a hard man; it's not easy to catch him showing any emotion but the tears were rolling down his cheeks. He had risked everything for me; he had given me everything. This was for him.

As we sat there – me with ice on my knee – we talked about the game.

'You're such a brute, such a beast, that you didn't even notice that on the second goal, your leg was doing this . . .' he said, and he started gesturing with his hand, wobbling. 'When you hit it, you were falling, you couldn't stand up any more. You were in a bad way.'

He was right. When I saw the goal again, I saw that my knee had gone entirely. I had hardly trained with the team. Sofi had told me that I was 'bloody mad', that I hadn't realised what I was risking for the World Cup. Now it felt worth it. It even felt like I had won something back in England, like some people in England loved me *more*, not less, after what I had done against them. I think they appreciated and respected what I had done in coming back from the injury and scoring the two goals. If it had been another player who'd gone through everything that I had in England, I wonder if they might have gloated, rubbed it in. I didn't. But I can't deny that it was very special. Or that my emotions were all over the place.

I was carried around the pitch on my team-mates' shoulders. Before the game, I'd told Nicolás Lodeiro: 'I'm dreaming of beating England and scoring.'

'Relax, take it easy. . . your knee . . .'

'But that's the way I dream it.'

It was like a film.

But the end was not the end. There was more. Sofi was right. Walter was too. We had beaten England but my confidence in making it to the World Cup was superficial and that became clearer than ever before after the England game. Playing against England, beating England, scoring two goals despite the injury, somehow made the risk seem more real, not less. It brought it to the surface. I'd been terrified; the tension had been unbearable. All those questions: Will I get there? Won't I? And what if it goes wrong? Liverpool will kill me. What about the cartilage? I trusted in Walter entirely and without him I wouldn't have made it at all, but the doubts inevitably built up. Then when I came back to play, there was no easy first step. Instead there was England and the obligation to win. The fear and the tension had been there before the game and it wasn't leaving me afterwards. There should have been an explosion, a release. But, oddly, there wasn't. The two goals, the victory, didn't settle me. Instead, the tension grew.

In a World Cup, there is no escape; it doesn't end until it ends. You win the game against England, you've still got all that emotion in your body, you don't sleep, your head's everywhere. And two days later you travel to face Italy and you have to win then too. You *have* to. Otherwise everything you have just done is worthless; all that effort, all the sacrifice. You want more, always. That has always been the way with Uruguay and it has always been the way with me.

The responsibility and the pressure is still there. You're playing Italy. That's even harder than England and it's still sudden death. You hardly have time to think, to breathe. You feel like bringing the shutters down, closing it all out for a while, but you can't. You don't have time for that and I think that is what damaged me for the game against Italy. I had all that tension inside and I couldn't find a way of letting it go.

I spoke to the professionals about this and I told them that at no time did I have the chance or the inclination to talk to someone, to unburden myself, to find a way of easing the tension. I didn't have the chance to shout and swear and let go. I had worked in isolation, desperate to return, away from my team-mates. I had Walter and Sofi but I didn't even talk to them. I bottled up the pressure. I needed to let it out but I couldn't. Or I wouldn't. I kept it to myself and I made things worse for myself.

I couldn't explain to anyone what went on in my head in the days before that game, in the month before it; all those things spinning round my head were mine and mine alone. 'Suárez this, Suárez that.' The season.

The injury. The worry. The work, day after day. Not making it to the World Cup. Making it to the World Cup. For Uruguay and for me, *the* World Cup. Losing to Costa Rica, powerless on the bench. Facing England. *England*. Scoring twice. The knee. The emotion. And then having to do it again two days later or it's all gone, taken away. And it's Italy. And the clock runs down and the chance comes and Gigi Buffon saves. And then it happens.

EPILOGUE: THE CALLEJÓN

When I was seven years old my field of dreams was the narrow back street that passed behind our home in Montevideo's La Comercial neighbourhood. At one end was the lemon tree that my grandmother had planted years before we moved to her tiny one-storey house, as my parents looked for work in the city. And at the other end were the grey imposing walls, the barbed wire and the turrets of the local women's prison. Wedged between the children's home that belonged to the prison and the row of lock-ups and workshops next to our house, was the bumpy gravel surface that passed as our make-do pitch.

The *callejón*, as we called it, was wide enough for our matches but too narrow to take any traffic. Set back slightly from the exhaust fumes and the noise of the buses and cars hurtling along Bulevar Artigas, it wasn't the open-country fields of Salto where we lived until I was six, but it was our refuge from Montevideo's perpetual motion. It was also the favoured location of another sort of traffic entirely. After dark the people passing through would be there to buy marijuana and cocaine; or to sniff glue or get drunk. It was the kind of place you wouldn't have wanted to wander into by mistake, but it was literally on my back doorstep and I was there night and day, playing football.

The older I got the more I noticed the drugs and the alcohol. The smell of marijuana would waft across from the groups of people who had come to visit the prison. Many would be trying to smuggle substances in, some would even be trying to get inmates out – there were several escape attempts over the years. A few of them succeeded too.

My big brother Paolo, who was six years older, played in the *callejón* with his friends and I would join in. There wasn't a lot of space and I was one of the smallest. My brother's friends backed off at first when they saw the size of me but as soon as they realised I was fearless and more than useful there was no holding back. They were surprised at how well I handled myself – chest out, head down, crashing into the older boys and bouncing off the walls, never intimidated and always keeping my eye on the ball, fighting, scrapping for every inch.

If there were enough of us we would play lengthways from the Lemon Tree End to the Prison End with the ball constantly kept in play by the workshop shutters and the barbed-wire wall of the children's home. If there were fewer of us then we would play widthways, smashing the ball against the goals spray-painted on to the walls amid the graffiti either side of the narrow lane.

I missed playing barefoot on the green grass of Salto where we lived on Paraguay Street and where everyone's front door was left open and you played with your friends in the fresh air every day. Salto is like a village compared to Montevideo. Everyone knows everyone. And I started to play Baby Football when I was four years old in a side called Deportivo Artigas, managed by my uncle, my father's brother. The pitch was at the military base where my dad had briefly been a soldier and he played for them too. He was a tough left-back who kicked a lot of rivals but also struck the ball very well with his left foot. When my family was forced to move to Montevideo because my father was looking for work, my parents left with my brothers and sisters and I stayed with my grandparents because my uncle wanted me to play in a tournament. It was the perfect excuse. I didn't want to leave my home anyway. I loved playing football with my friends. For a while I resisted leaving Salto. I was already a rebel aged six. When I finally left I took the name of the town with me – I'm still 'El Salta' to many of my oldest friends.

Swapping the open fields for the back street was hard and it toughened me up. I would finish some games crying with beaten and bruised feet from playing with cheap sandals because I only had one pair of trainers and I needed to wear them to school.

Across the road from our old house in the neighbourhood where we played our games was the block where 'El Jefe Negro' Obdulio Varela once lived. 'The Black Chief' captained the nation in its finest hour, winning the 1950 World Cup in Brazil in the Maracanã. Not that I was too aware of this as a kid – charging up and down the back streets, my heroes were a little more contemporary.

We used to commentate as we played: 'And it's Francescoli on the ball, to Ruben Sosa and back to Francescoli.' The first proper boots I ever had were Adidas Francescolis – a birthday present from my mum in 1997 when he would have just been retiring and I would have been turning ten. Every time I scored I would scream the name of my idol and first real footballing role model, Argentina's centre-forward Gabriel Batistuta. 'Bat-is-tuuuuut-a!'

When we couldn't play football in the *callejón* then we would play indoors. If we were sent to our rooms it was supposed to be lights out and sleeping, but we would make a ball out of screwed-up newspaper inside a sock and we would practise acrobatic volleys or diving headers with the bed as a landing pad. We broke the bed in the end. The desire to play football, whatever potential obstacles were put in our way, was insatiable.

We would also play a kind of homemade Subbuteo with bottle tops painted in team colours and old shoeboxes for goals. If our mum threw the game out because we'd been misbehaving then we would improvise again; this time with folded cardboard players and a button as the ball.

And if we weren't playing, or improvising, then we'd be watching football. The 1994 World Cup finals were the first I remember, with Italy and Brazil contesting the final and Roberto Baggio missing a penalty. I remember Romário and Bebeto with the famous 'cradling the baby' celebration. In 1997 Uruguay played the Under-20 World Cup final against Argentina in Malaysia. We were incredibly proud to have Uruguay in the final, albeit the Under-20s, and we would be up at 5 a.m. to watch Fabián Coelho, César Pellegrin, Marcelo Zalayeta and Nicolás Olivera play the final against

Argentina. I never have any problem understanding the way the fans feel about this sport because I only have to wind the clock back to those times and the feelings all come flooding back.

Leaving Salto wasn't all bad. There is a club in every neighbourhood in Montevideo and Nacional was mine. The two most successful clubs in Uruguay – the teams that dominate football there – are Nacional and Peñarol, and we were a family divided. It is said that Peñarol were the club of the railway workers and Nacional the team of the élite, but I didn't see it like that. What is true is that Nacional are the biggest, although my brother Maxi would disagree. He supports Peñarol. Maxi was one year younger than me and we were inseparable. We argued about football from dusk until dawn with our mother as the reluctant, overrun referee of most of our disputes. Going to games was the biggest battle. He wanted to watch Peñarol and I wanted to watch Nacional. The compromise was to go to Peñarol one match day and to Nacional the next but I was never much into compromises.

I would say: 'Why do I have to put up with going to Peñarol if I don't want to?'

'Well, if you want to go to Nacional then you are going to have to go with your brother to watch Peñarol.'

Whenever I went to a Peñarol game I would stay very quiet. I imagined that people had no idea I was there as a Nacional fan reluctantly accompanying my brother although there were times when they could probably work it out. I remember one game when Peñarol were playing Racing in a Copa Libertadores match at the city's Centenario Stadium. There in the huge concrete bowl that hosted the first World Cup final in 1930 I was doing my best to hide but I was dying inside, surrounded by Peñarol supporters. I was only at the game so that I would be able to go to the next Nacional match. What I hadn't realised until I was inside the stadium was that I had Nacional socks on.

Peñarol scored and I had this big chunky kid to one side of me and my brother and my mum on the other. My mum was a Peñarol supporter too. As Peñarol scored everyone was jumping up and down and singing apart from me. 'Chunky' next to me says: 'Why aren't you celebrating? Peñarol are winning.' And so I started bouncing up and down a bit with my brother who was doing his best not to laugh knowing full well that the last thing I wanted to be doing was celebrating Peñarol winning in the Copa Libertadores, especially with my Nacional socks now in full view. It was hell.

It was a similar story when we asked to be mascots and my mum told us: 'Okay, no problem – you can both be mascots but you have to go along one week and be a mascot with your brother at Peñarol and then another week you can both be mascots at Nacional.'

My boys' team shirt at Urreta was a bit like the yellow and black stripes of Peñarol so I put their kit on so as not to have to wear the Peñarol shirt. The only shirt I wanted to be wearing was the white and blue of Nacional.

In some ways it became worse for my brother because when I later went to play for Nacional he came and played with me in the same youth system. I would wind him up even more than he teased me. I found a Nacional flag in a park on the way to school once and presented it to my brother in the playground in front of all his friends. He did his best to maintain the pretence that he was 100 per cent Peñarol but it became impossible once word got out that he was playing for the other side.

On the days of the *clásico* one sibling would be crying while the one alongside him would be shouting each goal in his ear. And if your team lost you never heard the end of it. My dad Rodolfo supported Nacional and my elder brother Paolo does too. I have one sister Giovana who supports Nacional and another Leticia who supports Peñarol. So we had four for Nacional and three for Peñarol. My youngest brother Diego got cajoled and pressured by both sides but we were always going to end up winning and so he supports Nacional too.

Maxi and I were not always on opposing sides. My uncle had found me a place at Urreta when I was seven and Maxi joined when he was six. Much of Uruguay's football success is owed to Baby Football – the intensely competitive six-a-side leagues played by boys from age five until thirteen, on football pitches about a third of the size of a full size pitch. At first glance this youth football model looks similar to that used around the world, but in Europe they encourage almost a no-contact sport at that age. Baby Football in Uruguay is nothing of the sort. It's physical and it's aggressive and the parents and coaches take it so seriously that some mothers and fathers even keep their children away from it because they believe some of the fun is lost due to the intensity. Some even consider it dangerous. It instils a ferociously competitive streak from an early age and it reinforced in me the lessons I had already learned from the street – that you play to win at almost any cost.

Urreta's neatly enclosed ground, with its tiny three-bench grandstand at one end, now has a lush green playing surface, but back then my brother and I would spend our evenings sliding around on its unforgiving gravel pitch. It was about ten minutes away on the bus when we had the money for the bus fare, and a half-hour walk when, as was the case more often than not, we didn't.

I can still remember us keeping each other company on that walk to Urreta's ground, zig-zagging through Montevideo's grid of streets in the cold and dark, walking fifteen blocks to train. When I finished the under-nines level at Urreta the father of my team-mate Martín Pírez invited me to come and play for the boys' team at Nacional. Urreta would not let me leave; it was my first transfer tug of war.

It was silly really. Urreta had very little claim over their young striker. They were a neighbourhood team and the biggest club in Uruguay – *my club* – was calling me. It was an opportunity I had to take. But Urreta were adamant that they did not want to let me go. I think the final exchanges went something like:

'Well, I'm going anyway.'

'Well, if you're going then you have to give us all the kit back.'

'Of course you'll get your kit back but I'm going to Nacional.'

My brother went too and so from the thirty-minute walk together to Urreta we were now taking a forty-minute bus ride to train with the three-times Copa Libertadores champions. Training started at 7.30 p.m., but we came out of school at five o'clock and we knew that until six o'clock we could still travel for free on the buses as long as we had our school tunics on. So we would arrive one hour early just to avoid having to pay a bus fare and then get a lift home from one of our friends' dads when training finished at 9.30 p.m.

At that stage, I was still going back to Salto every summer to play a tournament in my old home town. I was teased for my big-city accent back home just as I had been teased in Montevideo for my Salto accent when I arrived there aged six. It was always great to go back but it was beginning to dawn on me, and everyone else, that perhaps I was now a little bit better than the rest of the players in my age-group.

My uncle Sergio Suárez was the one who had got me playing competitively when I was only four years old. It was my uncle who taught me how to hit the ball properly and made sure I was playing matches from that very early age. The tournament was held every December during my holidays and I would stay in my grandfather's house for the duration. But when I was eleven years old I was told that I wasn't going to play in that summer's tournament. I was at Nacional and we were champions. I was one of their best players so as far as the organisers were concerned I had outgrown the Salto tournament.

If I wasn't going to play in the tournament then that meant I was not going to go to Salto every year. It was the closing of a chapter of my life. I was sad but at the same time being told I was too good to play in the tournament had a positive effect on me. It was a sign. That was the first time I had ever thought: 'They're scared of me, that's how good a player I am.'

As an eleven-year-old playing for Nacional, I already had a fiery temper, I would get heated up over things to the point where I would cry if I didn't score goals. There were games when I never gave the ball to anyone else because a team-mate had scored a goal and I hadn't. I had grown up in an environment where no one gives you anything. If you want something you have to take it. As a country Uruguay has its very poor people; it has its poor people who at least have work and can try to scrape together a living; it has its working people, and then it has its rich people. I grew up in the second group. My parents and my brothers and sisters would make and sell whatever we could to make a living and survive. It was never easy.

I learned very early on in my life the value of work, and how hard we had to fight to get anywhere. You had to grab at every possible opportunity, no matter how small, fighting tooth and nail once you had it in your grasp to never let it go.

As well as work, focus was required – a single-mindedness that I always possessed and that helped me along the way. You have to be mentally tough. Talent is never enough.

Maxi was a better player than me. He played in my age group despite being one year younger. He was the technically gifted one. But he had a problem with the company he kept. I managed to stay on the right side of the tracks and he went the other way. It was a difficult time for all of us with the separation of our parents. My oldest brother, who would later make a playing career in El Salvador and Guatemala, had already left home to go and live with his partner and to us young boys it felt as though the family was breaking up. We were moving from one house to another quite a bit – all in the same neighbourhood – and there was no stability. We would spend time with one parent then live for a while with another.

I never really had the chance to sit down and speak to my parents and have that kind of conversation in which they might say to me: 'Listen, son, when you're bigger be sure to value what you've got'; 'Act like this'; or 'Never forget where you're from'.

They were separated, there were lots of us, some were leaving, my mum worked all day, my dad worked, so it was hard to learn from them in terms of getting advice about what life would be like, about how to handle growing up fast and about how to act when I made it. I would have loved to have had that conversation when I was a kid. I wasn't lucky enough although that was also because of the way I was. I think my brothers and sisters, or some of them at least, did have that kind of talk. But I rather looked after myself. And when I did almost fall, Sofi was there for me.

I had my blip at Nacional but I played on through my teenage years and I kept advancing. Maxi hit a wall. He stopped improving because he fell in with the wrong crowd. He knows, and all the family knows, that he was better than me. If he had been more focused and wanted it more then he would have progressed. Instead he preferred to go out to discos or he would disappear for a couple of days with friends when he was only fourteen years old.

As his brother, I always tried to help, talk to him, but we were both kids. I could talk all I liked and he was still going to do what all his friends did, not what his brother told him to do. Maxi's back playing football now and he's fine. He was never close to ruining his life, but he did enough to ruin what could have been a brilliant career. He knows the hard work that you have to put in to go a long way. He knows how I worked to make it. I think he is proud of what I've achieved because he knows how hard it was for us both and how tough you have to be sometimes.

You could also say that for a 'tough guy' I have shed a lot of tears during my career. I'm not ashamed to admit it – I cry a lot. I was that way as a kid and I haven't changed. I'm the guy who walks off the pitch in floods of tears when he knows the league title chances have gone; the one who cries when he is torn apart with indecision because he has said he wants to leave a club but now believes the move could make things even worse for him and his family; the man who cries when he has to get up at 7.30 a.m. to go and sit in a hotel and listen to lawyers discussing a verdict that he feels is inevitable and will stain his reputation for life.

I cried when Ajax fans said goodbye to me. And I could never understand why Jamie Carragher didn't do the same when he waved goodbye to Anfield for the last time as a player. Come on, a tear – at least one. I was crying for ten or fifteen minutes in the Amsterdam Arena when they gave me my send-off and I had only been there for three seasons. Carragher had been at Liverpool all his life when he retired and yet as he said goodbye he didn't flinch. Maybe the send-off on the pitch should have been bigger with a giant screen showing all his best moments at the club. The day that Stevie Gerrard retires I hope he gets the full works.

I would have liked to have had a farewell game at Liverpool and no doubt I would have been in tears. I'm an emotional person. I'm sentimental enough to have the words of the song that Sofi and I got married to tattooed on my back: 'Our time is short. This is our fate, I'm yours.' And I'm the guy who tries to dedicate the goals he scores to his loved ones to the point where the celebration lasts longer than the goal. I also have a tattoo on my leg: *Uruguay: Campeones de América* with the date of our 2011 triumph. I have tattoos of both my children's names and another that just says 'Sofi'.

The guy who tattooed my son Benjamin's name for me also did the tattoo on my back with the words to our wedding song. He's a huge

Liverpool fan and wanted me to do a tattoo on him. I told him I thought he was mad but he found a tiny un-tattooed space on his body.

'Do it there.'

I thought it would involve drawing an outline first and then going over it with ink. Nothing of the sort.

'Just do it,' he said. No outline, no practice run, just me, a needle and his flesh. So I did. An L, and an S, and a 7. Sofi recorded the whole process on her phone and it wasn't actually *that* bad.

I would have loved to have added a tattoo that marked Liverpool winning the league in the 2013/14 season, but it wasn't to be. I don't mind the fact that the image of me walking off the pitch at Selhurst Park will for many be the lasting one. In many ways that fits perfectly because it is a reminder of how much it meant to me and how close we came to doing something truly incredible.

That's not all people think about when they think of me, I know. For non-Liverpool fans it will also be the biting incidents and the Evra accusation.

Attitudes change with time and to get the Player of the Season award from the journalists in 2014 was special and then from my fellow players even more so. Wayne Rooney said some nice things about me before the 2014 World Cup; that he loved the way I played. His opinion matters to me. He knows what it is like to be out there on the pitch; he knows the pressures, the expectations and the microscopic analysis of your every move. Events in Brazil will have coloured people's judgements again. But I'll bounce back again to show people my better side. I am trying.

I would like to think that people respect me as a player. I have been criticised for things that I have done and for things that I haven't done. But I always pick myself up and get back to work, back to doing my job, a job which I love.

I knew when I returned to work this time that it would be in front of 98,000 people at the Camp Nou – about as far from the *callejón* as I could possibly have come.

October, 2014

ACKNOWLEDGEMENTS

I would like to thank Sofi, Delfi and Benja, who travelled this journey with me. They are my everything. I would also like to thank friends, family, team-mates, staff and fans who have always supported me, in good times and bad. They have been there throughout my life and they are here on these pages too. So many people have given me so much and I will always be grateful to them for everything they have done for me. My thanks too to everyone who has invested time and effort in helping me to tell my story, which I have tried to do with sincerity and affection. Without all of them, none of this would have been possible. Thank you all.

PICTURE CREDITS

INDEX

Abreu, Sebastián 75–6, 80, 85, 86, 211, 226, 227
Adam, Charlie 138, 174
Afelay, Ibrahim 62
agents 162–6
Agger, Danny 128, 129, 134–5, 173, 209, 210
Aguilera, Carlos 164
Ajax 14, 15, 36, 42–3, 44–5, 47–54, 55–6, 59–70, 98, 114, 115, 121, 123, 160, 229, 270
Alberto, Luis 209
Albín, Juan 29, 30
Alderweireld, Toby 63
Allen, Joe 174–5, 184, 209, 210
Alves, Dani 15, 153
Amoah, Matthew 91
Amsterdam Arena 66

Argentina 51, 77, 99–100, 101–2, 263
Arsenal 11, 13, 180, 182, 200, 201–2, 233
Aspas, Iago 209
Aston Villa 114, 124
Atlético River Plate 28
Aurelio, Fabio 119
Aventujuegos (TV show) 104–6
Ayala, Roberto 51
Ayre, Ian 203
AZ Alkmaar 51

Ba, Demba 216
Baby Football 3, 104, 261, 265
Baggio, Roberto 262
Baines, Leighton 136
Bakkal, Otman 4, 62–3, 64
Bale, Gareth 233

Barcelona 11, 12–15, 49, 175, 176
Batistuta, Gabriel 262
Bayern Munich 254
Beatles 111–12
Bebeto 186, 262
Belza, Eduardo 2
Benítez, Rafa 145, 175
Bergkamp, Denis 51
Birmingham 124
Borini, Fabio 184
Brazil 102, 241, 262
Brighton & Hove Albion 140
Buffon, Gianluigi 5, 258
Bundesliga 254
Burdisso, Nicolás 102
Busquets, Sergio 15

Cáceres, Martin 80, 102
Cahill, Gary 251
Cameron, David 199
Camp Nou 16–17
Campo, Noelia 104
Canavarro, Fabio 13
Cardiff City 131–2, 140
Carling Cup 140–3
Carragher, Jamie 113, 129–30, 270
Carroll, Andy 118–19, 143, 174,
 177–8
Castillo, Juan 87
Cavani, Edison 80
Champions League 5, 42, 48, 63, 98,
 115, 200, 201, 202, 218, 233, 234,
 235, 254
Charlton, Bobby 181
Chelsea 5, 8, 48, 49, 135, 142, 143–4,
 184, 189, 216–19, 221, 223, 231,
 233, 234

Chiellini, Giorgio 5, 9, 244
Chile 101
Clarke, Steve 125, 139–40
Clattenberg, Mark 73
Coates, Sebastián 36, 138, 179, 184
Coelho, Fabian 262
Columbia 41
Comolli, Damien 115, 138, 147, 149,
 155
concentraciones 78–9, 238
Copa América 99–100, 101–3
Copa Libertadores 28
Costa Rica 76, 249, 250
Coutinho, Philippe 153, 185, 188, 209,
 210, 212, 213, 214
Cox, Paul 185
Cruyff, Johan 69–70, 114
Crystal Palace 222–3
Cvitanich, Dario 50

Dalglish, Kenny 89, 115, 116, 117,
 123, 124–6, 127, 139–40, 141,
 143–5, 149, 155, 157, 158
Danubio 34, 163
De Boer, Frank 51, 63–4
De Gea, David 149, 179
dead-ball scenarios 178–9
Defensor Sporting 27, 29, 163
Delap, Rory 141, 142
Deportivo Artigas 88, 261
diving 39–40, 89, 132–3, 134–8
Downing, Stuart 138
dressing rooms
 Anfield 109–11, 209–10
 dressing-room rows 66
Drogba, Didier 138, 143
Dutch Cup, 2010 61–2

Dutch style of play 54–5, 67
Dutch Super Cup 48, 62, 98

Eguren, Sebastian 90
England 250, 251–3, 255, 256, 257
English style of play 130–2, 176
Enrique, José 89, 126, 172
Enrique, Luis 3, 13, 15
Eredivisie 41, 48, 70
Espanyol 13
Espósito, José Luis 19, 20, 163
Eto'o, Samuel 14, 72
Europa League 38, 52, 65, 124
Everton 122, 135–6, 143, 184, 205
Evra, Patrice 146, 147–51, 156–9
Exeter City 140

'fair play', concept of 71
fame 104–7
fans
    Ajax 64–5, 68–9
    Groningen 39, 44–5
    Liverpool 113, 207, 208, 236
Ferguson, Sir Alex 157
Ferreira, Carmen 248
Ferreira, Walter 239–40, 246–9, 251,
    252, 255–6, 257
Feyenoord 61
Figueroa, Elías 26
Flanagan, Jon 130, 209
Fonseca, Daniel 25, 29, 44, 163, 164–5
Forlán, Diego 76, 78, 81, 84, 94, 95–6,
    102, 103, 211, 227–8
Foster, Ben 179
fouls 39, 72, 102, 131–3, 138
France 76
Francescoli, Enzo 100, 240, 262

Fucile, Jorge 89, 94
Fuhler, Grads 26
Fulham 8

Gabri 49
Gardel, Carlos 100
Gargano, Walter 102
Germany 95
Gerrard, Anthony 140
Gerrard, Steven 11–12, 40, 113, 114,
    116, 158, 175, 180–1, 184, 193,
    194, 198, 202, 203, 209, 210, 211,
    215, 216–18, 219, 223, 226, 231,
    232, 236, 252, 253, 270
Getafe 29, 30
Ghana 75, 84–7, 88, 89–90, 91, 92
Ghiggia, Alcides 78–9
goal-less runs 139, 183–4
goalkeepers 89, 179–80
Godín, Diego 1
Golden Boot 236
Golden Samba 236
Golden Shoe 193
González, Alvaro 226–7
González, Nacho 80
Grant, Avram 49
Groningen 15, 26–7, 29–31, 32–6,
    37–46, 53, 58
group spirit 50–1
Guardiola, Pep 14
Guardiola, Pere 96, 115, 123, 200
Gyan, Asamoah 84, 85, 90, 92
gym work 56

handballs 5, 185–6
Hart, Joe 252
hat-tricks 69, 181–2, 183

Haughton, Ray 221
Hazard, Eden 233
Heitinger, Johnny 7–8
Henderson, Jordan 138, 157, 175, 209, 210, 235, 253
Henry, John 205
Henry, Thierry 14, 114
Herrera, José 81–2
Higuaín, Gonzalo 102
Hillsborough tragedy 112, 181, 212–13, 216
Hodgson, Roy 115, 181, 250
Holland 93, 94, 96
Hoyos, Jorge Hernán 41
Huntelaar, Klass-Jan 54

Iniesta, Andrés 13, 15, 96
interviews 40, 122–3
Italy 5, 8, 257, 258, 262
Ivanović, Branislav 4, 5, 6, 7, 106, 193, 199, 204

Jagielka, Phil 251
Jans, Ron 32–3, 38, 39, 40, 43
Johnson, Glen 119–20, 152, 157, 158, 172, 209, 210, 223, 236, 253
Jol, Martin 5, 8, 48, 58, 59–61, 63, 64, 65, 98, 229

Keegan, Kevin 123
Kelly, Martin 142, 177–8, 209
Kompany, Vincent 213, 214–15
Koster, Adrie 49
Kuyt, Dirk 110, 119, 121, 126–7, 140

La Liga 73, 254
Lasarte, Martin 28

Leiva, Lucas 119, 125, 209, 229
Lindren, Rasmus 62
Liverpool 7, 11–12, 14, 15, 37, 89, 107, 108–45, 160, 169–94, 198–225, 231–6, 254, 270
Liverpool FC (Uruguay) 26, 112
Lloris, Hugo 179
Lodeiro, Nicolás 87, 229, 256
López, Claudio 186
Lovre, Goran 122
Lugano, Diego 87
Luque, Albert 66

McCartney, Paul 112
McManaman, Steve 123
managers 237–8
Manchester City 142, 179, 180, 189, 198, 208, 213–14, 222, 223, 233, 234
Manchester United 65, 72, 143, 147–8, 180, 224, 233
Mansfield Town 185
Maradona, Diego 90, 161
Mascherano, Javier 15
mate 15, 35–6, 80, 195
Materazzi, Marco 3
Melwood training ground 112–13, 123
Messi, Lionel 13, 14, 15, 102, 160–1
Mexico 77, 101
Mignolet, Simon 210, 234
Milan, AC 63
money in football 34, 160–8
Montevideo 22, 26, 37, 241, 259–60, 263
Moses, Victor 210
Mourinho, Jose 125, 135, 218, 219
Moyes, David 135, 136, 184

Mujica, José 96
'mum motivation' tactic 211–12
Muslera, Fernando 89, 92, 102

NAC Breda 47, 48, 91
Nacional 12, 17, 19–20, 21, 23–4,
   26–9, 31, 36, 56–7, 60, 163, 164,
   165, 226, 227, 228, 239–40, 263,
   264–5, 266, 267
Nasri, Sami 214
NEC Nijmegen 48
Neville, Phil 135
Nevland, Erik 40, 53, 122
Newcastle United 193–4, 223, 236
Neymar 14
Nijland, Hans 26
Norwich City 181–3, 184, 216, 219

Oldham Athletic 187, 188
Olivera, Nicolas 262
Ostolaza, Santiago 27
Owen, Michael 137

Panenka penalties 85, 86
PAOK Athens 98
PAOK FC 69
Paraguay 99, 102, 103
Partizan Belgrade 38
Pascoe, Colin 187
Pastore, Javier 102
Pele 161
Pellegrin, Cesar 262
Peñarol 34, 263–4, 265
Pereira, Álvaro 77, 85
Pérez, Diego 102
Peru 87, 101, 102
Philippou, Pedro 110

Pinkster, Herman 69, 70
Pique, Gerard 13
Pirez, Martin 266
Pírez, Wilson 19, 20, 21, 27, 163
Player of the Year Awards 62, 231–3,
   271
pre-match routines 209
Premier League 12, 132, 254
   2013–14 207–25, 234–5
PSV Eindhoven 4, 8, 62, 63
Pulis, Tony 134, 141

racism issue 144, 146–59
Rakitic, Ivan 15
Real Madrid 13, 254
Rebollo, Mario 55, 82
referees 71–4
registration rights, selling 162–4
Reina, Pepe 89, 110, 119, 125, 127,
   157, 170, 171, 220–1
Revetria, Guillermo 75, 81, 84, 85
Rijkaard, Frank 49
Ríos, Egidio Arévalo 80
Rodgers, Brendan 14, 169, 170, 171–2,
   173–4, 175, 176–8, 179, 185, 187,
   189–91, 203, 204–6, 211–12, 215,
   232, 235, 236
Rodríguez, Maxi 119, 142
Romario 262
Ronaldo 186
Ronaldo, Cristiano 160–1
Rooney, Wayne 271
Ruddy, John 182
Rush, Ian 181

Salah, Mohamed 234
Salas, Marcelo 186

Salto 22, 24, 37, 88, 261, 263, 266–7
scams 161–2
Schuster, Bernd 30
Scotti, Andrés 102
Scudamore, Richard 12
Senderos, Philippe 8
Shankly, Bill 113–14, 209
Shaw, Luke 233
Shelvey, Jonjo 180
Silva, Bruno 34, 35–6, 39, 40, 44, 121, 229
Silva, David 214
Silva, Martín 80
Škrtel, Martin 128–9, 173, 179, 180, 187, 205, 210
Slavia Prague 48
smoothies 195, 197
Soldado, Roberto 30
Sosa, Rubén 100, 262
South Africa 76, 82
South Korea 83
Spain 87, 96
Spanish style of play 14–15, 16, 175, 176
Stekelenburg, Maarten 60, 93
Sterling, Raheem 184, 210, 235
Stoke City 127, 134, 140–1, 142, 234
strikers 59–60, 192–3
Sturridge, Daniel 72, 137, 185, 188, 189, 191–2, 193, 194, 209, 210, 236
Suárez, Benjamin (son) 186
Suárez, Delfina (daughter) 4, 12, 65–6, 99, 101, 186, 253
Suárez, Diego (brother) 265
Suárez, Facundo (brother) 166
Suárez, Luis

Ajax captaincy 60, 61, 62, 64, 121
biting incidents 4–6, 9, 16, 62–3, 64, 193, 199, 200, 244
boyhood football 8, 259–60, 261–2, 265–6, 267
courtship of Sofi 18–32
diving 39–40, 89, 132–3, 134–8
education 22–3
eight-game ban (2011) 65, 156
'El Salta' nickname 32, 261
emotionality 25, 223–4, 269–70
on fame 104–7
family background and issues 22, 34, 57, 166–8, 268–9
first trip to Europe 25–6
friendships 37, 229–30
goalkeeping 89
goals tally 193–4
Golden Boot 236
Golden Samba 236
'Grumpy' nickname 55, 110
handballs 5, 88, 89, 90–1, 92, 93, 97, 185–6
hat-tricks 69, 181–2, 183
heroes 226–8, 262
hunger for winning 6, 7, 57–9, 64, 68, 102, 265, 268
irritableness on the pitch 7–8
keepsakes 69, 226
knee injury 240–2, 245–9, 250–1, 256
languages, learning 39, 40, 61, 120–2, 151
Liverpool captaincy 187–8
on managers 237–8
marries Sofi 65, 69
on money in football 34, 160–8

nine-match ban (2014) 1–3, 10–11, 13
patriotism 100–1
Player of the Year Awards 62, 231–3, 271
playing career see Ajax; Barcelona; Groningen; Liverpool; Nacional; Uruguay
pre-match eating and drinking 195–7
pressure, reactions to 8, 10, 257–8
psychological therapy 9–10
racism issue 144, 146–59
on referees 71–4
seeks to leave Liverpool 11, 199–207, 231
self-discipline 33
seven-game ban (2010) 63
signs for Ajax 42–3, 44
signs for Barcelona 11
signs for Groningen 31
signs for Liverpool 108, 115–17
style of play 54, 56, 59, 60–1, 67, 131, 173–4, 190–1
superstition 187, 220–1
tattoes 270–1
ten-match ban (2013) 4, 199
trademark celebration 185–6
work ethic 167, 268
Suárez, Maxi (brother) 263, 264–6, 268, 269
Suárez, Paolo (brother) 260, 265, 268
Suárez, Rodolfo (father) 22, 163, 165, 166, 167–8, 261, 265
Suárez, Sandra (mother) 20, 22, 23, 166, 262, 264
Suárez, Sergio (uncle) 267

Suárez, Sofi (wife) 4, 9, 10, 12, 13, 16, 17, 18–32, 33–5, 45–6, 65–6, 69, 75, 76, 77, 78, 82, 83–4, 92, 97, 98, 99, 101, 148, 156, 157, 164, 186, 196, 233, 253, 256, 270
Sunderland 137, 234
superstition 220–1
Suso 124, 184
Swansea City 169–70, 174, 194

Tabarez, Oscar 1, 2, 37, 41, 81, 102, 235, 243–5, 249
tactical debates 66–7
Tassotti, Mauro 3
team-talks 61, 62, 126, 188, 211
ten Cate, Henk 48, 49
Terry, John 114
Tevez, Carlos 102, 180
throw-ins 141–2
Torres, Fernando 116, 118
Tottenham Hotspur 114–15, 124, 233
Touré, Kolo 179, 210, 223–5
Touré, Yaya 214, 233
trademark celebrations 185–6
training 54–6
  at Ajax 53, 55–6
  at Barcelona 15–16
  at Groningen 53
  at Liverpool 117, 125–6, 128–9, 176–9
Twente 41, 47–8, 62, 70, 98
Tyson, Mike 4

Urreta 264, 265–6
Uruguay 36–7, 41, 55, 75–8, 80–8, 90–7, 101–3, 241, 243–5, 249–53, 262–3

Uruguayan style of play 55, 67–8
Utrecht 58

Van Basten, Marco 48, 49–50, 51–3,
    54, 58
Van Bronckhorst, Gio 93
Van der Vaart, Rafa 114
Van Persie, Robin 181, 193
Varela, Obdulio 148, 261
Velame, Hugo Alves 34–5
Veldmate, Henk 43
Vermaelen, Thomas 60
Vertonghen, Jan 60, 61, 62, 70
Victorino, Mauricio 86
Vidić, Nemanja 72
Vitesse Arnhem 38

Wembley Stadium 142–3
Werner, Tom 203, 207

West Bromwich Albion 180
West Ham United 177–8
Willian 234
winter break in football 254–5
World Cup 1950 78, 261
World Cup 1994 3, 262
World Cup 1998 51, 137
World Cup 2006 3
World Cup 2010 75–88, 89–97
World Cup 2014 1–3, 235–6,
    239–58

Xavi 15

young players 56, 161, 162–3, 228–9

Zalayeta, Marcelo 262
Zidane, Zinedine 3
Zubizarreta, Andoni 16

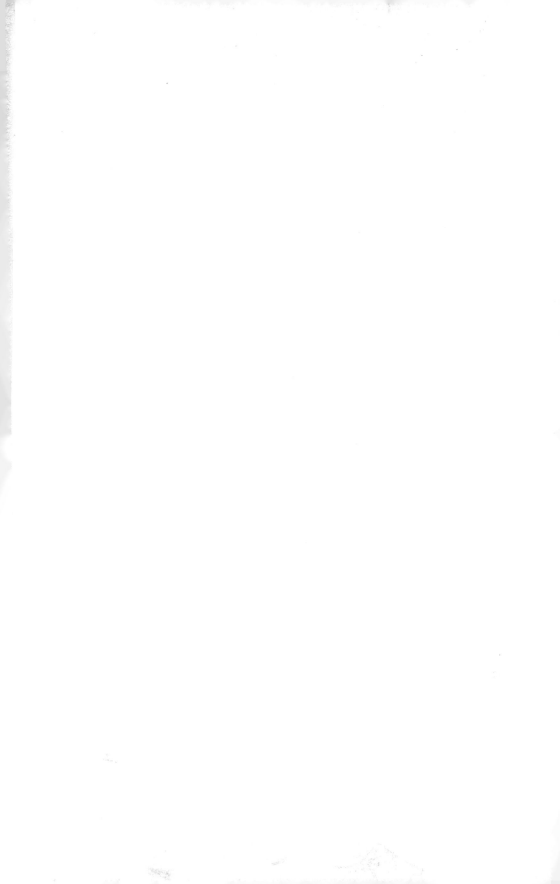